Children's Books for Grown-Up Teachers

"Appelbaum's thinking is at the leading edge (perhaps several leading edges) of curriculum inquiry internationally."

Noel Gough, LaTrobe University, Australia

"Peter Appelbaum has written an enormously erudite and important book about learning and teaching. Weaving together theories of curriculum, popular culture, literary engagement and pedagogy, he insightfully shows how deep insight emerges from the detours of teaching, and that the teacher's task is not to specify curriculum but, rather, to occasion learning. This book is an intellectual tour de force that will be of great interest to both beginning and experienced teachers."

Dennis Sumara, University of British Columbia, CA

Teachers and prospective teachers read children's books, but that reading is often done as a "teacher" – that is, as planning for instruction – rather than as a "reader" engaged with the text. *Children's Books for Grown-Up Teachers* models the kind of thinking about teaching and learning – the sort of curriculum theorizing – accomplished through teachers' interactions with the everyday materials of teaching. It starts with children's books, branches out into other youth culture texts, and subsequently to thinking about everyday life itself. Texts of curriculum theory describe infrastructures that support the crafts of inquiry and learning, and introduce a new vocabulary of poaching, weirding, dark matter, and jazz. At the heart of this book is a method of reading: each reader pulls idiosyncratic concepts from children's books and from everyday life. Weaving these concepts into a discourse of curriculum theory is what makes the difference between "going through the motions of teaching" and "designing educational experiences."

Peter Appelbaum is Associate Professor at Arcadia University, where he coordinates programs in Curriculum Studies and Mathematics Education, and directs the Strangely Familiar Music Group. His other publications include *Embracing Mathematics: On becoming a teacher and changing with mathematics* (Routledge); *Popular Culture, Educational Discourse, and Mathematics; Multicultural and Diversity Education;* and (*Post) Modern Science (Education)*.

STUDIES IN CURRICULUM THEORY
William F. Pinar, Series Editor

Appelbaum
Children's Books for Grown-Up Teachers: Reading and Writing Curriculum Theory

Eppert/Wang (Eds.)
Cross-Cultural Studies in Curriculum: Eastern Thought, Educational Insights

Jardine/Friesen/Clifford
Curriculum in Abundance

Autio
Subjectivity, Curriculum, and Society: Between and Beyond German Didaktik and Anglo-American Curriculum Studies

Brantlinger (Ed.)
Who Benefits from Special Education? Remediating (Fixing) Other People's Children

Pinar/Irwin (Eds.)
Curriculum in a New Key: The Collected Works of Ted T. Aoki

Reynolds/Webber (Eds.)
Expanding Curriculum Theory: Dis/Positions and Lines of Flight

Pinar
What is Curriculum Theory?

McKnight
Schooling, the Puritan Imperative, and the Molding of an American National Identity: Education's "Errand into the Wilderness"

Pinar (Ed.)
International Handbook of Curriculum Research

Morris
Curriculum and the Holocaust: Competing Sites of Memory and Representation

Doll
Like Letters in Running Water: A Mythopoetics of Curriculum

For additional information on titles in the Studies in Curriculum Theory series visit www.routledge.com

Children's Books for Grown-Up Teachers: Reading and Writing Curriculum Theory

Peter Appelbaum
Arcadia University
Pennsylvania
USA

Routledge
Taylor & Francis Group

NEW YORK AND LONDON

First published 2008
by Routledge
270 Madison Ave, New York, NY 10016

Simultaneously published in the UK
by Routledge
2 Park Square, Milton Park, Abingdon, Oxon OX14 4RN

Routledge is an imprint of the Taylor & Francis Group, an informa business

© 2008 Taylor & Francis

Typeset in Minion by Wearset Ltd, Boldon, Tyne and Wear
Printed and bound in the United States of America on acid-free paper by
Walsworth Publishing Company, Marceline, MO

Library of Congress Cataloging-in-Publication Data
Appelbaum, Peter Michael.
Children's literature for grown-up teachers : curriculum theorizing for a pedagogy of
response to global consumer culture / Peter Appelbaum.
p. cm. – (Studies in curriculum theory)
Includes bibliographical references and index.
1. Children's literature–Study and teaching (Elementary) 2. Education,
Elementary–Curricula. 3. Consumption (Economics) I. Title.
LB1575.A66 2008
372.64'043–dc22
2007023949

ISBN10: 0-805-84928-9 (hbk)
ISBN10: 0-415-96483-0 (pbk)
ISBN10: 1-410-61812-9 (ebk)

ISBN13: 978-0-805-84928-8 (hbk)
ISBN13: 978-0-415-96483-8 (pbk)
ISBN13: 978-1-410-61812-2 (ebk)

Dedication

In memory of Stella Clark

Contents

Preface

Teachers and prospective teachers read children's books, but that reading is often done as a "teacher" – that is, as planning for instruction – rather than as a "reader" who is engaging with the text. I offer a model for the kind of thinking about teaching and learning, the kind of curriculum theorizing so essential to our work, accomplished through our interactions with the everyday materials of our teaching. We start with children's books. From there we branch out into other youth culture texts. Finally, we think about how we read everyday life as a text of curriculum theory that describes the kinds of infrastructure that support the crafts of inquiry and learning. We develop a new vocabulary along the way. But what I am most interested in is the method, not the results. We each pull different concepts from children's books and everyday life. Weaving them into a discourse of curriculum theory is what makes the difference between "going through the motions of teaching" and "designing educational experiences."

In *Cherries and Cherry Pits* by Vera B. Williams (1996), Bidemmi lives on the floor above our narrator. They visit back and forth a lot, and Bidemmi loves to draw, so when she opens the door, we're standing right there with a marker of some kind or color she doesn't yet have: we see her peeking out in outrageously rich water colors on the facing page, and know that we're in for a treat of a story. The pictures switch from real-life water color to Bidemmi marker, and we learn of a man coming home from work with a bag full of cherries. "Dee Dee, Dennis, Duane, Dorrie," he calls. "I got something here for you." Then they come out. One sits on one of his legs, and one on another. One leans right in-between. And Dee Dee, she climbs round in back and leans over his shoulder. Then he opens the bag and pulls out a cherry.

He puts one cherry in each of their mouths and another and another ... really red cherries, too. And there they sit eating cherries and spitting out the pits. And before you can even ask Bidemmi any questions about that story, such as how come the names of all the man's children begin with D, she has another piece of paper ready and is drawing. The white woman on the train holds a big black pocketbook on her lap. In the pocketbook is a bag. She starts each story with a small detail, like the shoelace on a shore, a running shoe, or a boy, a boy who looks like her brother, a boy who is holding onto straps in the subway, with glasses like her brother. And in his pocket is a present ... Bidemmi herself in her favorite beret, in her favorite beret walking up the stairs one at a time, walking up the stairs onto the street where, what do you know, there's a truck, a truck holding cherries. The stories unfold like the revealed details of her drawings. And in the end, people and parrots and whole crowds of people from Nairobi and Brooklyn, Toronto and St. Paul, are standing in front of airplanes, eating cherries and spitting out pits, eating cherries and spitting out pits.

Option 1: Kindergarten through Grade 2. Stories of cherries and cherry pits. Exquisitely decorated and deceptively simple, the book alternates between the narrator's spare descriptions and evocative watercolors, and Bidemmi's own captivating tales and vivid, imaginative drawings. The book's title refers to Bidemmi's stories, all of which involve folks "eating cherries and spitting out the pits, eating cherries and spitting out the pits." What about all those pits? Bidemmi has an "important plan." She will plant them in her yard so they will grow "until there is a whole forest of cherry trees right on our block." Williams' latest work is another glowing tale of the transformational power of a child's creativity and love.

Option 2: Metaphors abound in this fantastic tale of eating cherries and spitting out the pits. Indeed, as I read, I conjure up images of routines and the security of family. How might I share the warmth of my family time with everyone in the world? Surely all this love of my family sitting on and around my Dad when he comes home from work, fooling with my brother when he brings me a cherry on his way home – the kind of love shared between an old white woman and the parrot waiting for her in her apartment – surely all of that love will overflow into the outer world beyond my family, beyond the boundaries of home, through the seeds of growth that are revealed in the physical act of spitting out our cherry pits. We can plant these pits, and many trees will grow, and all of those cherries on those trees will attract people from all over the world, people who won't resist the chance to come together in one big spectacular cherry party!

And what can be made of the seeds of love planted in the classroom that might contain this book in its library? Will moments of coming together and sharing time feel like eating cherries, full of juice and fun and hugging and talking, leaving seeds of future times together in their wake?

Or will the seeds planted in this classroom be more like those in Mitsumasa Anno's *Anno's Magic Seeds* (1992), able to grow into a plant that subsequently produces two new seeds, one of which can satisfy a person's hunger for a full year? In this magical tale, the farmer cleverly abstains from eating a seed one year, leading into a fascinating story of increasing seed production that changes with the unfolding patterns of his life. Happy-go-lucky Jack enjoys several years of easy subsistence until he decides to fend for himself one winter and plant both seeds. The next and each successive season begin a geometric progression of harvests: two sprouts produce four seeds (one of which he eats), three plants produce six seeds, five yield ten, and so on. In no time at all, he has a bountiful surplus and shares his wealth first with Alice, who becomes his wife, and eventually with their son. Even when a hurricane devastates their crops and storehouse, ten seeds are saved and the family begins anew. Anno illustrates the multilayered story (and its mathematical operations) with his trademark spare, clear watercolors, using metallic gold circles to represent the stored seeds and red circles for those that are consumed.

Unlike the abundance captured in the images of squirting, juicy cherries and seeds that grow into trees and trees and trees, serving to lure airplane-loads of new friends from all over the world, the model depicted in *Magic Seeds* is one of scarcity. A school in a world of scarcity conjures up students desperately working to survive, struggling for access to limited fields of knowledge (Jardine *et al.* 2006). And we hope that nobody is left behind. Delayed gratification, like the farmer who does not eat for a year in order to increase his future harvests, becomes the dominant motif. There is a kind of promised vision of abundance in delayed gratification and other forms of harvest growth, yet these forms of abundance do not carry with them the same sense of excess and celebration found in the delight of a cherry. They are more like the accomplishment of speedy multiplication algorithms than the generativity of an idea like balance, found on a see-saw, across an equation, in the relationship between adjectives and verbs in a poem, or in the flow of classroom discussion among teachers and students.

Once we make this kind of shift in our reading, from story to classroom practice, we are doing the joyous and challenging work of curriculum theory. And this is what the book in your hands is all about: children's books are remarkably good for curriculum theorizing. The best of them are rich in metaphor and generous with their ethical stance. Quickly and profoundly, they make for both good reading and good thinking. They help me reaffirm my teaching as an ethical stance with the world (Block 1999).

Nicolas, Where have You Been?, by Leo Lionni (1978), seems like it *must* have been inspired by one of the teaching groups in my undergraduate elementary education course. We work for three hours per week with groups of eight to ten children, leading them through mathematics inquiries that are designed to accomplish the Philadelphia School Districts' benchmarks in mathematics and language arts for the second six weeks of the school year. Like the field mice at the edge of the meadow, the children began their inquiry projects looking for special things – "the sweetest and juiciest berries" – in this case, questions that would jump-start rigorous mathematical inquiries and lead to numerous opportunities for writing and reading. But, also like the mice in this story, all they could find at first were the equivalent of pale pink berries that were neither sweet nor juicy. And, to make a long story short, the children and the teachers blamed the birds, those flying around in surveillance above them, for hunting and pecking and stealing all of the good questions. They were living in a regime of scarcity, unable to identify the abundance before them, and their frustrations came to life in a "war on the birds," a full-scale, all-out rebellion against those perceived to be swooping in from above, scarily wielding their claws. True to the fabled story of Nicolas, these children and their teachers benefited from a single child bravely exploring with the birds what their lives were like. One of the ten children brought their mathematician's notebook to the university supervisor, and asked for a berry or two to store in the notebook. The supervisor first offered a worm instead of a berry or nut, but quickly learned from the child what she was seeking. A few days later, sitting on the floor with the group, the supervisor swooped in from above, landed on the ground, and chatted about mathematics and learning, questions and berries, and left a happy clan of mathematicians hard at work on important projects.

Curriculum workers in ED 502 Curriculum Foundations at Arcadia University feel a lot like *Frederick*, the eponymous hero in another of Lionni's (1967) modern fables for our time. All of their colleagues are scurrying around, frantically collecting the last vestiges of data and funding before the coming of the cold, hard winter months. They are working day and night. Meanwhile, the heroes of *our* tale, like Frederick, gather colors (for the winter is gray), and words (for the winter days are long and many, and we'll run out of things to say). The mice are collecting corn and nuts and wheat and straw; the curriculum theorists are gathering sun rays for the cold, dark winter days ahead. The field mice survive on their stored supplies for quite a long time, just like our colleagues who make it through most of the school year on their data and hard-won extra grants. But when it comes down to it, the leadership is in the hands of Frederick. Readers from Amazon.com declare:

> In a community narrowly focused on efficiency, one mouse stands apart and concerns himself with art. Frederick notes the wonder of the world he lives in, and takes the time to assimilate it. While his cohorts may grumble at this behavior, when the dreariness of winter overtakes them they are grateful for Frederick's words. Frederick's poetry is seen as an essential supply for survival.

> In a children's bookstore, I once heard a father tell his son to put back a picture book because it was "garbage." Maybe he saw the shocked look on my face, because he started lecturing me about how children today need to learn a lot of things and they don't have time to waste on fairy tales and other stories.... Unfortunately, his point of view is becoming more common. It looks like this generation of children is going to grow up in a world that cares more about their ability to memorize facts and formulas and regurgitate them for standardized tests than it cares about their ideas and imaginations.... Leo Lionni's books – especially Frederick – are great antidotes to that narrow mindset.

> I don't think there's a better book about the importance of nurturing the imagination than Frederick. When Lionni first wrote it, in 1966, it

became an instant classic. Today it's not just a great children's book, it's a crucial one.

I can't think of a better argument for curriculum theory, expressible best by readers of children's books. And so the idea of *this* book came about. In the same way that themes of magic and planting and the inadequacy of planting as a metaphor of abundance – and imagination as the most important resource for survival – have popped up in this preface, each book I read conjures up images and concepts, deconstruction of other concepts, and generative narrations that can be brought back into my classroom work. I share my readings of these stories here, not so much to introduce the ideas that were generated, but more importantly to invite you to join me in this kind of work. Once we get started, I warn you, it's pretty contagious. And the habits of thinking about classroom teaching and learning often leak out into other areas of one's life. For example, children's books don't only mean published material on paper between two covers any more. They also mean the other stories that permeate children's lives: online, in shopping malls, at the zoo, in the alley behind the supermarket, and so on. Please join me, and let me know what you're thinking as we read these texts together.

Acknowledgments

Tana Hoban's first book for children, *Shapes and Things* (1970), uses photograms – photographs made without a camera, by placing an object directly on photographic paper under darkroom conditions, then exposing it to light and processing it in the same way as a photographic print. Her creative approach and photographic expertise raise the relatively simply photogram process to a fine art. Many people have been like a photogram process for *my* ideas over time, similarly exposing them under varying conditions of light and development that reveal the understated beauty of pure shape, new ways of "seeing", and "thinking", much in the same way that Tana Hoban's work helps us to discover new meaning in ordinary, everyday objects. As I discuss in Chapter 4, this metaphor of "seeing" for thinking has particular ideological functions that suggest the need for alternatives. Nevertheless, the analogy feels apt here: I have much to thank these people for. Conversations and critical reading are the greatest gifts someone can receive, and have made this book possible for me to write. Just as Tana Hoban reconstitutes in white on black the everyday black-and-white ... the images both material and dematerialized, revealing a startling beauty in the familiar, so have my ideas and processes of working been turned into what art they may claim by my encounters with others.

First on my list of thanks are my editor Naomi Silverman of Routledge, Taylor & Francis, and Bill Pinar, my series editor, for not losing faith in this book, even as every deadline came and went. I truly hope it was worth the wait! Naomi's consistent support and patience made the difference in the end. I would also like to thank Bill Pinar and the International Association for the Advancement of Curriculum Studies for getting me started on this project; my first chapter was originally a paper for the very first IAACS conference at LSU in Baton Rouge, Louisiana, and its inclusion in the subsequent monograph from that conference (Truiet *et al.* 2003) gave me just the right kick-start to continue the folly of children's books as curriculum theory. The 2006 Second World Curriculum Studies Conference in Tampere, Finland, gave me the final push to finish the manuscript for the book six years later.

Alan Block is the closest thing to a genuine study partner and mentor I have ever had. Our phone conversations over the years, our mutual sharing of writing drafts, and Alan's regular question, "So what are you reading now?" have been the most consistent sources of intellectual nourishment and prodding I have ever had the opportunity to experience. Alan's friendship has been a cherished nomadic epistemological standpoint, throwing me off my paths to wonder and dream, only to stay on the trail of inquiry. The best elements of my work are inspired by Alan's statement that teaching is "an ethical stance one takes with the world."

The so-far five-year collaboration with Leif Gustavson, co-teaching and co-writing, has been a fundamentally life-altering process. The most original of my ideas are as much Leif's as my own at this point, as evidenced by our co-written chapter outlining how the new curricular concepts developed in this book have been integrated as habits of mind and body in our work with pre-service and in-service teachers.

My two-year fellowship at the Psychoanalytic Center of Philadelphia, administered by Dr. Bruce Levin, and under the mentorship of Dr. Robert Kravis, was critical to the development of the ideas in this book. I especially want to thank Mimi Rogers, Pat Dougherty, and the rest of the Center's City Schools Forum. I thank as well the University of Cape Town and its Department of Academic Literacy, chaired by Lucia Thesen, and the Spencer Foundation, for funding my residences in Cape Town, where revitalizing and challenging conversations with faculty and staff helped me to flesh out and elaborate a number of the chapters in this collection. I further extend my appreciation to Christine Keitel, Eva Jablonka, Astrid Gebehr, and the Freie Universität Berlin for hosting me during the final completion of the manuscript.

The Bergamo Conference on Curriculum Theory and Classroom Practice of the Journal of Curriculum Theorizing has played a powerful role in my growth as an artist of curriculum studies; in particular, each chapter here owes much to the audiences and friendly conversations in-between sessions. The members of the Critical Issues in Curriculum and Cultural Studies special interest group of the American Educational Research Association have been equally supportive and generative in sponsoring and attending conference sessions that laid the groundwork for ideas that later evolved into themes in this book. Arcadia University, Provost Mike Berger, and Dean Norah Shultz have supported my research and travel to national and international conferences with professional development and other travel funds. I extend special appreciation to Noel Gough and David Kirshner for their probing interactions with my work over the years, serving in many ways as the mentors I might have had in graduate school but have been fortunate to find in them years later. Joe Kincheloe, John Weaver, Toby Daspit, Karen Anijar, and Elizabeth Heilman gave me that much-needed encouragement along the way by including early versions of my work in their edited volumes, and Dennis Sumara provided both an example of engaged reading for imagination, interpretation and insight, *and* that last-minute push on the final version of the book. Donald Blumenfeld-Jones, Karen Ferneding, Celeste Snowber, Bob Klein, Erica Dávila, Karen Clark, and Christine Miller have each spent innumerable hours with me talking about those important things and possible projects that provided the framework for crazy ideas that later found their way into this book. Thanks as well to Joan Fox and Kate Shapero of the Project Learn School in Philadelphia for the wonderful weekly lunchtime discussion group, which challenged me to work through the implications for classroom pedagogy, and for ceaselessly feeding me amazing concretizations of curriculum theorizing.

My final thanks go to Belinda Davis, Noah Appelbaum, and Sophia Appelbaum. I am forever in love with and grateful for my family not only for being themselves and supporting and nourishing me, but also for serving as co-researchers in one or more of the projects that surface here.

I dedicate this work to my dear friend Stella Clark, and her family, Jesse, Eammon, and Kevin Naidoo. Our loss of Stella as a friend and family member and as a well-spring of intellectual innovation continues to reverberate interminably. Each poetic image, from poaching to the feed to re-zooming reminds me of Stella, our friendship, her teaching, her unique ability to pinpoint precisely what issue of language and ideology is implicated; Stella and Kevin dancing from the living room to the kitchen of their beautiful home in Rondebosch, Jesse asking a member of the opposing debate team after the match if he honestly believes in capital punishment, Eamonn keeping everyone focused on the latest episode of Afrikaans soap opera; Stella as a devoted mother, teacher, scholar, and colleague, who established no boundaries of separation between any two of these roles.

1
Introduction:
Weirding and Poaching

A new discourse of educational theory: weirding, poaching, the feed, vision stinks, cyborg selves, consumer culture, dark matter, jazz, aliens. A project seemingly doomed from the start: why would anyone want to adopt a "novel" and therefore possibly initially unclear discourse for thinking about and working through classroom practice? Well actually, while this book could be thought of as an argument on one level for doing just that, what I have in mind is something different. Sure, I argue for these new terms, but my main purpose is to advocate a method more than to promote my results. More important than these terms – although I do indeed hope to show their relevance and usefulness, especially in the later chapters – is my illustration of how I got to them.

Teachers read children's books all the time. But we read them as curriculum materials; that is, we read them as potential literature for our students. We don't read them for ourselves. At first, like others, I thought of these books as experiences for youth, asking such questions as, "Is this the right level of difficulty?," "What themes will my students be grappling with if they read this book, and how might they relate to such themes when connecting to their own everyday life experiences?," "What curricular content goals could be addressed through this book?," "What might my students learn about voice, audience, narrative structure, genre, and so on through interaction with this book?" My next step was to think about using children's literature in courses for prospective and current teachers. So my questions changed a little: "Which educational issues can teachers think about by reading this book?," "What issues can readers of this book grapple with regarding their students' lives?" Soon, however, I found myself reading these books as themselves, not as curriculum materials. I couldn't help it. They are so good! I enjoy them as books, not as tools for my work! I noticed that my mind would wander as I personally thought about images, concepts, metaphors, depictions of the lives of youth, and philosophical questions that arose in these works of literature. And, as we formed literature circles in my courses, the pre-service and current teachers in my classes found that they, too, could develop ideas about teaching and learning through their discussions.

This book is an invitation to join me in an enterprise. I welcome you to a method of curriculum theorizing: read children's books for yourself, not for the potential they hold for others. Not only is this fun, and not only does this give you an excuse to indulge in the guilty pleasure of reading works of literature that are quick and easy to get through – in fact, I argue, you can think about the ideas in these books and use them to help you find more meaning and purpose in your practice as a teacher. You, too, can develop a set of terms that can be used to make sense of what is happening in your classroom. Treating children's and young adult books as literature opens up a world of intellectual inquiry and personal growth.

At one point in my work with teachers, I encouraged them to use any popular culture texts as curriculum theory resources. In developing clinical interview skills we would pay attention to the kinds of questions that worked well on television and radio talk-shows (Appelbaum 2001). Which ones led to the guest speaking in paragraph-long stories about how they thought about ideas, and which ones seemed to shut down the conversation or shift the focus away from the guest toward the host? Analyzing talk-show strategies would help us work in the classroom as "hosts," enabling our students to metaphorically take on the roles of special guests. What is it like to visit a shopping mall on a day when your life has changed in some way? Is there a curriculum of the mall, in terms of the types of experiences, which we might translate into the classroom, so that analogous social experiences might support similar decisions, accomplishments, and feelings of satisfaction or personal growth? My aim was to provide busy teachers with little time for academic scholarship tools already at hand for improvisational reflection and refraction on the nature and purposes of their work.

Some teachers find the metaphoric application of popular culture and everyday life exciting and productive. Others devalue such resources, either through a reproduction of the cultural dichotomy between high and low culture, or simply because they do not have the time in their busy lives to watch television or visit a mall. In response to the latter concern, I continue to push my colleagues to think about the experiences they already have in their everyday lives as resources for curriculum theorizing. For example, when one is cooking, why not consider the differences between following a recipe and inventing your own dish out of the ingredients you find in your kitchen? Why not experiment with slight variations in quantities to discover for yourself the difference between a cake and a cookie, a soup and a sauce? Ideas from such reflections might be brought to bear on analogous elements in a classroom: suppose the essay to be written is a cake or a cookie, or the students approach composing a poem as a sauce instead of a soup? What if the teacher is a cookie in her actions while the students are cakes, or vice versa?

However, I have also come to understand a powerful and positive professional orientation to teaching and learning that tends to make it harder to use

TV or shopping, or cooking and so on, as curriculum theory texts, harder than teachers' manuals or teacher resources, or even children's literature: teachers naturally want to spend their limited time on more overt resources for their work. Why watch a lousy television game show for inspiration when one could digest five to ten potential lesson plans on the internet, or plan a new unit around a recent Newbery Medal winning children's book? Indeed, why should I insist on *not* spending more time exploring the curriculum materials more readily sanctioned in the school curriculum? I have found over the past decade that teachers not only enjoy reading children's literature for their students, but moreover also delight in reading these books for themselves. Reading for ourselves is something often missing in our work, which so easily focuses on planning what others will read.

I write about my own reading of such books. I intentionally read them for meaning rather than technique, even though ideas for technique and organization pop up occasionally in my writing. My own personal reasons for this focus have to do with my position with respect to curriculum. There is already so much out there telling me what to do and when that I do not need to think so much about such things. Instead, what I crave is meaning and the underlying purpose for my work. I need a discourse for talking about this less overt and critically important aspect of my craft. In the end, what I have created for myself is a new discourse of teaching, one which I have begun testing out over the past few years, and find extremely helpful both for planning and assessment. When I work now as an educator, I use this new language to think about units, lessons, assessments, and so on. My plans and assessment include poaching, weirding, the feed and consumer culture, alternatives to vision and perception as the dominant metaphor for knowing, dark matter, improvisation, ways of working, and identification with the aggressor. Like the French philosopher and social theorist Michel De Certeau (1984), I have noticed that my reading produces "gardens that miniaturize and collate a world"; like him, I feel "'possessed' by [my] own fooling around and jesting [which] introduces plurality and difference" (p. 172). De Certeau writes that a reader is a novelist, "oscillating in the nowhere between what he invents and what changes him" (p. 172).

Reading and writing in this sense is a method of *currere* (Pinar 2004), a shift from analyzing the content of the curriculum (from the Latin: the racetrack) toward the experience (the running of the track); it is a systematic and self-reflective study, using youth culture texts to interrogate the relations between academic knowledge and one's own life history, in the interest of both self-confirmation and social reconstruction (p. 35). Looking back, I affirm Pinar's four steps or moments in the method of *currere*, the regressive, the progressive, the analytic, and the synthetic. Flipping through the pages of my writing, I see those moments where I have re-entered my past to enlarge and transform my memory, as in my tales of reading to my children, or in my stories about my classroom, as a teacher or earlier as a student, practices central to the regressive step. I see as well examples of the progressive moment, which involves looking forward toward what is not yet the case, meditatively imagining possible futures. I describe schools that sanction poaching, schools that weird curriculum, mathematics classes that center improvisation; I conflate curriculum and science fiction in terms of their mutual concern with possible futures; and so on. The analytic moments of this project took me into an intensive engagement with the daily life of the classroom rather than serving as an ironic detachment. And the synthetic moments, when at their best, have felt to me like "a coursing, as in an electric current" (Doll 2000, p. vii, quoted in Pinar 2004).

Yet further questions are generated by this experiencing of *currere*. On the one hand, my reading is informed by a wide range of ancillary reading that my students and the readers of my writing likely do not share. What does this mean for my audience and for others who might be interested in experimenting with this kind of way of working as a curriculum worker? On the other hand, my reading of such literature destabilizes the canon of curriculum theory as complicated conversation: who are these interlopers that I place at the center of the curriculum theory landscape, one might ask, and why do they belong here when they haven't asked to join the conversation in the first place? Finally, one particular aspect of my technique is that I arbitrarily select the works of literature that I consult. What are the implications of this, given the expectations of systematicity and coherence in academic scholarship?

In the words of Gilles Deleuze (1994), reading such works and writing about them as curriculum theory might be conceived as a form of stutter, a "stop" in the development of curriculum conversation. The gap that is created by any form of disruption of thought evokes awareness, making knowledge possible, just as emptiness might be understood, not as an absence, but as a potential space to be filled.

In what follows, I invite you to read some of these texts along with me, both for the ideas that I develop and for the processes I go through in connecting the themes, images, metaphors, and plot developments of the stories that are told to classroom practice, through analogies with teaching and learning. If I could claim a "method" that I am espousing, I would evoke Paul Feyerabend's definition of "science" as a "collage" in contrast with a "system": science, he writes, has conflicting parts with different strategies, results, and metaphysical embroideries; both historical experience and democratic principles suggest that science be kept under public control; scientific institutions are not objective, nor do they or their products confront people like a rock or a star (Feyerabend 1995: 143). Scientific institutions and their products:

> often merge with other traditions, are affected by them, affect them in turn. Decisive scientific movements were inspired by philosophical and

religious (or theological) sentiments. The material benefits of science are not at all obvious. There *are* great benefits, true. But there are also great disadvantages. And the role of the abstract entity "science" in the production of the benefits is anything but clear.

If that is what we mean by "science," then this book is my call for a new "science of curriculum." Indeed, the phrase, "Weirding and Poaching," is inspired by European mathematics educator Hans Freudenthal's (1978) similar call for a new science of (mathematics) education, *Weeding and Sowing*. My first conception of my work here was as a sort of postmodern update of Freudenthal's rallying cry, in which the post-colonial, globalized consumer-mediated culture demands a shift from the agrarian, romantic notions of farming and cultivation of the young toward a more contemporary and future-oriented collection of transitional concepts. I'll get back to this later on in this introduction, but for now I'll simply say that our metaphor undergoes startling transformations. Weeding in order to isolate the individual student and make it possible to carefully cultivate him or her, feeding just the right amount of prescribed nutrients in the proper environment, is "supplanted" by weirding, which connotes images of distortion, disorientation, and displacement. Sowing the field of knowledge with potential concepts that can be grown by the student as a garden in his or her own right is similarly supplanted by poaching, which in its origins has more to do with innovative and artistic gleaning than with criminality and law-breaking, but in its contemporary definition heralds a new sense of presence in the merger of science and creative expression.

Freudenthal was searching for "the situation where – in quest for paradigms – we are not struck with blindness by our explicit knowledge" (Freudenthal 1978: 214). If reading children's books for utility in interpreting and imagining educational possibilities is a science, then, according to Freudenthal, recognizing such work as "science" will neither depend on a clean-cut definition nor on a complete set of characteristics. Science, after all, is delimited more carefully from other domains of human activity by criteria such as relevance, consistency, and publicity. Early on I decided, following Freudenthal, that the truth of my efforts in this method of *currere* was not really relevant to the method, "because truth is a property of statements, whereas science as an activity is not a treasury of truth but a method of asking questions" (Freudenthal 1975: 1). Relevance, on the other hand, is not only a property of statements, but also of problems and methods, and is more crucial as such. Relevance as a property of definitions, notations, concepts, classifications, and more globally, of problem complexes, theories, domains of knowledge, and so on, has become a fundamental criterion of my readings and applications of young adult and children's literature.

Consistency, Freudenthal's third criterion for science, at first seems connected to truth, but more importantly emphasizes an attitude which faces consequences, as a property of action and patterns of activity, those practices that ask relevant questions and pursue promising leads. Consistency is sometimes confused with its meaning in formal logic, as a logically closed system; in contrast, this criterion is employed by Freudenthal as a repository of organizing devices. In this way, consistency moves away from the less attractive, rigid model of science that many have mistakenly taken from cartoon conceptions of logic and general theories in physics. Even "physics is like a shop of mini-theories supervised by, though not derived from, general theory," writes Freudenthal (p. 1). Officially, according to the rhetoric, science as an ideal (i.e., the kinds of science we are referring to here in this new notion of a science of curriculum) is publicly accessible to everybody who agrees to learn its language, and in the long run neither schools nor prophets succeed in monopolizing a domain of science – though sometimes it may be difficult to decide whether a particular science means more than the language in which it is expressed.

Relevance, consistency, and publicity are criteria through which science contrasts itself with its "fringe" – pseudo-science and non-science. How does my work with children's literature constitute itself as *currere*, as opposed to pseudo-*currere*, or non-*currere*? The fringe of curriculum theory is a social danger worth studying in its own right. To extend the metaphor of a science of *currere*, I again refer to Freudenthal, who writes that flying saucers, the mysteries of the Cheops pyramid, and the paragnosts are not serious problems for science; Nazi pseudo-scientific racism, however, was a menace to mankind, and new pseudo-sciences may endanger humanity even more (c.f., Davis and Appelbaum 2001; Winfield 2005). Pseudo-science, Freudenthal continues, often sounds like a protest against public science as far as publicity means public recognition and is suspect to public coercion. It may also be a danger to serious "science" because pseudo-scientific infections may cause a cancer-like growth in serious science; language borrowed from pseudo-science may be abused in other scientific venues, for example, when terms like function, information, model, and structure, which originated in mathematics, become meaningless when translated into some other sciences. It is essential that *currere* does not fall into the traps of pseudo-science by carefully monitoring its appropriation of methods.

Thus, to borrow from multicultural educators Donaldo Macedo and Lilia Bartolomé (1999: 125), "it is important that educators not blindly reject teaching methods across the board, but that they reject uncritical appropriation of methods, materials, curricula." When an educator reads a text of any kind as a tool for making sense of her or his work, she or he needs to reject what some (e.g., Macedo and Bartolomé) call the "methods fetish" so as to create learning environments informed by both action and reflection. In freeing themselves from the blind adoption of so-called effective (commonly called "teacher-proof") strategies, teachers can begin the reflective process, which allows them to re-create and re-invent teaching methods and materials. By always taking into consideration the sociocultural realities that might limit or expand possibilities to humanize education, for example, teachers can keep in mind how methods are social constructions that grow out of and reflect pedagogical implications of asymmetrical power relations among different groups.

Pseudo-science falsely focuses on methods as solutions. Well intentioned, we often look for the latest method – could reading children's books *as* curriculum theory be "the answer?" Methods promise that they may magically "work." We sincerely want to create positive learning environments, for example, for culturally and linguistically subordinated students; specific instructional methods promise to resolve, say, perceived academic under-achievement of subordinated students as a technical issue (Macedo and Bartolomé 1999; Appelbaum 2002b). Solutions become technical. In contrast, the "new science of curriculum" that I call for with the "method" I espouse in the following chapters is a kind of method "against method," in the sense that it is a challenge to technical solutions. Rather than assume that teachers and materials are "the best they can be according to scientific research," I believe we need to identify, interrogate, and change our biased beliefs and frag-mented views about subordinated students; that schools, as institutions, are basically *not* fair and democratic sites, but rather, ideological apparati that dif-ferentiate opportunities and resources. Further, I believe that a science of *currere* must examine the assumptions behind beliefs about children who experience academic difficulties, and the presumptions that such students must be prescribed "special" forms of instruction that solve the problems of "their" failures. If nothing is fundamentally wrong with schools, then under-achievement is best dealt with by providing teachers with specific teaching methods that promise to be effective. However, the one-size-fits-all instruc-tional recipe reinforces "a disarticulation between the embraced method and the social-cultural realities within which each method is implemented" (Macedo and Bartolomé 1999: 122). A myopic focus on methodology often serves to obfuscate the real issue: for example, why do subordinated students disproportionately experience something other than success, often in fact reproducing asymmetrical power relations?

Science must be distinguished from "technique" and its scientific instru-mentation, technology. Science, writes Freudenthal, is practiced by scientists, and techniques by engineers, which in our context would include people like doctors, lawyers, cosmetologists, and teachers. The question is not which chil-dren's books to read and how, or even whether or not we need the actual books. (Here in this work my "children's literature" is expanded beyond the normal sense of this term to include television, computer-based communit-ies, and the creative practices of youth, in addition to stories published on paper carried in the hand between a front and back cover.) Instead, if know-ledge and cognition are primary for the scientist, then, writes Freudenthal, action and construction characterize the work of the engineer, though in fact his or her activity may be based on science. Historically, technique often pre-ceded science. "Western" medicine, for example, was a technique with some background philosophy before it was codified and institutionalized as "science," and even today there are intellectual activities that call themselves science while they are little more than technique with a little technology and a huge amount of background philosophy. I have in mind here curriculum development and design as placed in the canon by Ralph Tyler (1949/1969). Of course, technique can be a good thing, and indeed, in some pages which follow, I will be found reflecting on the power of technique to instigate aes-thetic practices. Technology is a collection of valuable instruments. However, their background philosophy has no right to behave as though it were scientifically justified, and both should be carefully distinguished from science.

The caricature of science is a set of practices that provides a picture of the world (Rorty 1981). We need something else. Not a picture of humanity nor a picture of society, as advocated in his pre-postmodern sensibility by Freuden-thal, although his notions that these things are related to matters of "faith" is right on. He meant to reconnect the activity of the engineers of the world with a rational expression of faith, by which he thinks of philosophy, in the mode of inquiry that sees philosophy as steering technique. What I bring to this dis-cussion started by Freudenthal is Joanna Field's (1957) earlier idea of the gap into which a new thing will fit. If the new thing is knowledge, we can, she writes, "plan the question, frame the question, work on deliberately planning the empty space into which the new knowledge was to fit" (Field 1957: 104). Or, if it is to be a new invention, a new way of doing things, Field suggests we can plan "the practical need that the invention must satisfy; even though before inventing it one obviously could not say what the exact nature of the solution of the problem would be." In the classroom, as I discuss in Chapter 8, neither the teacher nor the student can plan precisely what the real function or will of creativity can or should be. Yet either can say that the business of the will is to provide the framework within which the creative forces will have free play. In the context of science and pseudo-science, we can think about the relationship between the technique and the technology. Along with an unceasing interaction between a technique and its technology, there is no sharp boundary between them. "The practitioner noting down and analyzing his experiences or the theoretician advising and briefing the [practitioner], do not do science; on the other hand so much fundamental and paradigmatic knowledge can arise in the course of practice that everybody gladly recognizes it as science," writes Freudenthal (1978: 20). And Field points out, "It is said that no art school can teach you how to paint,"

> But the art school can and does provide the frame, it offers regular times and places and materials for creation. And by the willed act of registering as a student and attending at the proper time one can, as by a protective frame, free oneself from the many distractions of trying to paint at home.
>
> (Field 1957: 104)

In other words, crafts form another source of our present techniques. I am longing for the lost craft of reading as theorizing. I have learned this from thinking about the youth cultural practices that young people engage in as creative practitioners in their everyday lives. In Chapter 10 I write with Leif Gustavson about how we translate the ways of being that such youth embody as they pursue their popular culture crafts into the classroom. Yet there is a more fundamental way that my interaction with youth cultural practices has informed the "method" of *currere* illustrated by each of the chapters in this book. Youth are involved in popular culture practices in the same ways and with the same intensities that Picasso was involved in painting, or Mozart was involved in composing. They have the kinds of skills that we want them to have in order to be able to work at a high and complex level. For example, if you watch somebody play a video-game or choose an outfit, you can see them demonstrating knowledge, comprehension, application, analysis, synthesis, and evaluation, the full range of higher order thinking according to Benjamin Bloom's taxonomy of learning (Bloom 1956). In my reading of children's literature, I am honing the craft of reading as an educator, as a curriculum theorist. How can this be the sort of engagement exemplified by youth absorbed in serious pursuit of perfection in their graffiti, use of lip balm, personalization of clothing, organization of MySpace blogs, and collection of iPod playlists?

Commitment interwoven with method

Abraham Joshua Heschel (1966/1959) noted a half-century ago that teachers often complain about the listlessness and the lack of intellectual excitement of their students. He asked, "Is it the fault of the students?" (p. 46), describing the sequence of what is required in schools as a call for information to be digested by the student, questions presented by the teacher, and answers to be supplied by the student. Evaluation in this context focuses on the students' "ability to answer questions rather than to understand problems" (p. 46). The truth, argued Heschel, is that the valid test of a student is his ability to ask the right questions. And he suggested "that we evoke a new type of examination paper, one in which the answers are given – the questions to be supplied by the student" (p. 46). I confess a strong agreement with Heschel, one that cannot be unraveled from the method of *currere* I advocate. I believe with Heschel that our system of training tends to smother the sense of wonder and mystery, to stifle rather than to cultivate the sense of the unutterable. "I shudder to think of a generation devoid of a sense of wonder and mystery," he so elegantly declares, "devoid of a sense of inadequacy and embarrassment. I am terrified at the thought of being governed by people who believe that the world is all calculated and explained, who have no sense either of quality or of mystery" (Heschel 1966/1959: 47). This book takes Heschel's anxiety as its fundamental premise: we are fostering a type of person who lives by borrowed words rather than by one's own innate sense of the unutterable, by the stirring in one's own heart which no language can declare.

My students are *not* listless and lacking in intellectual excitement. As Leif and I describe in Chapter 10, the experience of "work" in our classes is informed by the habits of mind and body students bring with them to the investigations and experiments they develop and pursue. This is informed by the notion of poaching that I introduce in Chapter 2, by the infrastructure of weirding that I chase in Chapter 3, and so on. And I do usually evaluate my students – when evaluation rather than more meaningful feedback is necessary – according to their ability to ask questions, as opposed to providing answers. The readings that follow provide an example of my method that is also influenced by the ways in which I accept teaching and learning to be apprehended but not comprehended, "within our reach but beyond our grasp" (Heschel 1966/1959: 47). If my readings offered explanations they would seemingly make us "strong" but, I believe, they would not make us "noble."

> Is it not our duty as teachers to share the awareness of the ineffable, to cultivate stillness in the soul? Stand still and behold! Behold not only in order to explain, to fit what we see into our notions; behold in order to stand face to face with the beauty and grandeur of the universe.
> (Heschel 1966/1959: 47)

In this sense, my *currere* is both method and philosophy, both practice and polemic. More than a stance, I conceive of *currere* as an embodied social and cultural practice. My passion is to work in a particular way because of my personal and theoretical commitments. What are the practical, concrete consequences of the ways of working and thinking that unfold? I draw on Lawrence Grossberg's (2003) description of the politics of Deleuze and Guattari, "grounded in an ethics of life itself as immanence" (p. 6). I use this philosophy of immanence to help me trace lines of flight through and beyond the chaos of teaching and learning, the lived experience of groups of teachers and pupils working together in classrooms, between what is for me an unfinished present and the already begun future. The notion of immanence for me differentiates what I need to think about as a teacher and curriculum worker from the transcendence of theory that is often offered to teachers and policymakers. In this sense reality is composed of a multiplicity of processes, as "becomings." Here thinking and reality are inseparable, as are metaphysics and ethics. The main rule that I take from Deleuze and Guattari (Deleuze 2001; Guattari 1995; Boundas 1993; Deleuze 1993) is to defy the lure of the transcendent (Huebner 1999) by opposing all structures, hierarchies, totalities, and unities; I refuse any reduction, accepting instead the variety of events that comprise reality, and in so doing, subtract any "one reality" that seems to predetermine where the lines or connections are or must be, so that it is possible to (re?)draw multiplicities of lines of connection and determination. It would be silly to argue against this rule as undermining itself, given that it is itself a line. It's not. The rule simply means, as Grossberg writes, "don't not let anything stop you" (Grossberg 2003: 2).

Now, I don't see Grossberg's rule conflicting with Deleuze's stuttering "stop," which actually opens up possibility; the stutter of reading as writing a world is really a craft of not letting anything stop me, one of a series of tools of *currere*. My work is a search for tools, voices, and concepts that will allow us to understand the making of the present as the becoming of the future. And this, in turn, is what I urge you to consider for yourself. Can we find, in Grossberg's terms, "a way through the chaos without constructing prisons (whether same old ones or new ones)" (p. 8)? The practical might usually be associated with activities capable of being described in terms of objectives and assessment. Yet acts that occur within the inner life – a thought, a moment of sensitivity, a moment of stillness and self-examination, an effort to interrogate the politics of a discourse that presumes a unitary self, a feeling of spiritual insight – are supremely practical. Thoughts are tools, and coming up with new ones can lead to a "pragmatics of concepts" that refuses formal systematicity even as it chases a science of curriculum.

Such a philosophy is not distant from the daily life of classrooms, but *in* the classroom even as it is outside of it, seeking something other than the closure that we have in our silliness mistakenly used as the line from here to there, from question to answer. What if we did something else, something that might at times feel and sound like answers, yet also taste and look like new questions? To explain is to "flatten out," leading to prediction and control, and maintaining a dualism between theory and practice; the "'proof of the pudding' is in the practice" (Macdonald 1995: 174). Reading children's books for the metaphors they release provides a supremely practical technology of understanding. James Macdonald writes that the "fundamental human quest is the search for meaning and the basic human capacity for this is experienced in the hermeneutic process of interpretation of the text (whether artifact, natural world, or human action)" (Macdonald 1995: 176).

Like curriculum theorist Dennis Sumara (1993, 2002), what I am doing is reading children's books and young adult novels as *literary* text. Sumara contrasts the experience of a literary text with expository texts whose function is to explain or tell; literary texts do not give experience, but invite the reader into a potential experience. I think literary texts are tools for Deleuzian lines of flight, because, as Sumara suggests (Sumara 1993: 155), they enable the aesthetic reading of being drawn into language that can fulfill a formulative function, which is for my project far more important than the efferent reading he juxtaposes, a sort of reading that dwells in the world of instrumental communication. This contrast is critical to the "method" I am espousing here, which asks for teachers to shift momentarily from the instrumental function of texts as "good curriculum materials" toward the hermeneutic process of *currere*.

In the end, however, what is happening here, I believe, is that the reading of these texts makes it possible for us to rewrite the text of school. Indeed, as the curriculum scholar Alan Block (1988) pointed out some years ago, "reading is the process by which reality is consumed; writing is the very production of that reality" (p. 23). To learn to read is to learn to interpret another's text, and this is certainly an important thing to know how to do. But to learn to write is to "weave a conception of the world" (p. 23). This to me is truly what *currere* is all about. To live in the world of schools is to read the texts of others, to apply others' prescriptions and follow their directions; to *be alive* is to write one's own text for what teaching and learning is all about, what Heschel and Macdonald and Block together proclaim as the supremely *practical* work of curriculum theorizing. This theorizing profoundly affects what I and my students are doing and thinking about in the classroom, once we read children's literature in order to write our own school text. We read, as does Dennis Sumara (2002), because reading helps us to experience what is necessary to reconsider what we think to be true about our personal worlds of experience, for imagination, interpretation, and insight.

Alan Block reads the meta-narrative of the text of school, in which "teachers" is the name given to the delivery system of curricular content. The teacher's role, in this commonsense discourse, is prescribed by his or her place in the hierarchy, leading students to a determined answer, outside of the activity which they initiate, at best catalysts who remain unchanged by a particular situation (Block 1988: 35). The philosophy of immanence traces lines of flight through the chaos of teaching and learning, the lived experience of groups of teachers and pupils working together in classrooms. All language is called into question in what Block describes as the "writerly text," so that it might initially feel as if there are no longer any hierarchies, codes, or master analysts. Actually, though, he explicates the ways that the hierarchies of the school text deny the writerly quality of the school text even as they prohibit the writing of the text, by settling meaning, determining signifieds, and closing off and denying access to the signifiers that are the raw materials of the writing text. "The vocabulary code establishes a hierarchy which announces meaning; determines access to materials for writing even as it condemns that writing" (p. 35). The act of appropriating concepts and metaphors from literature disconnected from the school text disrupts the meta-narrative. At least, it has the potential to do so. I am highly aware of the ways that this book could be perceived as irrelevant drivel by those who are reading the school text and hoping this book will be a useful tool for doing so. Reading glasses help me read. But new metaphors help me read new things differently, to write new meanings, and I value them over my treasured glasses. I agree with Block (1997) that "the discipline of school that has invented children denies the act of creation and in that denial commits an execrable act of social violence" (p. 171). To deny imagination is to deny the very act of creativity that makes the self, always becoming, possible, to perpet-uate the hate that results from the inescapable discrepancy between subjective and objective. School is structured by and about boundaries (p. 172), and this makes "writing" or "painting" a new text impossible, causing us to hate our-selves when we need to split in two between the boundaries and our thought-dreams of what is possible, what might be. Can we still create an environment where the student is constantly a creation of him or her self, where the school is the place where teachers and students write the text of school? The image requires more than thinking of reading as changing the lenses through which we see the text; it requires that we honestly read as writers. I believe the chap-ters that follow are helping me to do this. I refuse the lines of direction that move from hierarchy to teacher as delivery system, and choose the lines of flight offered by the writerly reading of the literary text, whether this text is a young adult novel, a picture book, the text of youth cultural practice, or the literary text of online communities.

Pragmatic concepts

I start with *poaching*, which indeed is the core of what I am doing. In my work I am poaching concepts and metaphors from literary texts, and bringing them back home into the world of curriculum, where they become the raw compost for teaching and learning. There are two important ideas to be taken from *currere* centered in poaching. The first is that learning may be understood as the act of poaching, a clever sort of problem-solving raised to a high art, in which one needs to take what one is entitled to in ways that require elaborate strategies and complex social relationships. The second is that learning, like poaching, must be dangerous, because, like poaching, an act vital to one's very survival has been twisted in recent history into a seemingly criminalized notion of steal-ing someone else's property. The "answer," if there is a question embedded in this situation, is not necessarily returning to earlier notions of stewardship of the land, and analogously to a romantic nostalgic conception of teaching as stewardship; what tales of poachers reveal to readers is the spark of life that has been made possible through the complications of criminalization; the danger at once raises the stakes by introducing the threat to life itself as well as requiring the complex problem-solving strategies. I find, in the end, that poaching is the essence of a vital curriculum, and in the end, of "becoming."

However, in writing my text of poaching, I have come to understand two other important ideas in refreshing ways. First, poaching helps us to understand how we may inadvertently perpetuate gendered conceptions of learning and the relationship between knowledge and self-understanding. Second, a requisite analysis of the ways that poaching manifests itself in the usual school narrative highlights the need for curriculum to think a little differently about time and space. I find that we use spatial imagery to think about, and hence establish, time in schools. Because both teachers and students poach time (because, as noted above, poaching is a vital act of life), but also, because they tend to create time in spatial ways, they lose the sanctity of time, and in the process desanctify the space of learning. What if we sanctioned poaching as the primary grounding of *currere*? Chapter 2 posits a curriculum that does just this, and therefore sanctifies time and space. Poaching is the starting point for a new world, for new lines of flight.

How, then, might we sanction poaching? One idea I suggest in Chapter 3 is to *weird* curriculum, rather than to weird the content of the curriculum, which is what I see happening more routinely in classrooms. My interrogation of curriculum as hypertext understands its origins in the rise of "attention" as a component of modernism. As the architectural historian and critical theorist Jonathan Crary (1999) comments, a great deal of critical analysis of modern subjectivity during the twentieth century dwelled on the idea of "reception in a state of distraction," as articulated by the German critical theorists of the early twentieth century. Crary elaborates on the paradoxical intersection that has permeated modernism and beyond, between an imperative of attentiveness within the disciplinary organization of labor, education, and mass communication, and a kind of ideal of sustained attentiveness as a constitutive element of a creative and free subjectivity. There is a way in which seemingly qualitatively different notions of attention, such as a "cultivated individual gazing at a work of art" and "a factory worker concentrating on the performance of a repetitive task" become examples of a purified aesthetic perception inseparable from the processes of modernism that made the "problem of attention" a central issue in new institutional constructions of a productive and manageable subjectivity. Within education, the prime objective became over the past century the art and science of gaining and holding students' attention, so that they can learn. Once their attention is attracted, the subject matter of the curriculum is expected to carry them through to the learning objectives. Yet, more recent work, such as Gloria Ladson-Billings' (1997) studies of effective teachers, shows that the most successful curriculum is enacted when teachers focus on instruction and the work at hand, rather than on management techniques such as gaining and holding attention. My reading of several series of children's books in Chapter 3 introduces my working idea that it is not so much the content that needs to be specially marked in some way in order to attract attention, but that the narrative within which the content is embedded needs to be strangely modified or oddly presented if the content is to be more successfully understood. That is, instead of weirding the content of a lesson in order to attract students' attention, we would be better off weirding the narrative of which it is a part.

As I develop my ideas about weirding and poaching, several contextual issues arise. The first is the role of perception as a metaphor for knowing and coming to know (epistemology and learning); the second is the image of the "feed" that the internet provides (the relations among consumer culture, technoculture, and identity); and the third is the complexity of understanding the dark matter of education (the unconscious) and how it interacts with the jazz of curriculum (creativity and freedom). Chapter 4 deals with the ideology of perception in educational discourse and practice, and the search for alternative analogies. We often think as if knowing or understanding is "seeing," and even if we try to use a different sense as our model, we end up relying on visual images to talk about the other senses anyway, so that in the end we reproduce the hegemony of vision. But, as Nancy Farmer's *The Ear, the Eye and the Arm* (1994) evocatively portrays, especially powerful senses do not necessarily make human beings into super-heroes. For example, a character who has super-sensitive hearing is just as much disabled by the constant noise and information pouring into his brain and distorting his perception of his surroundings as he is able to hear small whispers miles away. In other words, even if we wanted to use the image of perceptual enhancement as our metaphor for learning, we might still be wary of whether or not we are achieving our goals for our students. Given the limitations of sensual enhancement translated into education practice as prosthetic magnification, we may wish to employ alternative images and language.

M.T. Anderson's clever novel *Feed*, J.K. Rowling's highly successful *Harry Potter* series, and interviews of children about Saturday morning television left over from the days of *Cartoon Network*'s 24-hour animation offerings provide the impetus for my interrogation of consumer culture, technoculture, and identity in Chapters 5, 6, and 7. In the world of the internet literally implanted in our nervous systems, only a minor shift in my mind from what we currently experience, advertisements and information pop up in front of us at all times, whenever there is a potential association. We also hear each other inside ourselves as instant messaging becomes a simple matter of thinking what we want to say to another person, "chatting" them. Youth refer to each other as "units." Perception is destabilized by the onslaught of sights, sounds, and any other impulse or input from the internet, the "feed," even going so far as to offer website locations where one can malfunction, "go mal," and disorient perception, as a sort of drug substitute. What we are looking for, I believe, are our own "feedpacks" that allow us to coexist with the feed but not really in it, categories that not only coexist with the problematic concepts and practices, but which also subsume them in a way that displaces – literally robs them of their place. One trajectory that I associate with critical pedagogy offers three "nomadic" opportunities: youth leadership, voice, and participation in democratic institutions. Imagine teacher education and curriculum theory blurring together in the actions of youth leadership, and the evocation of voice as a characteristic of democratic participation. Instead of quibbling over the idea of "technology of vision" I problematize, or suffocating in the deluge of "commodification," "teacher/ education/curriculum/theory/practice" would use some technologies of vision, looping in and out of commodification and cultural resource work, understanding but not being confined by object relations, toward student leadership within democratic forms of institutional and community organization. Neither "selling out" nor "buying in," such a political turn can be both postmodern and the "pause that refreshes." I suggest that we embrace consumer culture, object relations, and the ideology of perception but also leave them to do what they wish while other important conceptual work is accomplished by recognition of difference, disparity, and desire (Todd 1997). These three "D"s are outcomes of events instead of causal origins of entrenched problems. In casting them as outcomes, their identification offers possibilities for coalitions and multiple levels of possibility that cut across the lines of difference and power. Rather than standpoints in a Cartesian universe, disparities are enunciations.

As a teacher I celebrate children's perceptions of their own choices of entertainment. What we may fear as negatively impacting on children I find in interviews to be something substantially different. If we use technoculture and cyborg metaphors to look at the selves of pedagogical practice, the research becomes a technology of vision which splits what is observed and analyzed into a spectrum of technoculture. In contrast, if we employ technoculture and cyborg metaphors as a mode of enunciation with which we speak and write a story of pedagogical practice, the research becomes a technology of sign systems, power and the self, and of production. This is not to say that such stories do not exist and are not rhizomatically linked in innumerable ways with the one that appears in this book. They may be more likely to be found in other spaces, and told by other characters from the story I choose to write. Nevertheless, cyborg selves become a technology of morality when they enunciate a hierarchy between knowing oneself and taking care of oneself, and this is something that I find increasingly important to think about as I work with my students. The gundam or *animé* hero surfing and breathing technoculture lunges for self-care and begins to know his or her self *through* the act of self-care, discovering self-potential and realization. The machine-self of the invisible man shuns self-care in the process of self-knowledge. The cyborg teacher is positioned in a web of possibility that presents links to any technology of vision, enunciation, self-knowledge, or self-care, and is itself in relation to such technologies imbricated in extended webs of possibility, power, signs, and production. Technoculture is a node in the web, a region of the möbius strip, a character in a saga, and in this respect becomes yet one more line of flight in *currere*. While new tools of perception can hone and extend perception, curriculum is only present in the intergenerational, which distinguishes the picaresque adventure from the educational encounter.

Dark matter, which I write about in Chapters 7 and 8, is a term I borrow from astronomy, inspired by parallel readings of Sheree Thomas' (2000) analysis of speculative fiction in the African Diaspora, Phillip Pullman's (1982) *Count Karlstein*, and Sharon Flake's (1998) *The Skin I'm In*. Theories of motion and the expansion of the universe require us to infer that most of the universe's matter does not radiate (it provides no glow or light that we can detect). In one sense, this dark matter (called dark because it is the light that is missing, not the matter) is something we might try to look for, using different tools. In another sense, it is a secret (buried) treasure that we seek to find.

In yet another sense, such dark matter may be hypothesized by us as an aid in avoiding something else that we don't want to think about. The secret treasure of learning is always present in the educational discourse. What is the key to unlocking learning? When does it happen? How can we find it? Perhaps this secret treasure is of that latter form, a kind of dark matter that we can't find because in our search for it we no longer have to think about other things that we would rather keep in the dark. Often, people need to use various forms of "defense" to help maintain our unawareness of disturbing thoughts or feelings. Ego-defense, which I claim this is related to, is concerned with the emotional logic of dependency grounded in the social fact that early life requires care to survive, and the authority of the Other in order to learn. Because of this connection, I use Chapters 7 and 8 to think about how we develop skills of meaning-making through the use of objects (things, people) in our environment from those beginning moments of life. Things and actions get identified with meanings and become symbols. The problem of this human condition for educators, writes Deborah Britzman (2006), concerns how we may encounter the spurious nature of identifications as also defying literal correspondence, causality, or even – to come full circle with the quest for a new science of *currere* – any explanatory power. My reading of two books by Chris Raschka, *Charlie Parker Played Be-Bop* (1992), and *Mysterious Thelonius* (1997), along with a third, *The Skin I'm In*, by Sharon Flake, leads me to the conclusion that each student is a collection of potential futures that carry with them the trace of their signs into a design process. At the heart of the design process is the shift from thrownness to using the material and tools at hand to do something that one can positively value: the good designer does not deny constraints, nor does she allow herself to be trapped or paralyzed by them; instead, she finds a new way of looking at them, a new language that shows the possibilities for response, i.e., for design.

Finally, I take the discourse of weirding and poaching into a discussion of my daily work, sharing the ideas that have developed in my collaboration with my Arcadia colleague, Leif Gustavson. By studying the ways in which youth work in their everyday lives, we have looked with our students for classroom structures that encourage youth to use these same practices and ways of working in school. The goal is to translate the habits of mind and body that enable students to be proficient in crafts outside of school into the school experiences, so that the same habits of mind and body can become part of their life in school. At the same time, even as we celebrate youth cultural practices, we can both recognize those habits that are shared with practitioners of disciplinary ways of working, refine them, and contribute new skills and techniques to students' ways of working outside of school. We have developed an effective *infrastructure* that enables our student teachers to learn about the ways in which their students work creatively on their own, and to bring those ways of working into the classroom experience. They then juxtapose such creative practices with ways of working as a mathematician and writer, to introduce criteria that promote youth application of creative practices as forms of engagement with the school curriculum, and to document how the students are meeting performance objectives. In the process, I believe, we sanction poaching, weird curriculum, and support improvising by students and teachers, while also enabling teachers to make decisions based on concepts such as identification with the aggressor, the feed, and dark matter. I do not mean this chapter as "an answer" to the question, "What should I do?" or, "What is the right way to teach?" but as an illustration of how the *currere* of reading children's literature as curriculum theory texts is for me inherently practical.

As curriculum theorist Dwayne Huebner (1999) noted, the task of curriculum theorizing includes laying bear the structure of being-in-the-world and articulating this structure through the language and environmental forms one creates. We can take seriously Huebner's notion that the descriptive and controlling functions of language are significant vehicles for developing and introducing new conditions into the environment. There are, I presume, numerous ways to do this. No "method" should or could be prescribed. Grossberg's one rule – defy the lure of the transcendent, and don't let anything stop you – is accomplished by seeking, in curriculum scholar Ted Aoki's (2005) words, "curriculum in a new key," in yet another scholar of curriculum, Marla Morris' words (2004), the rule is approached through heretically continuing to rethink and redo one's "(un)frames of reference" (p. 83); and the rule requires Huebner's notion of a "new language." In this book, such a new language led to startlingly different forms of classroom organization, growing simply out of the reading of youth culture texts and children's literature as curriculum theory.

2
Poaching*

The elevator in Raubinger Hall is very slow. Everyone is always waiting, waiting. Will it come? Why does it take so long between each floor? More than anything else in my work these days, this elevator dominates almost every experience. If it's not just slow, but out of service, I will have to trudge up and down two flights of stairs lugging a cartload of manipulatives to each class. If it's merely taking its time again, I'll spend several minutes complaining with the rest, sharing impatience and anger. I find myself repeating advice that I heard back when I was an undergraduate music major; then, too, there was a frustratingly slow elevator. Alvin Lucier, a professor and composer, would wait with us and suggest that we celebrate our technology: accept this treasure that the elevator gives us, of time. Time to relax, to think, to not have to be doing anything else but waiting and then riding the elevator. The elevator experience was a musical composition, a pattern of pauses and movements in time and space. A delicious opportunity to experience. So now I find myself talking to students I have not yet met, other faculty racing late to class on the third floor: take this treasure, I say; enjoy this moment in time. We're all crazed with speed and things we have to do, but here we have something that we can take as ours, a time away from all else and all the demands of others that encroach on our peace, a time that is only for us. By taking the elevator in this way, it is no longer an eternal wait; it is a moment that we cherish.

Some years after that music phase of my life, as I was a graduate student in mathematics searching for meaning and purpose in my efforts and life's work, I had possibly my first and only genuinely religious experience. Reading Abraham Joshua Heschel's *The Sabbath*, I was not only reading about the Sabbath as a place in time, as a treasure waiting for me to seize and enjoy, but I was transported to another space thoroughly removed from my everyday life's thrills, fears, and obligations. We seem to need these kinds of oases these

---

*The original version of this chapter appeared in Donna Truiet *et al.* (eds.), *The Internationalization of Curriculum Studies*. New York: Peter Lang, 2003.

days. Indeed, many educators have suggested that schools can and should be such oases from the ennui or violence of everyday life (Greene 1982).

Heschel offers us the Sabbath, and many people do find that this place in time serves a unique purpose, while others pursue meditation, aerobic exercise, and so on. The interesting thing about these "treasures" is that they are not gifts or possessions: they are unowned objects waiting to be seized. And it is not enough just to take them. It takes a lot of effort to find them, even though they are there always to be seized. And we must put in an enormous amount of effort in order to seize them. It is as if something is holding us back, as if we are always acting not to find them, until we do; and then we know they were always there. Looking back, it was not the Sabbath that I took, but Heschel's beautiful meditation on the Sabbath. The Sabbath is not something we receive as a gift but something we must pursue as a treasure. Heschel's book is the treasure I possess, and I "own" the experience of reading this book; the Sabbath itself is something that must be embraced on my own through my own efforts.

This issue of "property," and of the need for serious labor in order for property to be recognized as owned, is deeply entrenched in Ameroeuro culture. And the idea that it is the basis for education has a long tradition as well. Rousseau (1979) recognized this for his education of *Emile*. For Emile to be happy, he must learn over time that "the best way to provide oneself with the things one lacks is to give up those that one has" (p. 81). Early in life, writes Rousseau, a child reaches out toward objects. A child is stretching "his" hand well before "he" can say anything, not yet comprehending the distance. At first, the lack of comprehension is like an error of judgment.

But when he complains and screams in reaching out his hand, he is no longer deceived as to the distance; he is ordering the object to approach or you to bring it to him. In the first case, carry him to the object slowly or with small steps. In the second, act as though you do not even hear him. The more he screams, the less you should listen to him (p. 66).

In this parable of the object, Rousseau asks us to recognize the essential link between the labor of seizing objects and the ownership of the object. He believes it is important to accustom a child not to give orders either to people (to establish a taboo against owning people as objects to seize) or to things (for things cannot hear, can only be taken by one's own serious efforts).

Thus, when a child desires something that he sees and one wants to give it to him, it is better to carry the child to the object than to bring the object to the child. He draws from this practice a conclusion appropriate to his age, and there is no other means to suggest it to him (p. 66).

Hence my theoretical leap that a teacher should never give the knowledge and skills to a student as a gift. If school is a place in time, then this place cannot be owned in this way unless it is taken as such an object. We can carry children to the space, but they themselves must take it. It turns out in the end that it was always there, and that we just did not see it yet. But it is in another real sense only there when we take it.

In my family these days, the Sabbath occasionally takes on this role. More routinely, however, our "Sabbath" is found in the evening ritual of reading before bedtime. We read every night with both of our children, Noah, almost 11, and Sophia, who is 6. We have been reading for as long as I can remember. This is not bedtime reading, although it may have started out that way, and it does continue to be part of a slow winding down toward going to sleep. Rather, it is a time outside of time. All four of us are all together, in one bed, and we take turns reading a book ostensibly for one child and then the other. All four of us read and listen to all of the reading together. As parents, we bring our children and ourselves to the reading. Each of us on our own, however, must "take" the reading for ourselves; it is at this point that the reading is there.

Rousseau does not share our enthusiasm for reading together. He warns that it is the "companion of his games" (p. 159) that the child approaches. It is instead the "severe and angry man" who takes him by the hand, speaks gravely, and takes him away into a room of books.

> What sad furnishings for his age! The poor child lets himself be pulled along, turns a regretful eye on all that surrounds him, becomes silent, and leaves, his eyes swollen with tears he does not dare shed, and his heart great with sighs he does not dare to breathe.
>
> (p. 159)

But perhaps he thinks we parents are trying to teach a love of books, rather than merely allowing the books to be taken together, as Rousseau and Emile are together, "never depend[ing] on one another, but [always agreeing]" (p. 159). He warns us that "Our didactic and pedantic craze is always to teach children what they would learn much better by themselves and to forget what we alone could teach them" (p. 79). In this spirit our reading books is one of our games, our love of books is what we parents alone could teach our children about who we are.

But what can the child learn about herself? What is hers and hers alone? Rousseau notes for us how difficult this is, because so very little of what is around a child genuinely belongs to the child. A child cannot understand her clothing, her furniture, her toys, as property in the sense that Rousseau means, because she cannot fully comprehend how they came to be clothing, furniture, toys, or how they came to be "hers." To say that they were given to her, and that is why they are hers, is no better, since in order to give, one must already have; besides, a gift is a form of convention, something only learned through years of enculturation. Property is thus something exterior or anterior to a child.

Therefore Emile, and all children by extension, need to learn about property. Emile is encouraged to see himself in the garden he has created. He has taken possession of the earth by planting a bean, by returning every day to care for his garden, by investing his time and labor, his effort, finally his person there. "There is in this earth something of himself that he can claim against anyone whomsoever, just as he could withdraw his arm from the hand of another man who wanted to hold onto it in spite of him" (p. 98).

> One fine day he arrives eagerly with the watering can in his hand. Oh what a sight! Oh pain! All the beans are rooted out, the plot is torn up, the very spot is not to be recognized. Oh, what has become of my labor, my product, the sweet fruit of my care and my sweat? Who has stolen my goods? Who took my beans from me? This young heart is aroused. The first sentiment of injustice comes to shed its sad bitterness in it. Tears flow streams. The grieving child fills the air with moans and cries. I partake of his pain, his indignation. We look; we investigate; we make searches.
>
> (p. 99)

It turns out that the gardener did it! But he, too, is furious. He had planted his melons on this land, had come back after investing labor and time to see his melon patch ripped asunder and some beans there instead. This was his property, and should not have been taken by anyone else. "In this model of the way of inculcating primary notions in children one sees how the idea of property naturally goes back to the right of first occupancy by labor" (p. 99).

I want to tie all of this together. On the one hand, something is ours when we take it through labor and not when it is given to us. This is what constructivists mean when they say that learners need to construct their own knowledge. A child takes objects, both physical and symbolic, and in the process takes ownership of these objects; at the moment of taking, the child owns knowledge that has always been there but was not "real" to her before the taking. On the other hand, the very place in which such labor unfolds is not a place of learning until it is taken as such. This is what Herb Kohl (1991) means when he writes about the role of assent in learning. A student is not *in* school until the moment in which she takes a place *at* school. When an adult and a child together take a place as theirs, danger lurks in the adult's first occupancy by labor. The property belongs to the adult.

Rousseau negotiates a deal for Emile. He can work the land as "his" garden in return for sharing half of the produce with the farmer, but more importantly for making sure that he respects the farmer's labor and thus ownership of the melon crop. He must set aside his garden in a space not yet worked by the farmer. The labor in the taking of the land is, in the end, more important than the right of first occupancy. And it is upon this principle that modern pedagogy is based. As long as the child labors herself, we trust that she can take possession of knowledge. Still, we come back to the notion that the earth is not a garden until one takes it as a place in which to make a garden. Just as Emile gets the idea for taking a space as a potential garden from noticing farmers already working the soil around him, so do we hope that our students will get the idea of taking a place as school by watching others. Here is the principle that guides all barriers to modern pedagogy. What happens if Emile never thinks it interesting that farmers are doing all this plowing and sowing and watering and harvesting? What happens if a child does not take school as a place for learning?

In our nightly reading at home there is no such issue, I believe. This is because we are in a place where people do not "not take" "sitting around with books and decoding the words and talking about what they mean" as reading. Now this reading is not always the object that I describe above. Sometimes we are merely going through the motions, and this special place in time is lost, we can't find it anymore. But at other times we know it is there, and it has always been there. There are special books that have been the focus of these times, maybe because of their specialness or maybe because of what we came to the reading with at that time. It will be hard to know why they are special. However, I can recall two books that seemed to resonate particularly well, and also seem – probably without randomness – to speak to the issue of property and ownership and, in the end, how our relationship with the taking of objects is intimately bound with who we are and how we learn. They speak as well to the issue of losing that place and finding our way back, our way back home.

For Sophia and me, the book is Roald Dahl's (1982) *The BFG*, a story about a little girl named, coincidentally, Sophie, who meets a big, friendly giant, and how they together save the world from bigger, evil giants and make it possible for all the boys and girls to have beautiful dreams. For Noah and me, the book is another work by Dahl (1975) that includes a cameo appearance by the BFG, *Danny, the Champion of the World*. In this book, a boy named Danny finds out that his wonderful father is even sparkier than he thought when he learns about the beauty of poaching that he can share with him. Of course I believe these books are about more than these brief descriptions. They are first of all about my relationship with my children. How Sophia loved to listen to me reading *The BFG*; how the BFG may or may not caricature a father, every girl's big, friendly giant who towers over her and frightens her at first, but quickly comes to be known as a protector against scarier, more menacing giants, and then to be the provider of all good dreams. How Noah didn't want me to stop reading *Danny, the Champion of the World*, and I, in cahoots, stayed up with him past midnight (on a school night!) to finish it; how the father in the story fulfilled his destiny as teacher for his son according to Rousseau's prescription (this one didn't hire out a *philosophe* like Jean-Jacques, relishing his own responsibilities); how my son read the last page, that every boy deserves a father who is sparky, and then declared, "Like my dad's sparky!" How poaching is not the violation of labor Emile learned from Rousseau, but instead an essential challenge of life requiring careful and skillful planning, analysis, and problem-solving skills; how poaching is in fact the "spark" of life.

We need to unpack a lot of what these books are about, including the problematic gendering of these images, of the role of girls and boys and who does the poaching, who is the listener, and who the actor. For now, I want to ask, what is it that enables us to read Dahl as a shift in our taking of poaching? As Alan Block (1999) has written, "The space – seemingly an objective locus – itself has been redefined by the entrance into it by someone whose action changes the potentialities of the space" (p. 23). Block quotes the Mishnah: "If one sees an ownerless object and falls upon it. and another person comes and seizes it, he who has seized it is entitled to its possession." The landowner in Danny's world takes some pheasants as his own; Danny, his father, and it turns out almost everybody in town, lay claim to these pheasants because they come along and seize them. Hadn't Emile's farmer earned his garden by seizing the land, working it with his labor? Danny, our modern Emile, lives in a place where the landowners no longer work their land but merely fall upon it. Danny's (and our) classed society understands poaching in a new light. The Mishnah, according to Block, had it right all along: a field may not acquire absolutely for the owner; what is left must be considered unowned and so findable, available for the taking. Gleaning is what Danny does, and in gleaning he avoids the plight of the sharecropper Emile, who no longer owns half of what he makes.

Sophie, too, is a new kind of poacher. Her name, synonymous with Emile's lover, the everywoman for Rousseau, evokes true wisdom – (Just this year, my Sophia noted in her "Proud to Be Me" book that she's "special" "because my name means wisdom") – and genders this wisdom in its juxtaposition with Danny, the new Emile. She's the companion for the BFG, poacher and giver of beautiful dreams.

Reading poaching

Ordinary usage of the word "poaching" carries a bad connotation. Crafty thieves who have no respect for wildlife, poachers are typically represented as disregarding licensing fees, ignoring wildlife and its habitat, and thieving for profit or ego (National Anti-Poaching Foundation). Law enforcement agencies go to elaborate lengths to capture poachers (Tisch 1997; Bartz 1999). Yet beneath the rhetoric of sportsmen as the true conservationists and poachers as destructive criminals lurks a romantic intrigue of squirrelly, outrageously clever artists of camouflage, deception, and ingenuity.

"I've seen animals stuffed in hubcaps – turkey breasts, stuff like that," said Jeff Babauta, a wildlife officer with the Florida Game and Fresh Water Fish Commission (GFC). "I've found hogs and deer underneath the hoods" (Tisch 1997).

It is this romantic aspect of poaching that Michel De Certeau (1984) captured in *The Practice of Everyday Life*:

Far from being writer-founders of their own place, heirs of the peasants of earlier ages now working on the soil of language, diggers of wells and builders of houses – readers are travellers; they move across lands belonging to someone else, like nomads poaching their way across fields they did not write, despoiling the wealth of Egypt to enjoy it themselves.

(De Certeau 1984: 174)

When Sophia, Noah, Belinda, and I are reading together, suggests De Certeau, we are "not here or there, one or the other, but neither the one nor the other, simultaneously inside and outside, dissolving both by mixing them together, associating texts like funerary statues" that we awaken and host, but never own. Far removed from the bricolage of constructivism, welding conceptual bridges and monuments to our masters, we poachers – crafty as ever – take ownership of things that have been withheld and locked away in others' fields and forests; we carry these things to new places, new contexts.

In *Danny, Champion of the World*, nasty Mr. Hazell stocks his woods with pheasants in preparation for hosting a fancy hunting party for his rich, important friends. As a single parent, Danny's father hasn't gone poaching for years, staying home with his son instead. But one day, the yearning is too great and he walks the six and a half miles to Hazell's wood.

"I have decided something," he said. "I am going to let you in on the deepest, darkest secret of my whole life."
"Do you know what is meant by poaching?"
"Poaching? Not really, no."
"It means going up into the woods in the dead of night and coming back with something for the pot. Poachers in other places poach all sorts of different things, but around here it's always pheasants."
"You mean stealing them?" I said, aghast.
"We don't look at it that way," my father said. "Poaching is an art. A great poacher is a great artist."
"Is that actually what you were doing in Hazell's wood, dad? Poaching pheasants?"
"I was practicing the art," he said. "The art of poaching."

(Dahl 1975: 28–29)

Granddad was a "splendiferous" poacher who "studied poaching the way a scientist studies science" (p. 33). Back in those days, people poached not only because they loved the sport but because they needed food for their families. "There was very little work to be had anywhere, and some families were literally starving. Yet a few miles away in the rich man's wood, thousands of pheasants were being fed like kings twice a day" (p. 30). But to say that people poach for food is to miss the point. "Poaching is such a fabulous and exciting sport that once you start doing it, it gets into your blood and you can't give it up."

A thief would go into the woods with a gun, shoot some pheasants, and drag them home. A poacher practices elaborate schemes, perfecting strategies and techniques for months and years, experimenting on roosters and calculating the interests and fears of the pheasants themselves. Danny's father inherited a number of these intricately developed secrets from his own dad. The "horsehair stopper" is completely silent.

> There's no squawking or flapping around or anything else with The Horsehair Stopper when the pheasant is caught. And that's mighty important because don't forget, Danny, when you're up in those woods at night and the great trees are spreading their branches high above you like black ghosts, it is so silent you can hear a mouse moving. And somewhere among it all, the keepers are waiting and listening. They're always there, those keepers, standing strong stony still against a tree or behind a bush with their guns at the ready.
>
> (Dahl 1975: 35)

We'll come back to this image of the "keepers," like the real thieves with their guns, working for Mr. Hazell, and ask who or what the keepers might represent for education and reading. For now, though, let's stick to the elaborate art of poaching:

> "What happens with The Horsehair Stopper?" I asked. "How does it work?"
>
> "It's very simple," he said. "First, you take a few raisins and you soak them in water overnight to make them plump and soft and juicy. Then you get a bit of good stiff horsehair and you cut it up into half-inch lengths"
>
> "Here's what my dad discovered," he said. "First of all, the horsehair makes the raisin stick in the pheasant's throat. It doesn't hurt him. It simply stays there and tickles. It's rather like having a crumb stuck in your own throat. But after that, believe it or not, the pheasant never moves his feet again! He becomes absolutely rooted to the spot, and there he stands pumping his silly neck up and down just like a piston, and all you've got to do is nip out quickly from the place where you've been hiding and pick him up."
>
> "Is that true, dad?"
>
> "I swear it," my father said. "Once a pheasant's had The Horsehair Stopper, you can turn a hosepipe on him and he won't move. It's just one of those unexplainable little things. But it takes a genius to discover it."

My father paused, and there was a gleam of pride in his eyes as he dwelt for a moment upon the memory of his dad, the great poaching inventor.

This wasn't even the technique Danny's dad had used that evening, having chosen The Sticky Hat instead. Laying a trail of raisins to a little paper hat in a small depression in the ground, he smeared it with glue and filled the hat with more raisins. The old pheasant was supposed to come along, pop his head inside to gobble up the raisins, and the next thing find a hat over his eyes, so that he can't see a thing. Here too the pheasant will not move and can be gently collected on the way out of the woods. As with any art it takes practice, and this night, the first in many years, Danny's dad was out of practice.

A bricoleur is given a toolbox out of which she fashions new uses for the tools. Schools drill us in skills and intellectual tools, hoping that one day a few of us may use them in new ways. Instead, most of us leave disaffected, yet master our bricolage in the realm of popular and consumer culture (Fiske 1989b; Appelbaum 1995b); like the affichist artists of the 1920s, we scavenge the worthless trash of popular capital, and retool our clothes and images to meet the crises of our culture. We buy things to make a statement, and use these things we buy to make new statements. What would our lives be like if schools were places that foster poaching? There is no buying and selling, no consumer culture. Students would take as theirs the knowledge and skills that adults are immorally safeguarding for their own pleasures. Instead of waiting around for small gestures of generosity, waiting for paralleled gifts of knowledge, students would be refining and extending their crafts of poaching, of taking as their own these knowledges and skills.

Indeed, people are poachers. Poaching makes life "sparky." The keepers of knowledge protect that knowledge from students as Mr. Hazell's keepers guard his pheasants. And those keepers hide this knowledge so that it's hard to find; like the pheasants who disappear into the trees after twilight, knowledge in the classroom is made invisible by the rules and regulations of the school, the curriculum standards, and school expectations. Students and teachers play elaborate, intricate games in order to poach a place in these classrooms, and the playing out of these games becomes the fun of being there, indeed becomes the "real" curriculum of the school. Resistance theorists have presented a less optimistic view of these games. Here I offer a potentially more positive interpretation of resistance as poaching. The basic idea is that the treasure cannot be given to another person, because it is in the taking of that treasure that the spark is found, in the poaching that the meaning of the encounter is manifested.

A generous teacher tells students what they need to know. Then they know. Is it surprising if the students mock or dismiss what the teacher offers? Is it surprising if the child does not take what the teacher offers? If the child cannot take what the teacher offers? Danny learns that Mr. Hazell's token generosity is unwanted, because with it comes disrespect and physical threats. There is no need to serve him at the filling station despite the family's plight of poverty. Rather than take his money, Danny and his dad will take the pheasants he so unjustly keeps in his wood. They will take the pheasants Mr. Hazell is fattening up for entertainment and use them for a good purpose. In the process, however, the purpose is immediately transformed away from stealing or redistribution of resources toward the art of poaching itself, the process and method as opposed to the result. It is like the difference between "fandom" (Jenkins 1988) and "social activism." Fans buy mass culture products and may even reclaim in a bricolage the shards of popular culture, salvaging pieces of found material in making sense of their own social experience. In fandom, marginalized subgroups of a culture reread texts and rewrite texts in ways that pry open spaces for (women's, gay, bisexual) voices. Fans often cast themselves as loyalists, rescuing essential elements of the primary texts misused by those "keepers" who police the copyrights. Social activists, on the other hand, trespass the terrains of consumer culture and its keepers, not to reassert a fundamental truth or pre-existing nostalgia, but to glean what can be taken for parallel purposes.

We know that Danny attends school. Indeed, his father walks him all the way to town to get there (two miles each way). Yet it is Dad who is Danny's teacher. By the age of 8 he is a master mechanic. Now it is the walk to school that is Danny's real education, a time for looking and talking and learning about nature, and now, planning an extensive new method of poaching pheasants. Until now, Danny gleaned from the fields along the road things to take and study, he asked questions, and his father answered. Now he asks questions for which nobody knows the answer ("Why does the skylark make its nest on the ground where the cow can trample it?"), and this only peeks his interest even more. His questions have assumed a new role now that he has taken on the aura and excitement of a poacher. Before Dad let Danny in on poaching, he merely led his son to places of freedom where unowned objects could be seized. This alone made Danny's education special in its possibilities. But now there is the pleasure of the game: Danny can't just seize; he has to come up with a clever way to do it without being caught. It is Danny who comes up with a really big plan for poaching a really big number of Mr. Hazell's pheasants in a really great way.

Boys and girls

In *The BFG*, it is Sophie who comes up with the big plan, after her surprising initiation into something that might be poaching. But for Sophie, it is a big, friendly giant, not her dad, who carries her off into her new state of awareness. This BFG spends his days catching dreams and bottling them up. At night he blows them into the heads of sleeping boys and girls. We met the

BFG before, in a bedtime story Danny's Dad told as they were going to sleep in the old caravan behind the filling station. There was no Sophie in that version, but of course Danny didn't know her. Here we learn that the BFG enters a silent twilight very much like Hazell's wood: swirling mist and ghostly vapors: "It was ashy grey. There was no sign of a living creature and no sound at all except for the soft thud of the BFG's footsteps as he hurtled on through the fog" (p. 80). The BFG, too, has mastered the art of poaching. He waits quietly, a long net in his right hand. His colossal ears swivel out from his head and gently wave to and fro.

Suddenly the BFG pounced. He leaped high in the air and swung the net through the mist with a great swishing sweep of his arm. "Got him!" he cried. "A jar! A jar! Quick quick quick!"

He catches both the good dreams, the "winksquifflers," and the bad ones, "frightsome trogglehumpers," the former to give to someone, the latter to bottle up so that nobody will ever have them. The difference between these dreams and Mr. Hazell's pheasants, however, is that nobody is keeping these dreams from the BFG; he keeps them for the children. Sophie is not capable of catching dreams, and she never learns how. This really isn't poaching, and Sophie is not an initiated comrade. She's merely a companion. Unlike Danny, who asks more and more questions, and finds an increasingly Sparkier life with Father, Sophie is constantly confronted with her narrow-minded presumptions as a "human bean," and her need to practice polite acceptance. But her destiny is not a Sparky life. She has the loftier role of helping the BFG save all humanity from other giants, the ones who aren't friendly. Sophie gets him to mix up a special dream for the Queen of England, a dream designed to help Her Majesty understand what's behind the large numbers of missing children. She can talk to scary giants and queens, and she knows how they think. She is pleasant and inoffensive and can talk about anything; she is an effective go-between for those who act, even as she helps to define their actions. Like Rousseau's Sophie – and I claim the common name is no accident – this one wields power through her femininity, manipulating the big, friendly giants (men) behind the scenes, and accomplishing her work through them, using their brute powers and public images. She is a poacher of male public power in this respect, but not a public male. The BFG is likable while Mr. Hazell is not. The BFG is his own keeper and he is generous with his dreams, unlike mean Mr. Hazell, hoarding pheasants for the big showy shoot. The irony is that mean Mr. Hazell makes it possible for poaching to exist, whereas the benevolent BFG, doling out the right dreams and locking away the bad ones, winds up being the creepier of the two. Docile folks need to poach, and do not ever learn what they are missing. And who provides the oversight for the BFG? Who decides which dreams are winksquifflers, and which are trogglehumpers?

Sophie's world and Danny's world are not the same. Yet they share the

BFG. In both worlds, dreams are not constructed out of objects related to one's life. Dreams for these children are not the result of poaching but are breathed in as they sleep; dreams are gifts from a benevolent giant. What a creepy image! And this image is not at all the stuff of good dreams that I bring with me from my reading of Winnicott; dreams should be the creative use of objects to evoke the self (Winnicott 1984: 95). It seems that dreaming as poaching is a critical piece of the life project, and this lovable BFG has taken that project away.

The child who can manage dreams is becoming ready for all kinds of playing, either alone or with other children (p. 60).

"It is in the use of objects," writes Alan Block (1995), "that playing occurs; it is in playing that creativity is realized" (p. 23). Block, too, quotes Winnicott (1971: 101): "Every object is a 'found' object. Given the chance, the [child] begins to live creatively, and to use actual objects to be creative into and with."

Block (1995: 59) again: "The child must be able to use the dream creatively; it must be available for play."

Sophie loves the BFG "as she would a father" (Dahl 1982: 207). This "father" is the keeper of dreams, her dreams, and, since she cannot poach dreams, she cannot evoke a self. In the end she teaches the BFG to write not only stories but the story of her life from the beginning: she herself, in a grand twist of irony, is merely the dream of the BFG, as we see on the very last page:

> But where, you might ask, is this book that the BFG wrote?
> It's right here. You've just finished reading it.
>
> (Dahl 1982: 208)

But of course! We knew from the beginning that the BFG poached Sophie. He plucked her out of bed through the window and used her to dream his own new life.

Danny has a different fate. The specter of the BFG haunts his dreams too. Luckily, however, he has learned the practical, poaching art of play. He is therefore able to write his own life. "It is not play to do with the object what it has been ordered to do; rather playing is to do with the object what we will because it is available for use" (Block 1995: 60). This is poaching. This is Danny's life experience. "The power to endow our world with our dreams is creativity. Our action creates the world, and then it is our world and not that of common sense" (Block 1995: 170). We leave Danny and his Dad, two poachers together, in the middle of their dreams, and we know, with Danny – the narrator of his own life story – that, after they buy just two knives and two forks, they will buy two more of each.

> And after that,
> We would walk home again and make up some sandwiches for our lunch.

And after that, we would set off with the sandwiches in our packets, striding up over Cobbler's Hill and down the other side to the small wood of larch trees that had the stream running through it.
And after that?
Perhaps a big rainbow trout.
And after that?
There would be something else after that.
And after that?
Ah, yes, and something else again.

(Dahl 1975: 204–205)

Everything is in place: I just know that Danny grows up to marry Sophie, exactly like Emile and Rousseau's Sophie. The poacher writes his life as a tribute to his Dad. The daughter's life is written by her big, friendly giant.

Should we try, as others have done using different terms in different contexts, to just say that poaching can and must be practiced as an art, studied as a science, by both boys and girls? This is first-stage feminism: poaching the male public presence. And it is not enough. It is little better for Sophie to live the BFG's dreams than it was to have him give her her dreams. It is crucial that her life story stopped, was arrested at this young age, before she could learn that what she dreams will change the world. She does not yet learn from her dreams. Only when she poaches to dream – what Danny has been given the opportunity to do all of his life – when she dreams as opposed to breathing in the BFG's dreams, will she evoke her self?

Time

At its best, our family reading is a place in which we each dream. It is a place in time during which we craftily take what is being kept by the keepers as our own, and in doing so evoke our selves. And when we're done with this book? We'll read another book. And after that some other one. And yes, something else again. As I said, this is our Sabbath in our secular life. Why should the keepers of the Sabbath guard it for the traditionally observant Jew? We've poached it. And in it we poach our dreams.

But we have a lot of work to do if we are to take this into the schools, if we are to explicate more carefully what it means to poach as a learner. Who, exactly, are the keepers? The adults? Do we paint school as children ingenuously strategizing ways to poach the knowledge that adults guard from them to no purpose? This indeed is the life project of children. We are always keeping things from them: she's not ready for this; he's not going to understand this. And in the end our most cherished treasures – our anxieties, our phobias, our prejudices, and hubris – are taken to new places to be used in new ways.

Poaching opportunities have been reduced to resistance in our schools, telescoped into the poaching of space, turning time into an object that can be given or taken. Teachers and students take sick days, leave early, arrive late. Students devise elaborate schemes for seizing school as a place in which they evoke their selves: they pass notes, plan their weekend, disseminate important information (where and when certain drugs are on sale, whether or not a hallway will be safe from violence after school…). Students and teachers perform, take the stage to be seen possessing the space: they become a person when they have taken the space. It is in the playing that the creative use of objects occurs. It is not enough to just release all control, to remove the keepers. In the end, we need to sanction the playing around the rules and regulations.

What all of these have in common is that they move away from people jockeying for space toward the possibility of poaching time. We know from Danny's book that you cannot just poach at any time of the day. One must wait for twilight, when the keepers will have a hard time seeing you, but the pheasants are still on the ground and poachable. Even trout must be poached at a certain time – in the morning, when they are visible but still asleep, is the carefully developed time for tickling them so that they can be seized. Poaching is not just taking things; it is playing, developing elaborate games for seizing things that are guarded and protected. But poaching is not just playing to poach what the keepers are guarding; it is doing this at the time that poaching is possible; it is the waiting for this time, and then taking it. I don't just use the elevator in Raubinger Hall: I anticipate the elevator ride in my car on the way to campus, as I walk from my parking space to Raubinger, as I push the button and still don't know how long I will have to wait. I can't just go to the elevator and ride it for fun: the slowness of the elevator must be important at the time I am racing to class, at the time when I am planning my busy day at the office, at the moment when I want to hold time in my grasp as a thing in space. It is just when I am wanting to take time as my own thing, to spend it as I wish, that this treasure can be embraced. The ride is a treasure at this moment, when I can take it as a thing in time.

To gain control of the world of space is certainly one of our tasks. The danger begins when in gaining power in the realm of space we forfeit all aspirations in the realm of time. There is a realm of time where the goal is not the "have" but to "be," not to own but to give, not to control but to share, not to subdue but to be in accord. Life goes wrong when the control of space, the acquisition of things of space, becomes our sole concern (Heschel 1951: 3).

And this is a lot of what is wrong with many of the schools I work in. "Reality to us is a thinghood, consisting of substances that occupy space" (Heschel 1951: 5). Blind to "all reality that fails to identify itself as a thing, as a matter of fact," we build school as a place in space, and knowledge as things to collect, receive, stick together. We don't see "time, which being thingless and insubstantial, appears to us as if it had no reality." Instead we are always grasping at time as a thing to have. We say, if only I had more time. There's not enough time for that. That kind of education, in which I let kids seize what Block calls "un-owned objects," and in which they choose these objects in the way that they themselves choose, takes "too much time." There's not enough time in the day, in the year, to cover all the things I am supposed to cover: we cover, we keep these things hidden because we can't grab time.

But we also say that this taking of "un-owned objects" is the stuff of creativity, the stuff of dreams, the evocation of self. Creativity is both playing and a realm of time. We should not go to school but wait for, anticipate, and cherish the time of school, regardless of where it is in space: it is a realm of time. Poaching is about time. It is not about getting the pheasants but about doing it in the "best" way, the cleverest way, and doing it without getting caught. "When looking at space," writes Heschel, "we see the products of creation" (1951: 100). This is why we think school is about the products. This is why we list objectives to catch and collect. Heschel continues: "when intuiting time we hear the process of creation."

A new Sophia, a school of time

So after four years of classroom research in which I had to continually throw over what I thought I had known about gender, in walks Sophia, who, with the help of her friends, lays down a new layer of complexity to the subject. In effect, Sophia enters and claims territory for herself. She prevents me from making the issue of what it means to be a girl in a primary classroom in any way static. She throws in my face what I thought I had known about girls in public. She reclaims the territory of her social world as unique aboriginal territory, and my place as a tribal member alters once again as I am forced to consider how our lives and our awareness of the world do and don't match.

(Gallas 1998: 146–147)

Another Sophia? This is no coincidence that Karen Gallas has brought to our attention. This Sophia is a poacher, not a woman educated for a male poacher. Where did she come from, and why is this teacher able to find her? I believe Karen Gallas can write about her because Gallas' classroom is a place where children can poach. It is a place where the teacher is not so sure that she can give anything to her children; a place where the teacher knows that children need to take things from those who keep the stuff of meaning and learning and use it for themselves.

As the years progressed, my concept of "teaching well" altered and good teaching became more than believing that I was covering important curricula and that children were mastering subject matter. I wondered what was the most important part of my work. Was it to get the content across, or to get out of the way of the very serious work that children do below the surface?

(Gallas 1998: 2)

Gallas writes:

> The classroom is like perishable art. It has an evanescence that makes it, for me at least, energizing and joyful, but also bittersweet, because the events are impossible to hold in time as a complete entity. Being a teacher researcher, however, has given me some capacity to grab onto fragments of the life that is streaming by me.
>
> (Gallas 1998: 146)

Here she is beginning to articulate the problems that emerge when we think that time is evanescence, temporality. Heschel tells us that the fact of evanescence flashes upon us when we pore over things of space. But it is the world of space, he writes, that communicates to us a sense of temporality. Time is everlasting, as it is beyond and independent of space: it is a space that is perishable. I learn from Heschel that things perish in time, whereas time itself does not change. Instead of coveting cultural capital, things in space that I can collect and hoard to be spent in the market of space, I should covet the things of time (p. 90).

We cannot solve the problem of time through the conquest of space, through either pyramids or fame. We can only solve the problem of time through sanctification of time (p. 101).

So if we could sanction poaching in school, we would sanctify time. We could say: these are the rules. Now, how do you want to get these things of space? You have to do it cleverly, and you may not get caught. The cleverer the better. Watch out! It's dangerous. You could get shot from behind, peppered in the legs at 50 yards, like Danny's Granddad.

> "You could go to prison for poaching," my father said.
> There was a glint and a sparkle in his eyes now that I had not seen before.
>
> (Dahl 1975: 31)

And be careful: There will be traps set to catch you: if you are out of practice you may wind up like Danny's Dad, with a broken foot at the bottom of a deep, dark hole. But, if poaching is sanctioned, the poacher feels as if she is champion of the world, and she will never have to fear giants among the giants coming to eat her up. She will write a different life, of her own, of eagerly hiking to new things in time.

The tricky thing is that evocation of self is not the same thing as self-expression. It is not as simple as making it possible for people in school to "be themselves." Heschel tells us that "the self gains when it loses itself in the contemplation of the nonself" (1951: 228). In terms of sanctifying time by means of poaching, I take this to mean that it is in the art of poaching that the self is in contemplation of the world. It is found in the pleasure of the poaching. And, in order to be ready to guide students into poaching, like Danny's Dad, the teacher must have been there before, by which we mean he or she must be at heart a poacher.

3
Weirding

Educators are "weirding" knowledge all of the time, because they believe it is motivating. This is part of a science of pedagogy that constructs the need for a technology of attention. Because students are not learning in a context in which they are engaged in some way, the educator has to manipulate the environment so that the student "attends" to a body of "content." One technique is to make the content into an attractor – something that attracts attention. All other activity in the environment is understood then as a distractor – something that pulls the student's attention away from the content of instruction. Within this approach to curriculum and classroom practice, knowledge must be "weirded" if it is to become an attractor. Otherwise the student will be preoccupied by inappropriate activity. In this way we can understand that motivation is essentially a task of weirding. Without weirding a student cannot behave as if she or he is motivated to attend, for otherwise there is nothing that stands out from all potential attractors to become the specific attractor of attention. The one attractor at once defines itself as attractor and all potential other attractors as distractors. There are thus contradictions inherent in this discourse of education: attractors are simultaneously distractors; distractors are pre-eminent attractors!

What I think is needed is a Deleuzian embracing and disjunction with the attractor–distractor binary. In saying this, I want to point out that I conceive of my efforts in two ways: (1) as a phenomenological project; and (2) as a form of action research. This is a phenomenological project because, in a way, what I am studying is what I perceive as the heart of curriculum theorizing: I want to claim that weirding is a kind of phenomenological "essence" of curriculum theorizing. That is, even as we might ridicule scientist theories and applications of motivation, curriculum theory as well subscribes to the practice of weirding. (Weirding is a common node of discursive action that may be a key to collaborative and innovative educational efforts.) Phenomenologically, I want to say that within the various arenas of curriculum work, weirding is a fundamental aspect of the "experience" of the work. As I read through the 2001 Bergamo program, for example, I collected no fewer than 30 presentation titles that interpellated their audience through a descriptive heading which called forth one or more synonyms for "weird" – for example, "strange," "monstrous," "odd," "im-possibly redemptive" – or that conjure a notion of the peculiar, uncanny, odd, unusual, bizarre, and so on, by juxta-posing concepts and terms in "weirding ways." It is in this respect that I suggest we can understand our own work more fully if we lay claim to the weirding project I outline in this chapter. The common Deleuzian analogy is to privilege the nomad over the sheltered or the homeless, to understand the nomad as neither sheltered nor homeless, yet both sheltered and homeless. Weirding is both marginal and mainstream; yet if we dwell on those ways in which weirding is neither mainstream nor marginal, we can enter a new form of curriculum theorizing.

In the second conception of my work here, I am performing a kind of action research within curriculum theorizing – by articulating a response to the contemporary state of curriculum theory through a Deleuzian tactic, by constructing a "path" independent of both the margins of educational dis-courses and the mainstreams of educational practices. In this respect, I am searching for a way to perform curriculum work that is neither marginal nor mainstream, and also might be understood by both the margins and the mainstreams. This book is a projection of my current phenomenological experience, of working neither in marginal terrain nor in the mainstreams of educational practices, yet involved in aspects of the margins and the main-streams. The research question requires a direction that is mutual to both the margin and the mainstream efforts, yet is independent with its own trajectory.

I asked Sophia, during the summer between second and third grade, why she liked Dan Greenburg's *Zack Files* books. "Because they're weird," was her enthusiastic reply. And indeed these books are weird, I guess. They are playful stories in which something strange and out of the ordinary happens to fifth grader and ten-and-a-half-year-old Zack. In almost every introduction we are warned that something gross, or spooky, or creepy is going to happen; indeed, as Zack says in most of these introductions, "weird things are always happen-ing to me."

"You think you've got problems?" begins Book 12 in the series.

> I mean, I don't know if you do or not. But if you do think you've got problems, well, they're nothing compared with mine. Not unless you ever got stuck in a parallel universe. Or you had a Hawaiian volcano goddess put a curse on you. Or you ever started turning into a cat.
>
> (Greenburg 1998: 1)

Within a few pages we find out that Zack and his best friend Spencer do a lot of crazy things together, that they once entered an ice-cream recipe contest with a recipe for "Cashew Cashew Gesundheit" flavored ice-cream, that Spencer seems very smart (and that he invents a lot of things that cause some of Zack's adventures), and that Zack has accidentally drunk Spencer's "disappearing ink" – thinking it was lemonade. Astral traveling, peanut butter and jellyfish, You scream, Eyes scream, fame and fortune and a picture in the newspaper, a busy phone, running out of breath, and jumping around screaming like a maniac, all happen in a mere six-and-a-half dizzying pages of text. The exclamation marks are everywhere! And has this book gotten our attention, or what?!

Like Dahl's *Danny, the Champion of the World*, Zack's adventures also include a sympathetic Dad who at first goes crazy with some of the things that go on, but always ends up enjoying the wacky opportunities; often, he is a somber, rational interpreter of the things that go on, which, in turn, helps both Dad and the reader to appreciate the reality of the weird things that Zack experiences. Sometimes, we discover that Dad has even had similar adventures himself, such as slipping into the parallel universe where things are not quite the same.

In its zaniness and in its continual overload of stimulation and weirdness, the *Zack* series shares a variety of characteristics with other recent children's literature. For example, the Lemony Snicket series of "Unfortunate Events" in the lives of the Baudelaire children warns us at every opportunity of the terrible, unpredictable, and surprising turn of events that is about to come to pass in the story. Then many multiple plot lines converge in strange ways to lead the children into their next adventure. I think, though, that the excitement and interest that these series offer is not so much in the constant demands to attend to an overload of surprise, but in how they change the way that the story is experienced. Even repetitive volumes of similar plot lines do not make them less interesting, because the books continue to turn an ordinary story into an amusing entertainment through a weird form of storytelling. We might say that the way of telling the story is weird, not the story itself. What makes these books popular is that they recognize the naturally weird aspects of life. A person shouldn't shun the weird or dismiss the abnormal: she should embrace life *as* weird, to accept the weird *as* normal.

> Strange things happen to Zack Greenburg. There's no doubt about it. The question is "why?" Why should this affable 10-year-old, average in every way, be a magnet for what scientists call "paranormal experiences?" The reason is actually quite simple: weird things happen to Zack because Zack knows something most other people don't: that life is weird – full of the odd, the spooky, the inexplicable – and the startling fact is, anyone can see it who is willing to open their eyes and look.
>
> (Pazsaz Entertainment Network 1991–2006)

What if, instead of weirding knowledge (in order to attract students' attention), we preferably thought about weirding *curriculum*? We could use the node of commonality to communicate with most (mainstream) educators, because they have already been immersed in a weirding discourse. But we would shift the discourse. This could mean shifts in practice! – shifts that would be, I hope to imagine, "good." Weirding curriculum instead of knowledge requires a serious interrogation of curriculum theorizing. It demands its own form of weirding, its own set of attractors and distractors. It is a sort of deconstruction of curriculum practice by the tools of curriculum itself, turning in on itself to re-twist concepts and practices through this act of weirding. By shifting the discourse I mean a kind of surreptitious redefinition of common language through curriculum theorizing. By using common terms in ways that seem to have overlapping definitions through use, but which also stretch the usage-implied definitions of these words through the weirding practices, I hope to bring along with me people who like the words and are afraid to adopt new discourses. "Weirding curriculum" becomes a way to engage with everyday educational practice and action research on a theoretical level that in turn potentially affects those everyday practices and the meaning of words used to describe such practices.

Think of this another way: curriculum theorizing is too often misunderstood as theorizing *about* the content and/or theorizing *about* the courses of study offered by an educational institution, along with the relations among these courses of study. *Currere*, from which curriculum derives – *to run* – emphasizes the experiential nature of curriculum – the running of the track rather than the track itself. Now, it often seems theoretically efficacious to perform a phenomenological experiment "on" the curriculum: one looks at the courses of study, or even the experiencing *of* the courses of study, bracketing out, as a phenomenologist would say, the presumptions of the everyday, in order to precipitate a kind of pure experience of curriculum. In doing so, one "weirds" the knowledge, or one weirds the politics of the institution, or one weirds the role of the teacher, and so on. I am asking us to entertain a different sort of focus. In weirding the experiencing of curriculum, one changes the practices of curriculum theorizing.

Questions for a beginning

- What is the difference between weirding knowledge and weirding curriculum?
- Why is weirding knowledge harmful while weirding curriculum is not?
- Why would the shifts in practice be "good" (Donald 1992)?
- How relevant is the possibly related literature on the uncanny, on queering curriculum, and on practices of "othering" (Butler 1989; hooks 1996; Letts and Sears 1999; Morris 1996)?
- In fact, how is this project different from these other, related projects, and, if it is different, can it be taken in a way that avoids critiques that it is colonizing these already existing intellectual terrains?

What is the difference between weirding knowledge and weirding curriculum?

When we weird knowledge we make the knowledge strange and wonderful. (Or, uncanny, peculiar, odd…) This is the language of, for example, much of science education, in which the wow factor is employed to hook students into the lesson, and to carry them through the amazing new ways that exist to speak about the wonders of the natural world. This is also the language of maintaining engagement. If, for example, a third-grade teacher wants to help students to maintain their attention long enough to complete a grammar worksheet on nouns and subjects, she might create sentences with blanks that must be completed into a possible story, a story that itself is peculiar or fantastic. The child, amused by the unfolding story, will continue to complete the drill exercises because her or his attention is affixed to the worksheet. A side-effect of this teaching strategy, however, is that the attractor is not always the specific curricular content. It can often be the case that the student is attending to the pyrotechnics of the science demonstration rather than the scientific principle that underlies it; or that the child is attending to the amusing story rather than the attributes of nouns and subjects. Such a discourse is central as well to critical pedagogy practices; Ira Shor writes,

> As part of a liberatory culture, critical teaching challenges the limits on thought and feeling. A critical classroom pushes against the conditioned boundaries of consciousness. The enveloping realm of the routine is extracted from its habitual foundations. When the class examines familiar situations in an unfamiliar way, transcendent change becomes possible. Such an animation of consciousness can be formulated as *extraordinarily reexperiencing the ordinary*. This key rubric locates an empowering theory of knowledge in the re-perception of reality.
>
> (Shor 1987: 91)

Zack Greenburg and the Baudelaire orphans extract routines from their habitual functions: Zack is a problem-solver who loves science. Regardless of the wacky, strange things that happen to him, the science is always there as a well-treasured bag of tricks even as the paranormal may be bending and twisting that very science. Violet Baudelaire is the ultimate bricoleur, an inventor who plies her developing engineering skills in high-pressure circumstances; Klaus Baudelaire loves to read about anything, and his reading helps him and his siblings solve problems as well. Sunny Baudelaire, a baby, may seem too young to have a particular interest, but she consistently "cuts to the chase" and takes charge when her older, sophisticated siblings are lost in the details of science and its cultural context; I mean this both literally and figuratively, as Sunny's sharp teeth are often the tool she employs. As has been argued elsewhere, readers of science fiction and cyberpunk learn more contemporary science than students of science learn in school (Gough 1993).

While these books are "fun," school curriculum tries to fabricate "fun" as a motivational "hook" into the stodgy "school science." The mistake, for school science, is that it tries to weird the science, rather than be brave enough to take on the task of weirding the curriculum of science.

> There is a typography of "fun" in science education discourse. Its marker is the exclamation mark (!), which is a signpost in the terrain of fun. Words used by the host of a program or by characters in side-bar cartoons frequently help in identifying the typographical category, as one of SURPRISE!, TA-DAH!, IMAGINE THAT!, or LOOK! "Surprise!" generates an expectation that the viewer, web-surfer or student will respond with a form of curiosity. "Ta-dah!" initiates a magical element of science in which science is presented as a source of power for accomplishing something impressive, or impossible otherwise; the student, viewer or surfer is expected to want to obtain the power. "Imagine That!" evokes fantasy; there is presumed to be a natural appeal of fantasy which constructs this form of fun. Finally, "Look!" is associated with a base level of attention, in which extreme or unusual sounds, colors, etc., are deemed to be "fun" by their apparent difference with traditional school science.
>
> (Appelbaum and Clark 2001: 6–7)

Curriculum is different from curricular content. Again, as we have understood for quite some time now, at least since the reconceptualists (Pinar 1978), curriculum has to do with *currere*, with the experience of the encounter, of the processes of teaching, learning, assessment, and ethical events in an educational environment. Weirding curriculum entails an adjustment in the theorizing about the unfolding and enfolding experiences of those who are together called to relation in the educational processes.

In weirding curriculum we take the words we use to describe techniques and theoretical justifications and expand their definitions-in-context to include both the old and new meanings. Weirding itself would be a part of the practice. To help us accomplish this, I have included at the end of this chapter a selection of "postcards from the future," glimpses of family resemblances for a "weird" theory of curriculum.

One task of the curriculum worker as philosopher is to construct new concepts (Deleuze and Guattari 1996). This could be the work of the weirding curriculum theorizer as well. Another task of the curriculum worker is to design curriculum materials that meet the expectations of educators. This, too, would be the work of the weirding curriculum developer. But both of these sorts of tasks would be part of a larger project, a project that co-opts the discourses and practices, the words and structures, of common curriculum development, and uses it to deform such curricular materials into new forms.

Why is weirding knowledge harmful while weirding curriculum is not?

I claim that weirding knowledge is "harmful" in some ways. I also claim that weirding curriculum is not. In fact I claim that weirding curriculum can be "good." Thus I place ethical judgment at the center of weirding practice. Weirding knowledge is my insider's label for much of common curriculum practice. It is a term that can only be employed by those who have already accepted that their interests and practices are consistent with the fears and desires of the weirding curricularist. Thus by starting so early in my chapter with this discussion, I am inviting you to establish a kind of intimacy that requires a suspension of incredulity and an imaginative acceptance that there is indeed something to this. Such an embrace is a sign of the weird.

Weirding knowledge is harmful because it is a form of violence against children. Alan Block (1997) writes that our school structures commit violence on children psychologically while they further deny them the development of self and world. Weirding curriculum circumvents violence. The symbolic deformation is one of challenging our own assumptions about the nature of educational encounters and, because it is directed back upon the theorizer, it is not an act wielded upon the child. That is, because weirding is an intellectual act for the educator and not the child, it is not about the schooling, but about the curriculum theorizing. Block is inspired by a quote of Levinas:

> Violence is to be found in any action in which one acts as if one were alone to act; as if the rest of the universe were there only to receive the action.
>
> (Levinas, quoted in Block 1997)

Education has been structured by modernity to avoid confrontation with the ambiguities that children present; the unintegrated child threatens order and must be controlled. Education also promises future completion; Block describes how education creates a society of despair in its own name through the practices it enacts upon our children, by limiting that future, and by preparing children for a future that never happens.

The philosopher Alasdair MacIntyre (1984) once described the work of education as both essential and impossible, and teachers as the "forlorn hope of Western Modernity," because, he wrote, schooling demands that young people be taught to both fit into some social role and function that requires recruits, and to think for themselves. With this inchoate work of weirding I recognize that school is structured by boundaries that make creation of self, in Block's terms, difficult of not impossible: "World and self are made separate and the imagination – the wishes and dreams – are denied for the predetermined outlines of the other" (Block 1995: 172). Weirding asks us to find a conception of curriculum that makes it possible for the child to *use* the educational environment. It also places curriculum theorizing at the heart of questions about a community that includes curriculum theorizing and that is involved in the daily work of teaching and learning. It further values the kind of curriculum theorizing that decenters the "practical" everyday life of schools, because such intellectual challenges are focal in our efforts to reconceptualize and reconstruct our notions of pedagogy and curriculum. This mutually related but independent path is a nomadic epistemology, sharing discourse with school-based practice and theoretical practice; it is neither school-based practice nor theoretical practice; it might be praxis, but if it is, it is a praxis conceived of as its own independent trajectory. In MacIntyre's terms, we might say, given the post-Enlightenment imperatives of socialization and individuation as incompatible, that it will only be when discussion on "shared terms" is a feature of the roles for which students are socialized that it will be possible for the two imperatives to "go together." MacIntyre smoothly refers to this as the "educated public."

To understand a sense of "good" that is woven within this "educated public," and to imagine curriculum theorizing as threaded into this same "public," I turn to James Donald (1992), who weirds curriculum by questioning the opposition that is constructed by the discourse between socialization and individuation, or domestication and emancipation. Let us begin with an acceptance of the Foucauldian arguments that technologies of the self have pretty much *not* silenced or constrained the desires and self-governing capacities of people, but have instead attempted to attune them to political objectives. (In practice, writes Donald, this refers to identification with particular symbolic rules and grammars, and thus socialization into particular intellectual and academic subcultures (p. 142).) What is at issue is less about emancipation or liberation, writes Donald, and more about styles of participation, in which subjection and autonomy inevitably coexist.

One route out of this is Amy Gutman's (1987) notion about the "failure" of democratic theories to be "educationally complete." No democratic theory can offer practical solutions to all problems that afflict educational institutions, and must instead pose education as a question: the question of an authority that is always in question. (Who should have the authority to shape the education of future citizens?) This is a kind of Deleuzian response: the curriculum theorist would not try to declare once and for all what should be done in a classroom, or who should be designing the educational environment, nor would she even begin to think about what that educational environment might be like. A theorist might avoid completely the search for forms of education that support students' own design of the educational experience. She would instead be preoccupied with the kinds of popular involvement and professional accountability that would emerge from various sorts of participation by different members of the community in the decision-making processes. "Rather than wishing away conflicts," writes Donald, "inequalities and incommensurabilities; this approach should at least create a space for marginal and emergent voices in defining terms and setting limits to authority in debates about education" (p. 170).

The Deleuzian response to where "practice" is situated within curriculum theorizing that I am working with here is similar to the role of science in the *Zack Files*: it is both there and not-there. Every *Zack Files* reader knows what a tachyon is ("a tachyon is one of the tiniest things in the universe. Tinier than an atom, even. And it travels faster than the speed of light. A tachyon travels so fast, it gets where it's going before it starts out. If you were a tachyon, you'd never be late to school. You'd get there before you left home. I learned that in science class" (Zack Files Fan Club 1998); yet every reader can simultaneously suspend science (Zack can buy a real dinosaur egg that hatches into a baby dinosaur, travel through time, enter a parallel universe, adopt a talking cat that is really his great-grandfather – a lying one, at that – suddenly watch his 88-year-old grandmother hit 400-foot home runs every time she's at bat...) The playful science that is independent of reality and fantasy is what makes the books both "weird" and enjoyable entertainment. The role of the theo-rizer, learner, educator, becomes more of a process of becoming rather than a static identity, just like science shifts for Zack. One can both learn science through reading the books and also suspend reality, without getting confused about what is science and what is fantasy; on the other hand, perhaps science is now constructed as a collection of types of fantasy? For Zack, science and the paranormal are not incommensurable.

Donald's reliance on Gutman-style political theory would imply a "restless experimentalism" and a reconceptualization of the subjects at whom educa-tion is targeted. But I am not so sure it is the only direction for weirding cur-riculum. I only share it as a possible starting point for discussion. Because, as Donald asserts, education conceived in these terms implies that it is about being a citizen. It shifts our discourse in one (weirding? peculiar? odd?) way:

> to be a citizen is to be ascribed a certain status, it is not to be a particu-lar type of person. And yet, of course, modern education has consis-tently been allotted the task of sustaining social relations by creating psychologically adjusted, productive, enterprising and patriotic citizens. It is that attempt to reconcile the split between the pedagogic demands of citizenship and the enigmatic particularity of agency and subjectivity which, following Freud, I take to be impossible.
>
> (Donald 1992: 171)

How relevant is the possibly related literature on the uncanny, on queering curriculum, and on practices of "othering"?

The uncanny, the queer, and critical multiculturalism share some useful strat-egies with the weird. Indeed, the weird is often defined in terms of the strange, the odd, the bizarre, the peculiar, the uncanny, the eerie, the creepy, or the unusual. Curriculum as strange requires an existentialist's discomfort with one's existence (Greene 1973). To "strange" the curriculum means to recognize the dilemmas and conflicts that are constructed by one's curriculum, to embody the hope that blossoms within the angst of crisis established by the curriculum. Curriculum as odd sets forth the unreasonable and inappropriate aspects of one's curriculum. To "odd" the curriculum is to make it out of the ordinary, an anomalous or funny approach to the content. The bizarre curriculum introduces concepts of wacky, off-the-wall instructional and assessment strategies. To "bizarre" the curriculum and to "odd" the curriculum require a willingness to be singled out as so strange as to challenge others' sense of decorum. This in itself might justify the intent of the bizarre or odd curriculum; or it may lead the weirding curricularist to select a less socially challenging path. The peculiar curriculum is irregular, unusual, abnormal. As atypical or eccentric, the peculiar curriculum is not socially threatening like the bizarre or odd. In fact, it shares much with common curriculum practices by calling attention to itself. Because it supports the status quo, I argue it is inconsistent with the aims of a weirding curriculum. The uncanny, the eerie, and the creepy all introduce a spine-chilling sense of mystery and the supernatural. They are scary and frightening, alarming, maybe even sinister. These, even more than the bizarre and the odd, are threatening and may be difficult to implement. Yet their very scariness is what makes them alluring. They are excellent metaphors for the task of the curriculum theorist: weirding curriculum is not going to be easy; it is going to raise all sorts of fears and frightening fantasies. Finally, the unusual curriculum points to the fact that weirding curriculum will be remarkable even as it may be strange, odd, curious, extraordinary, abnormal, bizarre, or atypical.

But I choose to dwell a little longer on the uncanny and the queer, because these have made previous splashes in curriculum theory. The weirding curriculum might borrow from queer curriculum theorizing, sharing a joint effort to, as Marla Morris (1998) writes, "unrest" the curriculum (p. 285). By "making strange" gender, politics, identities, and aesthetics, curriculum as queer texts turns the everyday life of school inside out, upside down, backwards. Like queer theorizing, weirding curriculum seeks to open possibilities for transformation and change, and does its work through making the unseen visible. In the case of queer theory, the unseen is the odd or peculiar object of our gaze. Identity is reconsidered as the unseen "becoming" – the works in progress as opposed to the museum pieces: one says "I become queer in relation to my desires, fantasies, readings, reactings, writings, experiences," writes Morris. "A queer identity is a chameleon-like refusal to be caged into any pre-scribed category or role" (p. 279). Similar to queer curriculum theorizing, weirding curriculum shifts discourses. As Mary Doll (1998) writes, "I must work against the dulling tendency to make nice ... I must teach the nonnormal, be the nonnormal" (Doll 1998: 291). Doll offers four techniques of queering: the way of shock, the way of the joke, the way of the myth, and the way of the perverse. Are these synonyms for the way of the weird?

They may be. But before we compare weirding and queering more directly, let us also consider another joint effort that shares a great deal with the weird: the uncanny, or "unhomely." As Freud once implied, the feeling of the uncanny could suggest that particular organization of space where everything is reduced to inside and outside, and where the inside is also the outside (Vidler 1994: 222). The *unheimlich*. A word closely related to unhomely, but really not translatable to merely "haunting." The space of the mirror would meet some suggested conditions of the uncanny. The mirror is a space of "normal," binocular, three-dimensional vision, modified by being deprived of depth. This leads to the conflation, on the same visual plane, of the familiar (the seen), and the strange (the projected). Both familiar and strange, yet neither familiar nor strange. Uncanny. Dark spaces are other candidates for the uncanny. The dark spaces, we assume, might hide things, things might be hidden in the dark recesses and forgotten margins – all of the objects of fears and phobias that have returned with such insistency to haunt the imaginations of those who have tried to stake out spaces in order to protect their health and happiness. Indeed, "space as threat," as harbinger of the unseen, operates as a medical and psychic metaphor for all of the possible erosions of bourgeois and social well-being. We return to this theme in Chapters 7 and 8.

Othering, also developed further in Chapters 8 and 9, is yet another potential interpretation of weirding. As an existential project, curriculum can be, in Maxine Greene's (1973) terms, "estranging." The educator, as "stranger," cannot help but feel alienated and challenged by the commonsense presumptions of educational practices. Sharing the goal of "untelling" the narratives of normativity with queering strategies, critical multiculturalists seek to center the unseen. The realities we "see" in our school are understood as ways of making meaning, as the ways in which we comprehend possibilities, and our practices are interpreted as a sort of "theater of performance." Advocates of this orientation work first to "untell" essentialism, and to develop strategies that undermine essentialist hierarchies. They work to open up for students and teachers the fluidity of identity, and possibilities for their own lives that may also be used to interrogate the received stories about history and culture that come in the prepackaged curricula and materials that are available to them in and out of school.

A central feature of such curriculum work is a persistent effort on the part of teachers and students to always look at how people are represented as "types" or categories, and to understand how these types and categories imply affects on their own identities. This helps people think about how they perform their identities for others in varying contexts. For example, critical multiculturalists critique the curriculum that they study with their students. They also study popular culture experiences as parallel forms of "representation." They study with students how the school curriculum and popular culture forms of entertainment and information define an "order of things" for people – how to dress, how to eat, what to want, and in general how to be in the world. Instead of searching for the best curriculum materials or designing the best units of study, critical multiculturalists look for "interventions" (by which they mean points in the curriculum, moments in classroom interactions, places in the community or the school) where they can disrupt the representations, or where they can see the diverse locations of the multiple identities that are part of what they are studying (part of what they are doing together). Sometimes, as in the case of English professor DuBose Brunner (1998), they playfully talk about "in(ter)ventions," so that they can see themselves and their students as simultaneously, on the spot, inventing new ways to do things together in school, and out of school; they use words like this and play with them to provoke themselves and each other to think about how an intervention might also be an invention, how an invention of ways of talking or representing what they know might itself be an intervention into the inequities and problems of social life.

The series of unfortunate events in the lives of the Baudelaire orphans documented by Lemony Snicket places the uncanny and sublime directly in our face. At every moment, tongue in cheek, we are warned to put the books down, to avoid the horrible stories, to content ourselves with false ideas about potentially happy lives that these children might have been believed to have experienced if we only did not know what truly befell them. Weird as strange is the *modus operandi* of the books' humor, as when the children are put in charge of knowledge for a herpetological expedition, or when the baby sister is assigned to the job of administrative assistant at a boarding-school (and to make her own handmade staples in her off-hours), and so on. The evil Count Olaf and his cronies are weird as "others," and enact the weird as "unpredictable" in their many attempts to get their hands on the children and their presumed inheritance, as well as in their impressively clever getaways. Yet it is the remarkable children who weirdly remain calm and collected in the midst of adult horror and stupidity, who outwit Olaf and fend for themselves by achieving the odd, peculiar, and, strangely enough, normalizing and thus weirding the weird, within the perpetual uncanny. Uncanny, indeed, is the view of adults that we are subjected to as these books let us glance in the mirror and consider the images we can see.

In fact, how is this project different from these other, related projects, and, if it is different, can it be taken in a way that avoids critiques that it is colonizing these already existing intellectual terrains?

Weirding actually shares much in common with queering and the confrontation with the uncanny. It shares a great deal with critical multiculturalism as well. But its commonalities are most evident when queer theorists, students of the uncanny, and critical mulitculturalists are performing the practices of weirding. For example, it is not a core aspect of queer theory that one does more than reveal the unseen, nor is it essential that a student of the uncanny do more than look into the mirror, or stalk the darkness. Marla Morris is weirding curriculum when she writes about shifting discourses in *certain ways*: her contribution is a weirding of curriculum theorizing. She compares the binary of anti-queer and queer responses to the moral question of how to relate to others, or how to best live together, as a critical part of curriculum. The queer theorizing is to raise the question, to ask the unseen question. The weird theorizing is to seek a practice that unrests rather than preserves the binary. To look for queering practices that are neither anti-queer nor queer, yet are queering of curriculum, is to weird curriculum. Similarly, when Mary Doll uses shock, jokes, myths, and the perverse, she is neither queering nor anti-queering; yet she is weirding curriculum in order to queer it.

To see curriculum as an experience of mirroring, one that is both familiar and strange, but neither familiar nor strange, is to weird curriculum in order to make it uncanny. When curriculum is the experience of those dark spaces that hide fears and fantasies yet in doing so contain them and make them potentially "visible," it is weirding curriculum in order to make it uncanny.

And finally, to playfully introduce in(ter)ventions is to work along with but not within in-school and out-of-school identities and becomings, theaters of identity and untellings of normativity. In(ter)ventions would therefore be another example of weirding curriculum, in this case to make it critically multicultural.

Here is one more example: Donna Haraway's (1997) othering of the traditional scientist as a "modest witness" establishes a "peculiar" independent path of science as curriculum that is mutual to the "defenders of science" as well as those who work in the "cultural studies of science." In recognizing the power–knowledge relationships inherent in the construction of a scientist as a "modest witness" – a transparent conduit through which "reality" is communicated from the natural world into the language of science – Haraway helps us to understand relativism as "a simplistic modernist concept that assumes away power in the opinion making process" (Weaver 2001: 6). As John Weaver has noted, labeling someone a "relativist" not only announces a discursive power play based in the authority of modest witnessing, but also erases the role power holds in the thinking of cultural studies of science scholars. Relativism, on the one hand, claims no one person holds a direct and unmediated link to a transcendent authority that knows what truth is; on the other hand, it completely ignores how those with power construct and sanction legitimate ways of thinking. The cultural studies of science, as a practice of curriculum theorizing, is not interested in proclaiming the legitimacy of *all* opinions, but rather in the very power dimensions that relativists ignore.

The Bear

At this point I draw the crass conclusion that my audience is intrigued by weirding curriculum, and wishes to pursue more inspiring investigations. I offer a beginning list of adult literature that can help in thinking about the differences between weirding curriculum and weirding knowledge.

In the novel *The Bear Comes Home*, Rafi Zabor (1997) sets out to write in words the experience of jazz improvisation, to communicate the evolving relationship with music that the musician painfully and joyously brings to his or her life. Zabor does not twist the art/music/aesthetics into something different in order to help us understand what he has to say. Instead he makes the musician a "bear," a secretly intelligent one at that. He "weirds" the musician and not the music.

> As Rafi Zabor's PEN-Faulkner Award-winning novel opens, the Bear shuffles and jigs with a chain through his nose, rolling in the gutter, letting his partner wrestle him to the ground for the crowd's enjoyment. But as soon becomes clear, this is no ordinary dancing bear. "I mean, dance is all right, even street dance. It's the poetry of the body, flesh aspiring to grace or inviting the spirit in to visit," he muses, but before all else, the Bear's heart belongs to jazz. This is, in fact, one alto-sax-playing, Shakespeare-allusion-dropping, mystically inclined Bear, and he's finally fed up with passing the hat. One night he sneaks out to a jazz club and joins a jam session. On the strength of the next day's write-up in the *Village Voice*, the Bear begins to play around town and hobnob with some of jazz's real-life greats. A live album, a police raid, a jailbreak, a cross-country tour, and no small amount of fame later, Bear finds himself in love with a human woman – and staring down the greatest improbability of all.
>
> (Amazon.com a)

In another recent novel, *Girl in Landscape*, Jonathan Lethem (1999) writes of a young girl's coming of age. Lethem does not twist the experiences of adolescence into something weird in order for us to understand it in new ways. Instead, he places the girl in a new landscape, a peculiar planet of the "arch-builders" where viruses have altered everything about life and change on the planet. He "weirds" the landscape and not the girl.

> Science-fiction writers attempting coming-of-age stories have seldom risked showing the stew of loneliness, anger, and angst that really characterizes adolescence. Jonathan Lethem, on the other hand, avoids the plucky sidekick syndrome and instead gives us breathtakingly realistic Pella Marsh, a girl at that awful and wonderful crux in her life just before people start calling her "woman." Her broken family has just moved to a newly settled planet, with strange and passive natives and

the decaying remnants of a great civilization. Something in the alien environment soon enables Pella to telepathically travel, hidden in the bodies of inconspicuous "household deer," into the homes of her fellow settlers. She inevitably discovers the seamy side of humanity–loss of innocence eloquently portrayed. Don't read this book on a dark day, as there's not very much sunshine in here. The entire planet is covered with ruins: ruined towns, ruined hopes and dreams, ruined families. For a rare dose of SF realism, this is a fantastic read, full of raw (but not explicit) sexuality and the unhappy hierarchies of childhood. Forget about cheerful settlers moving in next door to helpful indigenous life forms. This is what the planetary frontiers will be. No matter how far away from Earth we may travel, we'll still be the same dirty, disappointing, beautiful monsters.

(Amazon.com b)

Curriculum as aesthetic creative encounter. Curriculum as coming of age. Curriculum as explorers interacting with the "new world" they are exploring. These books help us to set weirding curriculum in these contexts.

Postcards from a future of curriculum theorizing:

Strange
  Odd
  Bizarre
  Outlandish
  Eccentric
  Weird
  Weird and wonderful
  Extraordinary
  Out of the ordinary
  Peculiar

Odd
  Strange
  Abnormal
  Out of the ordinary
  Peculiar
  Anomalous
  Weird
  Funny

Bizarre
Strange
Weird
Peculiar
Out of the ordinary
Odd
Uncanny
Wacky
Unusual
Off the wall

Peculiar
Odd
Strange
Weird
Unusual
Irregular
Abnormal
Uncharacteristic
Atypical
Curious eccentric

Uncanny
Eerie
Weird
Strange
Mysterious
Creepy
Supernatural

Eerie
- Creepy
- Uncanny
- Weird
- Strange
- Peculiar
- Unnatural
- Supernatural
- Ghostly
- Ghostlike
- Paranormal
- Spine-chilling
- Frightening
- Sinister
- Alarming
- Scary

Creepy
- Sinister
- Frightening
- Eerie
- Scary
- Disturbing
- Spine-chilling
- Uncanny
- Weird
- Hair-raising

Unusual
- Strange
- Odd
- Curious
- Extraordinary
- Abnormal
- Remarkable
- Bizarre
- Atypical

4
Vision Stinks*

When we first meet the Ear, the Eye, and the Arm, the three eponymous characters of Nancy Farmer's (1994) delightful futuristic adventure-mystery for young readers, we are introduced to their unique talents of perception as simultaneously gifts and handicaps. They are indeed differently abled.

> We can hear a bat burp in the basement. We can see a gnat's navel on a foggy night. Hunches stick to us like gum to your shoe.
>
> (p. 46)

Yet Eye needs dark glasses to venture outside. Ear must fold up his ears for normal conversation, and don muffs to manage the outside world. Arm has no way to stave off the hate, greed, and anger he can feel from all directions, with only an occasional whiff of kindness softening the pain. Blessed with their peculiar afflictions – their mothers had drunk the plutonium-rich run-off water from a nuclear power plant when they were pregnant – the three men are uniquely positioned to recognize the powers of enhanced perception as well as the limitations this enhancement poses for them and for others. Wondering why General Matsika, Chief of Security for the Land of Zimbabwe, would need their assistance as detectives, Eye suggests, "perhaps it's a question of being too powerful" (p. 47).

For teachers, perhaps, there is something of a kinship with Ear, Eye, and Arm, for we are told we have powers that others do not yet possess: we can see what they do not yet see, we can hear what they do not yet hear, we can feel things that they cannot yet feel. In some cases, we can smell and taste what our students cannot yet smell or taste. Using the dominant sense of sight as our primary model for knowing and seeing as the metaphor for coming to know, we have the power to see the unseen, hear the unheard, and so on – to make the invisible visible, but only to us. This chapter explicates the following idea: as long as educational practice is restrained by these epistemological assumptions, we will only be able to understand our job in one of two ways:

---

*Parts of this chapter first appeared as "The stench of perception and its cacophony of mediation," in *For the Learning of Mathematics* 19(2): 11–18, July 1999.

as training folks in the art of using special technologies of vision; or as metaphorically strapping prostheses onto our students so that they can see. Unfortunately, I suggest, neither is enough to constitute education, which involves intergenerationality. I begin with three more quotes that, together with my reading of Nancy Farmer's *The Ear, the Eye and the Arm*, offer as good a starting point as any other, the first from Herman Hesse's *The Glass Bead Game*, the second from Donna Haraway's "Situated knowledges," and the third from Ralph Ellison's *The Invisible Man*:

In this course of instruction there were no concepts, doctrines, methods, script, figures, and only very few words. The Master trained Knecht's senses far more than his intellect. A great heritage of tradition and experience, the sum total of man's [*sic*] knowledge of nature at that era, had to be administered, employed, and even more, passed on. A vast and dense system of experiences, observations, instincts, and habits of investigation was slowly and hazily laid bare to the boy. Scarcely any of it was put into concepts. Virtually all of it had to be grasped, learned, tested with the senses.

(Hesse 1969: 42)

Throughout the field of meanings constituting science, one of the commonalities concerns the status of any object of our accounts to a "real world," no matter how complex and contradictory these worlds may be. Feminists, and others who have been most active as critics of the sciences and their claims or associated ideologies, have shied away from doctrines of scientific objectivity in part because of the suspicion that an "object" of knowledge is a passive and inert thing. Accounts of such objects can seem to be either appropriations of a fixed and determined world reduced to resources for the instrumentalist projects of destructive Western societies, or they can be seen as masks for interests, usually dominating interests.

(Haraway 1992: 197)

Then suddenly he fixed me with his eyes. "And now, do you understand?"
"What?" I said.
"What you've heard!"
"I don't know."
"Why?"
I said, "I really think it's time we left."

(Ellison 1947/1972: 86)

Technology of vision

Ear, Eye, Arm, and the characters in Hesse and Ellison, place vision and its dominant force in our perception of "the real world" at the forefront of our work. Indeed, I suggest that even other ways of knowing and coming to know act as "technologies of vision," extending the metaphor and thus manipulating our notions of that very "real world" we seem to think we see so clearly, so that everything ends up being something that we know because we "see it." How we see is influenced by our technologies of vision. I am using "technology of vision" in the sense of Michael Polanyi (1958), Paul Feyerabend (1988), and Donna Haraway (1992). Just as Galileo learned to use a telescope, I and the teachers I work with use new prosthetic theories; and the result is a similar collection of new metaphors and models. Far from understanding the objects of knowledge as passive and inert, my own practice assumes a volatile and aggressive mutation organism, the experience of which transforms permanently those who interact with it. Teachers are asked to comprehend content knowledge in the same fashion, for example, as a tool through which students are unequivocally mutated into people who "see the world through mathematical eyes" (Ritchart 1997), to "think like a social scientist," to "design an experiment like a biologist." Similarly, as policy is written, it constructs the nature of what it means to be a teacher (of mathematics, of social studies, of science): a teacher as a professional needs to "learn" the new policy and conform/adapt her or his practice such that it can be described in terms of the discourse of the policy. Policy positions the professional as ignorant of "best practice," devaluing the sort of learning emblematic of the boy in Hesse's apprenticeship narrative, an unarticulated, non-conceptual experience of the body. As a professor of education called upon to perform acts of professional development, I too am placed on this terrain in the midst of bewilderment. My experiences guide me, too, into a state of professional non-expertise as I am by my position in the configuration of policy and institutional practice constructed as an educator introducing a new prosthetic technology. I am ostensibly hired to train teachers in new technologies – math on the internet, CD-ROMs in the classroom, hypermedia presentations, performance assessment with technology. The pedagogical questions, remaining the same as "before technology," are seen, as I describe here, through a filter of metaphors. These metaphors continue to reconstruct the content knowledge itself in technological terms. In both cases, that of teaching new content, and in the problematic set-up of professional development, the stuff of knowledge is a prosthetic enhancement of vision. The primary model of knowing is that of seeing with one's eyes, and the dominant metaphor for understanding is vision. Content knowledge and policy are like ultramega-ray lenses surgically affixed to the eyes. Furthermore, the metaphor is inscribed in practice by the celebration in professional development of technology itself as a privileged focus of sanctioned and acclaimed "new knowledge."

We might say that the physical "technology" of a professional development workshop, the computers or PDAs, and so on, is an iconic representation; the skill-based tasks expected of the workshop are enactive representations; and the subject matter knowledge of the activities becomes in the process of the experience the symbolic representation of technology. A sealed cycle of mutual support elaborates the ideology of technology as it narrows the field of possibilities for constructing professional development, school mathematics, and the very notion of an educational experience. The context of inscription is that of technology as "superior," the improved being enhanced beyond simplistic "nature" or savagery (Appelbaum 1999). Hence prosthetic technology is an enculturation into a long Western tradition of colonialism, racism, and dehumanization (Adas 1989).

Ear, Eye, and Arm are detectives hunting down knowledge: the location and well-being of General Matsika's three children. As prosthetic extensions of the General and his wife, the detectives are perceptual enhancement devices. They see things, they hear things, and they feel things, and yet they always arrive at a place just too late – soon after the children are no longer there. Why is this? I believe that technology is simultaneously an aggressive agent of mutation and a mere prosthesis of vision. Perceptual enhancement only enhances what is perceivable, doing little to help one perceive what one is unable to perceive. For example, the point of a professional development workshop about "math on the internet," for me, is the potential enlargement of communities of inquiry and communication: to take one example, students across the globe can work on projects together, offer each other feedback on their ideas, and act as the originators of an activity (perhaps by sponsoring a web page that elicits submissions of various kinds from people surfing the net). Yet the most legitimized use of the net for teachers is the gathering of prepackaged lesson plans that do not transform the educational experience through technology at all. Instead of reflecting on possibilities for educational experiences with their students, teachers are trained to search with their eyes for something somebody else has done. Practice sends teachers on a perpetual wild goose chase for the intangible answer to an unknown question: the "answer," it turns out, is just beyond our reach, in the realm of the almost grasped. Like Ear, Eye, and Arm, we teachers arrive at the lesson plan just too late – right after our students have been there. The juxtaposition of transforming school subject matter, mathematics for example, through the net, with the realities of the actual technology available to the teachers who have been sent to this workshop by their school district, sets up a vision of the newfangled ideas as implausible, and the old-fashioned lesson plans as jewels. Thus the mutation effects are held at bay while the technology of curriculum is re-invented as new.

Some years ago I offered several times with my colleague and friend Rochelle G. Kaplan a workshop on "performance assessment with technology." The workshop focused on technology as the instrument of assessment by the teacher (videotaping group performance in classroom situations for analysis by the teacher), and technology as the instrument of performance by the student(s) (spreadsheets, graphing calculators, composed web pages) for assessment analysis by the teacher. In planning the workshop, we prepared discussions and activities designed to help participants think about issues of assessment and the notion of performance; we planned as well a variety of ways to help teachers think about the influence of technology on their understanding of performance assessment, performance, and assessment. Reflecting on the workshops afterwards, we found it extremely difficult for the participants to focus on the issues rather than working to develop technology skills. This is not because of a necessity for skill development prior to reflection or application of skills. Rather, it has to do with what Stieg Mellin-Olsen (1987) refers to as the problem of culture in education: the importance of the relationships among the pupil's own judgment of an educational situation she is part of, how this affects her learning behavior, and how this relationship might inform the designing of the learning situation. Placed in a position of "teacher," a person plans activities with a goal of conceptual growth over time; yet the people placed in the position of "pupil" are attending to the activity, to what they are supposed to do and how they are supposed to do it. The notion of a professional development "workshop" seems to preclude any form of conceptual growth or change, because the format of teacher-person and pupil-people is structured for training in skills and not for conceptual development. My entry into the institution of professional development proscribes my position within a cult of expertise that in turn thwarts the very notion of professional development. Some professional development programs stretch over time with a component that integrates practice with a dialogue on educational change; greater success has been reported in these cases (Ohanian 1992). Negotiations with school district personnel for such extended forms of professional development are cumbersome and problematic, however. Professional development as a cultural practice is so drenched in the ideology of vision that attempts to "take on its clothes" becomes of necessity an art in costume and camouflage. I have lately found it necessary to forgo such negotiations in favor of an examination of my position itself as potentially in conflict with my politics of knowledge. Can I construct alternative metaphors for the tasks of my profession and avoid the problematic job of mutation terrorist or prosthetic surgeon?

Epistemology of vision

Perhaps the reason why it takes so long for Ear, Eye, and Arm to achieve their goal is that it is not enough to simply perceive very well: perception is not everything. In Nancy Farmer's tale, we are glad for the extra pages and the added adventure. In the end, however, it is the spirit of the ancestors of Zimbabwe, the *Mhondoro*, who adds something extra. The *Mhondoro* first enters Arm, before finally giving Tendai, Matsika's eldest son, the strength to use his own hunches about another character, the She Elephant; it is the ancestors who provide the prodding, and our own wisdom that enables us to connect with others in the ways that are essential to the salvation of humankind. It is something independent of perception, and vision in particular, that we need to comprehend if we are to move past the limitations of the ideology of vision. My own attempts to reconceptualize pedagogy independent of perception, or vision – of epistemology – have not helped me that much. There have been numerous, remarkable attempts to offer alternatives to a Platonic notion of authentic vision as true knowledge. Most, however, remain within a hegemony of perception as essential to the comprehension of knowing and coming to know. Sartre's (1969) form of existentialism offers touch as a powerful challenge. We reach out into the world and feel those things we know; and the object *makes* us feel as we touch. We must direct our intention toward what we touch; but once we do, we are the object of experience, not the thing we touch. The magic of touch indeed has its enactment in education, primarily through the pedagogical use of 'tactile learning'; in mathematics education we talk of manipulatives. However, Sartre's project is undermined in the majority of tactile pedagogy. For example, in most manipulative-based experiences, the materials are claimed to embody a model of a mathematical concept, and students are supposed to be taught how to "feel" the concept. Michael Polanyi described Galileo's telescope as the icon of "tacit knowledge" learned prior to the experience of seeing with a telescope. In the same manner, students must now be acculturated to the way of touching mathematics through manipulatives. Often they are simultaneously taught how to "see" the concept in the material from a distance as well, thus returning the epistemology of touch into an epistemology of the dominant sight supported by touch. Much time in elementary methods courses and professional development workshops is spent convincing teachers to use manipulatives. How ironic is it that the manipulatives themselves may be the problem, adding layers of visual conundrums on top of what might have been simple conceptual understanding?

For me, the most accessible discussions of the ear, and listening as the model and metaphor of knowing and coming to know, are in feminist theory (Belenky *et al.* 1986), and, within mathematics education, in the exquisite work of both Julian Weisglass (1990, 1994) and Brent Davis (1996, 1997). This approach, which emphasizes the interactionist quality of listening to another person, is particularly pertinent to current reform efforts regarding the increase of communication in the classroom. As Davis notes, we tend to stand back in order to see, and to move nearer in order to hear. "Correspondingly," he writes, "there is an element of discomfort associated with being watched, but we generally want to be listened to – in part at least, because of the interaction afforded by listening" (1996: 37). Furthermore, participation as a "listener" or the "listened to" has a different quality from that of the "watcher" and the "watched"; "in particular, because we are unable to shut off our hearing with the ease that we can close off our seeing, attempts to *not* hear result in being compelled to listen more attentively." Yet, as Davis notes, a person's range of possible action, as described with the aid of listening as a metaphor, is determined by his or her structure: in an interaction with another person, how he or she acts is not primarily a function of the other person's actions (as in presumed transmission models of communication and teaching) but a consequence of his or her own structural dynamic. The ear within and part of the body is perturbed by the environment, but it is the structure of the living being that determines the changes that occur in it (p. 10). Interaction, then, is not "instruction": its effects are not determined by the interaction; but changes result from the interaction, determined by the structure of the disturbed system.

Significant in the work of Weisglass and Davis is their emphasis on listening as a form of "embodied action" as opposed to a technique of hearing. Weisglass presents a taxonomy of listening forms he designates as partially pedagogic; his alternative, dubbed "constructivist," encourages the talker to reflect on the meaning of events and ideas, to express and work through feelings that are interfering with clear thinking, to construct new meanings, and to make decisions. Davis similarly constructs a framework (1996: 53) of three comparative modes of listening differentiated by their features of attending to the one "listened to." *Evaluative listening* is the dominant mode of the detached teacher who rarely deviates from intended plans and judges contributions as right or wrong. More authentic forms of enactive listening are the responsibility of the learner. *Interpretive listening* requires a teacher to reach out rather than take in; listening becomes the development of compassion, increasing the capacity of the listener to be aware of and responsive to the interrelatedness and commonality across human beings. Finally, *hermeneutic listening* is messier in problematizing any differentiation between the "listener" and the one being "listened to"; participants are involved in a project of interrogating taken-for-granted assumptions and prejudices that frame perceptions and actions. Hermeneutic listening promotes "participation in the unfolding of possibilities through collective action."

I want to suggest that reform efforts tend to undermine potential hermeneutic listening when they promote increased student talk as a tool for assessment, a recent focus of much professional development (NCTM 1989, 1991, 1995, 2000). Workshops on alternative assessment practices or, for example, on performance assessment with technology, thus train teachers in the surveillance of students via evaluative listening. Greater pedagogical potential might be found in practices that create students as listeners and those listened to in one of the other two modes. Collaborative group work has this potential when not used for assessment surveillance and when listening skills are actually facilitated in the classroom, so that participants can begin to effectively engage in forms of interpretive and hermeneutic listening.

The relevance of a listening orientation for professional development may be found in Davis' point that the unfolding, enacted curriculum makes no attempt at optimization.

> Instead, the listening teacher works with the contingencies of the particular classroom setting. It is founded on the realizations that no learning outcome can be prescribed, no active setting can be controlled. But neither must we forgo attempts to influence (or fail to acknowledge our influence upon) what might come about. The key to teaching, in this conception, is to present a space for action and then to participate in – and through this participation, to shape – the joint project that emerges.
>
> (1996: 271)

In other words, a workshop designed to introduce new technology to teachers will have surprisingly little impact on workshop participants unless it speaks to the teachers' needs for enabling such enactive spaces within the peculiarities of their own styles of interaction and the particular circumstances of their classroom. (Remember here that "technology" in this context can mean any new set of practices or techniques, as well as specific electronic equipment: in any of these situations, the "technology" is a tool that promotes the attainment of performance objectives.) Moreover, such a workshop runs the risk of placing participants in the role of one-being-evaluated via evaluative listening if it must conform to expectations constructed by policy or district guidelines. I find myself placed repeatedly in such a position, in which participants bring expectations of evaluative listening to a workshop or graduate course that I anticipate as hopefully hermeneutic, at least interpretive, but never evaluative. Here lies one example of how I am positioned by practice in a role that is doomed to failure if my aim is to engage in a project of unfolding possibilities.

Epistemology of smell and taste

More challenging to current institutional expectations, and in need of further investigation, are the nose and the tongue as models, and scent and taste as metaphors. In one manner the counterpart to listening and the optimistic notion of hermeneutic conversation, smell, for Nietzsche, "sniffs out the cowardice of hypocrisy and decadence that lurk in those most-secret places into which neither eye nor mind can penetrate" (quoted in LeGuerer 1992: 185); instinct, not reason, has "the flair to scent out falsehood as falsehood" and reveal a facade of interpretive or hermeneutic listening as corrupted by evaluative aims. The links between smell and wisdom, mental penetration, and sympathy make it the sense of the psychologist, guided by instinct, whose action consists not of reason but of "scenting out" (LeGuerer 1992).

Nietzsche, Freud, Herbert Marcuse (1964), and Michael Serres (1998) raise the crucial counterpart to content knowledge as a technology of seeing or listening in noting the pleasure and intimacy that is repressed by the domination of sight and hearing over smell and taste. For example, mathematics as abstraction technology – a symbolic representation of a technological conception of experience, a technology in the sense of a thinking tool – does not abandon the idea of a person as a body in a caricature of prosthesis attached to a reasoning brain (the "invisible man"); nor does it deny the notion of a person as indeed a perceiving being (Lowe 1982; Merleau-Ponty 1964a, 1964b); instead, Serres (1998) recognizes, the particular technology constructed by mathematics as experienced in school breaks the body down into parts: seeing and listening are favored over tasting and scenting (see also LeGuerer 1992). The result is a perpetual lurking suspicion of the instigator of this bodily decomposition – the teacher – simultaneous with a harmful repression of pleasure and personal participation through the splitting of one's bodily perception of the world. Ear, Eye, and Arm each show us the implications of such perceptual splitting: for these characters, radiation *in utero* led to a sort of perpetual self-sustaining perceptual viagra for one of the senses. The toll this enhancement takes mirrors the potential of perception to both make things possible, but also to shut down opportunities; overpowered by the intolerable magnification of perception, the trio of heroes live a very marginal and chaotic existence in the dirty, smelly, putrid "Cow's Guts" section of the city.

> Arm braced himself for the assault of sensations from the street.... The others walked on either side of him as if to shelter him, but there was nothing they could really do. Arm almost cried out as the door opened and the tangle of emotions rushed in.... [He] had to suffer the hate, greed and anger boiling around the suburb known as the Cow's Guts. Only an occasional whiff of kindness, like a pale flower wilting in an alley, softened his pain.
>
> ...The streets rioted in all directions, twisting around in a confusing way. Newcomers always got lost, to the delight of muggers. Stolen goods were openly sold here. Drugs were bought as easily as bananas. Beer halls blasted music that made everyone's ribs rattle....
>
> Here, too, came the beggars after their day's work in the wealthy suburbs. Legless men pushed themselves on little carts. Women with milky eyes led children whose hands stuck out like wings from their shoulders.
>
> (Farmer 1994: 48)

I imagine the Cow's Guts is the only place for these men to live. On the one hand, in the Cow's Guts, "a person could have green wings and purple horns: no one would be the least surprised" (p. 49). On the other hand, it is only in the cacophony of the foul Cow's Guts that Ear, Eye, and Arm, so disassociated from their body as a whole that their very names are a sign of the body part that splits their perception from the world, can confront the "truth" that their life experiences have so far revealed to them. Their perceptual powers have certainly led to the repression of pleasure and participation in their life world as they lope from one case to the next. They have developed both a keen, critical perspective on life and society, and, in the process, a parallel, disconnected way of floating through that life, apart from the hypocritical and self-deceiving world of those in power and affluence.

It is in this respect that school knowledge reveals its stench: as a process of "truth" dominated by seeing and listening, it perpetuates in Nietzschean terms an environment of nauseating effluvia effervescent of the shady den in which such ideals are cooked up – ideals that stink to high heaven of falsehood, obliging so many students to hold their noses. My primary curricular field of mathematics, as the discipline most elaborately constructed as a process of "truth," is most odious indeed. Implications of the metaphor include following it further and reconstructing school knowledge in ways that emphasize other aspects of taste and smell. Why not begin with mathematics as a search for pleasure? Mathematics (or any other subject area for that matter) would be in practice a realm for scenting out, not just the foul stench of hypocrisy, but also the delightful fragrances of possibility or the unexpected. In Stephen Brown's study of problem posing and de-posing (Brown 1973, 1984) lurk potential tastes toward this sort of psychoanalytic use of school subject matter; therapeutically, the content area works to reclaim the sense of oneself as a moral acting being. Mathematics is for Brown transformed out of a technique that links means and ends, a tool for "solving it," into a collection of psychoanalytic activity through which one understands oneself and the subject matter in new ways.

My own description of sight and listening privileged over taste and smell, the splitting that occurs as a psychoanalytic crisis, could be understood in Brown's early work as a persistent bypassing of the type of activity that incorporates abstractions "out there" so that we begin to gain power over it and feel that we possess it in some important sense. Brown calls for an education grounded in making observations of a phenomenon, drawing implications from these (assumed valid) observations, using the phenomenon to imagine alternatives to it, negating some of the hypotheses, and posing new problems (Brown 1973). He writes: "If we persist in by-passing this activity" – by which I understand that we persist in the splitting of sight and listening over taste and smell, as opposed to his more wholistic engagement of all the senses –

> we desensitize ourselves to the point that we no longer "taste" the uniqueness among phenomena, and though they may be able to gain answers to questions, they become very much insensitive to what it means for something to be a problem and have even less of an understanding of what it means to have solved something.

> (Brown 1973: 271)

This "insensitivity" is another dimension of the splitting crisis. Mathematical knowledge includes a meta-knowledge of how one "does" the mathematics; developing skills in writing requires a meta-knowledge of one's personal, idiosyncratic ways of writing; working as a scientist is part of learning science beyond mere facts and models. One's relationship to the content knowledge of any discipline, and one's understanding of how this influences the conclusions that are drawn/reached become important considerations in and out of school. Other than this work by Brown, the field of mathematics education is ripe for greater comprehension of the plight of the student. In the area of writing, I recommend works by Jack Collom (1985; Collom and Noethe 1994); in science Margery Osborne (1999) and Angela Calabrese Barton (2003); and in language arts Nina Zaragoza (2002) and Karen Gallas (1994).

David Jardine and colleagues (2003) offer us a new conception of what would be basic to this integrative form of education, through a re-examination of what constitutes the "basics." In their view, the basics consist not of decomposed pieces of knowledge articulated through performance objectives, but of characteristics such as generativity, intergenerationality, recursion, and relationship. In the broader range of school knowledge beyond what Brown describes for mathematics we would hope for such a reconceptualization of curriculum. We begin by recognizing the ways in which school knowledge privileges sight and hearing over taste and smell. Touch, unique in its own ways, calls forth, like hearing, the notion that the perceiver is transformed in the process of perception. But this could have been claimed for sight all along. Surely the act of seeing requires similar bodily transformation and therefore may be understood as making a change in the seer. Yet instead of leading to a new sense of vision, hearing and touch reconstruct vision as the model for all perception, reinscribing the visual metaphor within this narrowly conceived hegemony of perception. What we are left with is a student who can see but who sees nothing, who can hear but hears little, and who can feel but feels hardly anything at all. Does this student taste or smell? Not in school. As Søren Kierkkegaard reflected,

> One sticks one's finger into the soil to tell by the smell what land one is on. I stick my finger into existence – it smells of nothing. Where am I? Who am I? How did I come to be here? What is this thing called world? How did I come into the world? Why was I not consulted? ... and if I am compelled to take part in it, where is the Director? I would like to see him!
>
> (quoted in LeGuerer 1992: 197)

Much like Ear, Eye, and Arm, we and our students are bombarded with too much sensory input, and don't know how to negotiate the cacophony, to make meaning out of our everyday life in and out of school. We put on conceptual ear-muffs, shut our eyes. But some of us, like Arm, need to be carried around like invalids by our friends, unable to negotiate life in the Cow's Guts. We are the epitome of school success. In fact, it is our careful embrace of school learning which leads to this miasma, very much like the episode from which my Ellison quote at the beginning of this chapter is taken. There the protagonist:

> has eyes and ears and a good distended African nose, but he fails to understand the simple facts of life. *Understand.* Understand? It's worse than that. He registers with his senses but short-circuits his brain. Nothing has meaning. He takes it in but he doesn't digest it. Already he is – well, bless my soul! Behold! a walking zombie! Already he's learned to repress not only his emotions but his humanity. He's invisible, a walking personification of the Negative, the most perfect achievement of your dreams, sir! The mechanical man!
>
> (Ellison 1947: 86)

The invisible man is traceable to his education, and his complete embracement of its promise, the subsequent chaotic interaction with the white man, and his excommunication from the world of school into the real world of the senses and his authentic education, much like Farmer's young characters, is a powerful indictment of schooling in our society. School had refined his senses as prosthetic attachments to a mechanized brain, the essence of the invisible man. So are Tendai, Rita, and Kuda invisible and anchorless when we first meet them, cloistered in their attractive home and meaningless repressed existence.

Still looking: for a way out of the ideology

I am arguing for a changing interpretation of school knowledge, technology, and professional development, one that does not reproduce the splitting crisis of sight and hearing over taste and smelling, and indeed, one that does not depend on an assumption of perception. One way through, out, around, or under might be to establish a sort of integrated perception epistemology that does not privilege some constellation of the senses over another. I have shared some possibilities in this direction; but by the end of this chapter I hope to convince you that this strategy is inadequate. Such an approach would nevertheless maintain school subject matter knowledge (for example, mathematics) as an object of reflection. My description of the work by Stephen Brown indicates one potential perspective. Weisglass offers a compatible process of professional development intended to help teachers with "the crisis of re-integration" (Weisglass 1994: 73) through constructivist listening to one another in dyads. As Ear, Eye, and Arm help us to understand, the perceptual enhancement does more than enhance our senses. It re-engineers us, mutates us into new and different beings. With our strapped-on prosthetic versions of Ear, Eye, and Arm's special "natural" wonders (in their case caused, of course, by a technological "mistake"), we are not just the same people with a cool tool. We now become new cyborg beings that experience especially good perception but associated handicaps.

Philosophers of education and curriculum theorists have routinely tried to escape the limitations of vision by using another metaphor of perception – popular examples, already mentioned here, include touch (also conceptualized as mediation by Sartre and existential curriculum theorists), hearing (see, under enactivism, e.g., Davis *et al.* 2000), and taste (Brown 1973, 1984). I claim this is hardly better, as these metaphors are still trapped in the same ideology of perception. Could it be that this approach merely clouds the issues in a new sense of "complexity" without giving us any guidance? I want to suggest that it is possible to avoid the conceptual collapse of perception and learning altogether by finding an alternative to school knowledge similar in some ways to what Brown proposes but which also avoids the reification of knowledge as a thing to which people relate or with which people do something. If particular school subject areas are understood as features of cultural practice and thus as a characteristic of professional action, we can enter the pedagogical encounter or professional development with knowledge as a mediating cultural process rather than as a technology. I am trying to make a distinction between the knowledge as the technology and the kind of knowledge that we 'see' with technology. Galileo's galaxy is only a certain technology for understanding the cosmos, because he used a prosthetic tool to construct it. School content knowledge can embrace the larger realm of cultural processes that include this technical knowledge, but also the richer, more complex other knowledges that we start to feel, smell, and taste once we move away from vision as the primary model.

The next step is to move beyond the reintegrated notion of perception itself, and work within an alternative universe of mediating processes. For example, mathematics might still be recognizable as a technology of vision, as a way of seeing the world; but, more importantly, it would be understood by the teacher, the curriculum designer, the administrator, the evaluator, and other members of the school community as a cultural resource for the construction and mediation of meaning and action (Appelbaum 1995b). This shift, from one of cacophony and stench, toward a vertigo of possibility and opportunity, is what I believe we are yearning for when Kierkegaard uses the (phallic – a possible connection to my discussion of gendered poaching in Chapter 1) image of sticking one's finger into existence, or when Jardine, Clifford and Friesen write about intergenerationality as basic to teaching and learning, and I believe it is also what Nancy Farmer helps us to think about toward the end of her novel, when Tendai allows the spirit of his ancestors to enter into his own existence.

The *Mhondoro* of curriculum

Enhancing perception is simply not enough to make a difference in the world. It turns out that all enhanced perception gets you is a stronger "sense" of what is at stake. Ear, Eye, and Arm, the detectives, are not just trying to find some missing children, even if that was what they were hired to do. These kids are caught up in a struggle for the heart and soul of Zimbabwe itself! All of the science and technology that has transformed the outward appearance of life in this potential future has left unchanged the central issues of politics and religion, which turn out to be about morality and ethics, and one's relationship to the generations who have come before. To confront the ultimate questions of evil and ethics – and indeed, as we find out in this book, to save the soul of the people – one of us needs the spirit of all those who have come before us to enter our souls so that we can act on its behalf. Why not just channel the energy and become a mediator for the forces of good in the world, as much religious thought suggests? Like the early New England settlers, should we fear that Ol' Deluder, Satan, rampant in the forest of our Massachusetts, and declare a requirement that every child be taught to read the Bible (or, in our more modern situation, perhaps include any sacred text, such as the *Koran*, the *Bhagavad-Gita*, Mary Baker Eddy's *Science and Health*)? Here lies the problem with mediation as the "solution" to my constructed "problem": enhanced perception merely produces an overwhelming cacophony of sights, sounds, feelings, and so on. As Davis and colleagues (2000) suggest, we get a different sense of the experience of education by working with the complexity of this cacophony rather than trying to make it go away. Yet is this enough? William Doll (1993) notes that a postmodern curriculum occurs when control is replaced by perturbation, difficulty, and complexity: instead of imposing possibilities and keeping all students on the same track, a postmodern curriculum would encourage diversity, multiple perspectives, and exploration. Curriculum in any subject area, in this sense, becomes a mediating process – "not of transmitting what is (absolutely) known but of exploring what is unknown; and through exploration students and teachers 'clear the land' together, thereby transforming both the land and themselves" (Doll 1993: 155).

To escape ideology is a pernicious task. How can we think about a curriculum not limited by vision without using metaphors of vision? Jayne Fleener (2002: 166) accepts the difficulties, hoping that a particular discussion of the ways metaphors are inadequate might be enough to help us move toward such a new curricular discourse. She notes that Doll suggests four ways of imagining (there's that visual metaphor again!) the curriculum as a self-organizing process: the curriculum should be rich, recursive, relational, and rigorous. She then works with metaphors to think about, for example, "richness," which "refers to a curriculum's depth, to its layers of meaning, to its multiple possibilities of interpretations" (Doll 1993: 176). The images Fleener conjures forth that we may associate with depth and layers include digging holes or peeling an onion.

> In digging a hole, we are digging deeper, going to greater depths through hard work. We hear similar words all the time, especially in sports. "Dig Deeper" implies trying harder, working harder, and tapping more of your inner strength and resources. Similarly, with onions, if we think of the curriculum as an onion, we only scratch the surface when we present topics superficially. Going to deeper levels might imply a more thorough and complete investigation of some particular concept, including making connections with other ideas. The phrase "mile wide and an inch deep" has been used to refer to the lack of depth of the American mathematics curriculum.
>
> (Fleener 2002: 166)

As Fleener points out, neither of these metaphors captures Doll's meaning of richness, because they both take as given content knowledge and assumed shared understandings of what we think is important for students to know in any particular field of study. If content is taken *as* the curriculum, this makes curriculum into a "thing." Both "digging deeper" and "going to deeper layers" are still treating the curriculum as a given thing rather than as a mediating process. The Mandelbrot set, Fleener suggests, is closer to what we are seeking, because it captures the process and emerging relationships of Doll's postmodern curriculum: "As we move around the edges of the Mandelbrot set, we see infinite complexity. While at the same time common patterns and relationships continue to appear" (Fleener 2002: 166). As Fleener notes in her further explication of images that serve Doll's conception, the importance of curriculum as a communication or meaning system has been overlooked for its potential to transform schools. Often, literature on school changes starts with changing administrative structures, power relations and mission statements. "Although not unconnected to the curriculum by any means, these approaches often fail to notice the ideas that perhaps changing what we expect students to learn and how we expect them to learn may in fact challenge the other structures" (Fleener 2002: 174). The Mandelbrot set is an image Fleener uses to help explain the possibilities for embracing complexity as we move from curriculum as thing to curriculum as process. She uses it also to represent the ways in which generations of curricula and reverberations within the set can enable us to rethink the role of relations between and among parts and pieces of the curriculum. In this image, the parts and pieces are clearly part of a larger holistic set even as they may appear to be unrelated when looked at closely. By conjuring this image, Fleener links her work in curriculum to that of Jardine *et al.*, who also struggle to find an alternative to a curriculum made up of possibly unrelated bits and pieces.

Jardine, Clifford, and Friesen's interpretive treatment of the basics mourns the ways that schools have lost the presence of all generations working together. Any living tradition of work, they write, requires the co-presence of all generations, because the truth of that work is inherently *inter*generational. This includes the presence of the new learners as well, so that their presence is essential to the well-being of that work as a tradition. They use two examples. The first is working in a garden with a 7-year-old. One doesn't send him off to a "developmentally appropriate garden." Instead the adult and the child go to the same garden and work together. This is very much what John Dewey (1915) meant by school teaching the occupations of life once industrialization had separated the generations in order for the adults to go off to work. Once the generations reach the garden and get down to work, each works as each is able – certainly not identical in ability, experience, strength, patience, and so on; *both* work *in the same place* doing some part of the *real* work that the garden requires, part of the continuity of attention and devotion that this place needs to remain whole (Jardine *et al.* 2006: 112).

How apt then that our work in question is written by a "Farmer!" Sure, these children have been kidnapped and therefore separated from the older generation, their parents. In this surface interpretation, the book is about bringing them back together. However, the larger context is that the children and their parents have been separated from each other all along, even as they lived in the same house. We can't just look for them – find them – in order to reunite them as a family. This is because, while they may appear to be lost, the more pressing issue is this lack of intergenerationality. And because of this, the task is much grander, requiring the whole nation as an extended family, and indeed, all of that nation's ancestors, so that the intergenerationality can be completely accomplished. It is only now that we can clearly see that the picaresque quality of this book, with Tendai, Rita, and Kuda meeting all sorts of isolated communities of outcasts and outlaws, is at the core of the very curricular meaning that is unfolding in our explication. The spirit of the ancestors, the *Mhondoro*, can only enter our world once the children have brought the pieces of this world back together through their encounters. The ability of some adults to have remarkably talented perception does not help the children to accomplish this important task, which they must do themselves.

"In an interpretive understanding of the basics, each person's work in the classroom is not treated as a subjective or interior possession, but is treated as something that happens out in the world, with others, in the presence of others and their work in this place" (Jardine *et al.* 2006: 112). In other words, each person's work is therefore taken up as adding itself to the richness of the place that we *all* find ourselves living in. In my reading of *The Ear, the Eye and the Arm*, the *Mhondoro* is a way of describing Gadamer's (1989) "increase in being" that arises when the intellectual and cultural inheritances of the curriculum are furthered through reading, study, analysis, and conversation. All of the conversations that occur in intergenerational learning add themselves to what had been previously understood, layering new interpretations upon former ones to form a parallel set of textual interpretations that model the generationality of life. Sometimes, I think, we confuse conception with perception when we think about teaching and learning. For Gadamer, interpretive exploration is not merely a question of a subjective variety of conceptions – a mistake we might be prone to make if we thought that learning was collapsible into perception, but more directly an issue of some phenomenon's own possibilities of being that emerge as it explicates itself in all of the potential variety of its own aspects. A phenomenon that is "looked at" by a teacher and a group of students together is a living inheritance, which includes all the ways that it has "gathered and collected itself" (p. 97) over time, and, in addition, our own explorations, leading to our own voices, objections and discoveries, as we stick our fingers into its existence.

Jardine et al.'s second example involves a group of people in a school exploring the meaning of numbers. The story allows them to question common interpretations of Piagetian developmentalism, where we presume a developmental line along which children's abilities might be strung. Piaget may be understood to be proposing something more analogous to evolution than linear progress, so that bodily and concrete manipulations of objects in the world ("like footfalls of the young child on a staircase counted out with each decent" Jardine et al. (2006: 117)) bear a family resemblance to some (e.g., mathematical) ways of thinking. Many different, discrete, concrete phenomena help to open a space around the other, making the other more comprehensible than it would have been without the co-presence of all its generations, i.e., all of its multiple relations. In this way,

> the halting steps of the young child do not need to be conceived simply as in need of maturation, refinement, and eventual replacement, or as some sort of proto-mathematics. Rather, these steps are paced out by one of us, one of our kin, and they articulate mathematical kinships and relations in ways that are irreplaceable in a full understanding of the whole of mathematics.
>
> (ibid.)

Children's literature often carries the message that it is the youth who can teach the older generations, even as the adults convey the wisdom of traditions. The book we are discussing here certainly has a thread of that same message. The details of Farmer's story are valuable, however, in helping us to think about the specific ways in which such mutual teaching and learning can unfold. A young child's steps down a staircase are not in and of themselves the adult version of numbers, but they are something far more important than that adult version of things. These steps of the child have the power to keep mathematical knowledge and mathematical ways of being in the world "in place, in relation" (Jardine et al. 2006: 117). They have the power to prevent mathematical operations from becoming "simply self-referential and self-enclosed, and all the consequent memory loss that ensues in the collapse into clear, memorizable (but not especially memorable) equations and operations" (pp. 117–118). The presence of the young child helps us to keep knowledge and meaning open to the arrival of renewal, and of difference. When we think this way we make mathematics, or any subject matter, a living tradition. Education becomes the renewal of memory!

I suspect this is what Stephen Brown (2001) is aiming at when he writes about purpose and meaning in mathematics education. (Again, while I am using mathematics as an example, I really have in mind any subject matter. Mathematics has that wonderful characteristic that people more readily assume it is immune from issues of value, morality, ethics, and so on. If we can change our conception of mathematics curriculum, surely we would have to change our conception of curriculum in general?) He writes, for example, that making something more concrete does little to clarify why it is that the idea is worth investigating in the first place (p. 86). What is needed, he declares, is a set of experiences that make clear why it is that "primitive" (*sic*) ways of characterizing numbers – such as using stones to convey how many horses there are in the village – have their shortcomings. (Place value was generated over time for a purpose, and that purpose is not revealed in learning how to handle place value problems in a meaningful way!) Brown continues to marvel at how readily his students see worlds he had never imagined, as they supposedly "misconceive" what he saw as the central focus. Pursuing their supposed misconceptions, not in order to fix them but to see where they lead, often leads to the exploration of valuable territory that nobody *in the world* has ever seen before. "If we teach with the expectation that errors, questions from left field, and confusions have generative power," he writes, "then we can appreciate that even supposedly naïve students are capable of changing the way we view any aspect of knowledge or experience."

Brown, like Jardine *et al.*, warns against viewing receiving the child's emerging meaning as depicting a progressive mode, juxtaposed with the adult teacher's imposed view, even if the teacher works with imagination, compassion, and concern for whether or not the child's meaning is understood. He returns to John Dewey, who recognized that this dualistic outlook masks an important commonality: we are too easily clouded by the assumption that subject matter furnishes the end at one end-point of the spectrum, while the child is the starting point at the other.

> From the side of the child, it is a question of seeing how his experience already contains within itself elements – facts and truths – of just the same sort as those entering into the formulated study; and what is of more importance is how it contains within itself the attitudes, the

motives and the interests which have operated in developing and organizing the subject matter to the plane which it now occupies.

(Dewey 1902: 345)

From the other end of this distracting spectrum, the subject matter specialist must see how academic studies are themselves experiences that "embody the cumulative outcome of the efforts, the strivings, and successes of the human generation after generation" (p. 345). In this way,

> the facts and truths that enter into the child's present experience, and those contained in the subject matter of studies, are the initial and final forms of one reality. To oppose one to the other is to oppose the infancy and maturity of the same growing life; it is to set the moving tendency and the final result of the same process against each other.
>
> (ibid.)

Dewey helps us to see that some of our confusion about education may originate in the silly assumption we make that the child and the curriculum are two separate things. When and why would anyone have sent us down the curriculum road with such baggage? What Brown takes this to mean is that we do not need to fixate on the child's interests, as some child-centered pedagogy has misunderstood, nor do we need to make any kind of compromise in the sense of teaching from the point of view of imposing a subject matter perspective while sometimes listening to the child. What he suggests is that however we structure the educational experience, we must keep in mind what is common between the two ostensibly different poles:

> we need to see at every turn that whatever we observe to be a subject matter perspective and whatever we observe about the meanings that a child imposes on the world, we would profit from trying to see these from an evolutionary perspective.
>
> (Brown 2001: 87)

So, for example, we would gain from asking questions of an epistemological nature, such as: What might this idea have looked like 100 years ago, 1,000 years ago? What might have inspired people to move beyond that idea? What forces might have prevented humans from altering their understanding of this idea? The point, for Brown, is to see every idea of a "naïve" learner as potentially evolving into something else. Furthermore, we would need to value the reverberations among and between questions and situations in which these questions come about. In mathematics, for example, school tends to present students with prepared problems to be solved. Better from Brown's perspective would be to move from a focus on creating problems out of situations or from recognizing situations for which a particular problem type is appropriate, toward trying to understand what motives some people have for creating some situations while others create different ones, or to why some kinds of created problems or situations are more appealing to some and not others. This, he suggests, begins to establish a dialogue, which enables people to reflect on what they value and how they think.

Here we have a reverberation of our own, regarding our own questions and situations. What leads us as educators to apply vision as our universal metaphor for learning and coming to know? Brown writes that communicating with others about "what we believe can be transformed from a problem to a situation" enables us to tell each other what we "see" even when we may not be stating it explicitly. How does vision creep into this important discussion of pedagogy? Brown is very interested in the ways in which new questions and ideas can be generated in mathematics. So he notes parallels between hidden assumptions in different situations. For example, he notes how most people do not notice that a typical definition of prime numbers takes for granted that the domain of natural numbers (those we count with) are salient, and in this way transformable into some other set. Likewise, centuries went by before anyone thought of recasting the axioms of geometry in ways that allow us to see Euclidean geometry as merely one kind of geometry: something marvelous had to happen in order for the questions to change from "how to prove the parallel postulate" to "how many different ways could we understand what parallel means, and how would this affect what we do in geometry." In seriously pursuing Dewey's plea for avoiding the subject matter–learner perspective dichotomy, Brown leaps to "seeing" an analogy between pedagogy and evolutionary knowledge, and therefore to the powerful notion of learning as seeing things differently from how one saw those things before, just as Fleener gives us the Mandelbrot set to help us think about a "thingless" curriculum.

As with the other chapters in this book, children's literature helps us to make new sense of curriculum and pedagogy. I want to present the idea that the *Mhondoro* of curriculum does not deny perception, but also does not find perception to be what is important. Tendai, Rita, and Kuda do not change or learn through denial of sensory perception in Farmer's tale. Indeed, they are forced through a variety of circumstances to see, hear, feel, taste, smell, and otherwise perceive *many new things*. We would all agree that these experiences are educational in numerous ways. So in the end, we must accept that perception *is* a kind of learning. This kind of learning synonymous with perceiving new things works best, we can tell, when the circumstances in which the new perceptions take place matter to the lives of the people perceiving. Here, for example, they are struggling for their lives. The important thing in this book, though, is that all of the new experiences are not enough. Seeing things, tasting things, and so on do not make it possible for the children to save themselves or the world as they know it; in fact, it is not clear to them until the very end that they are important in saving their world. If his experiences are his curriculum, new perceptions have merely prepared Tendai for the *Mhondoro*'s arrival. We can see in the climax of this work that all the previous preparation did not teach him much of anything of consequence. Instead, it is only through the *Mhondoro* that he has learned what is really going on in the world.

This is a truly fecund pedagogical point. Without experiencing the *Mhondoro*, we might accept the new perceptions made possible by all the picaresque experiences to be the essence of Tendai's education. This is my reading of Rousseau. In *Emile* (1979), Rousseau argues that the child must be removed from civilization in order to be prepared to re-enter it as an educated adult. He provides experiences that force the child to perceive anew the "real world" as nature has presented it; these new perceptions are the fundamental processes of education. In *The Ear, the Eye and the Arm*, we might find a similar message. The children must be removed from their everyday life and placed into the reality of less artificial worlds in order to re-enter the world of their parents, as truly educated people. In the same way that Rousseau allows nature to surprise the child and therefore to force him to make meaning out of these surprises, so do the various worlds that Tendai, Rita, and Kuda pass through challenge their expectations in ways that force them to see the society they are meant to be part of in a new light, so to speak. Jardine *et al.*'s garden analogy echoes Rousseau as well: Emile sows his own garden as part of a lesson in the value of work, literally and figuratively bearing fruit. One day he comes to check on the progress of his efforts only to find his garden ripped asunder. What has happened? What has led to this terrible fate? Rousseau had Emile intentionally plant his garden on land owned by another farmer, who saw Emile's garden as preventing his own hard work from bearing fruit. Such a surprise is a hard lesson learned through seeing his work represented by his garden in this new light. Tendai, Rita, and Kuda similarly "earn" how to be successful in each of their new worlds of hard work. In this story, as in *Emile,* the hard work does not always lead to the expected pay-off; plot twists force the children to understand their efforts in new contexts, and thus to seriously confront their beliefs about the world and about humanity. As Brown suggests, thinking about the relationship between problems they seem to need to solve and the contexts in which these problems are articulated is an educational encounter.

Yet these experiences are mere preparation, not education. In the interpretation I am offering here, "seeing things in a new light" is mere perception, as opposed to education. In *Emile,* we find out in the end that all of that education was barely enough. It is only through marriage to Sophie that education can truly occur. All pales in comparison with this new beginning:

> Finally I see dawning the most charming of Emile's days and the happiest of mine. I see my attentions consummated, and I begin to taste their

fruit. An indissoluble chain unties the worthy couple. Their mouths pronounce and their hearts confirm vows which will not be vain. They are wed. In returning from the temple, they let themselves be led. They do not know where they are, where they are going, or what is done around them. They do not hear; they respond only with confused words; their clouded eyes no longer see anything. O delirium! O human weakness! The sentiment of happiness crushes man. He is not strong enough to bear it.

(Rousseau 1979: 475)

I find a valuable set of lessons when I juxtapose Rousseau with Farmer. Rousseau places the father as the teacher in his fiction, and this teacher makes many careful calculations in order to create the most appropriate education. Note, too, that he maintains perception as synonymous with education, as when he sees the most charming of days "dawning," and the teacher can begin to taste the fruit of his efforts. Tendai, Rita, and Kuda either have no teachers, or have many different ones, however we wish to think about it. But their father is specifically absent, as is any other teacher, including the Praise Singer, who in some ways has filled this role in the past. The fact that the Praise Singer sets them off on their "quest" at their request is significant as a pedagogical act. But the primary message I take away from all of this is that there need not be a teacher. All a teacher would do is decide what perceptions the child is more likely to have than others. In this case, we see that a child sent off on their own, while a dangerous and frightening experience, also leads to just as many perceptions. This clearly implies that perception in general is not the result of the teacher, and instead is a fact of life. We all perceive things, as humans, all of the time. New perceptions in new places are important because they allow us, as Brown notes, to see things in new ways, a critically essential feature of a curriculum. Perceptions are essential for learning, but are not the embodiment of education: there is something more than perception that constitutes the difference between seeing things and growing as a person. Teachers may be powerful in ways that learners are not – for example, in being able to see and hear things that their students are not capable of – yet these perceptual enhancements are of little relevance, since it is the actual perceptions of the learner that form the substance of their experiences. A teacher might fantasize about controlling the precise sensations that enter the child, but such a dream is a mere distraction from the task at hand.

Furthermore, Farmer gives us the *Mhondoro* where Rousseau gave us the experience of marriage. We might find something of value in thinking about the similarities here; for one thing, Rousseau constructs marriage as part of the cycle of generations. However, the differences are more important in my mind. For Rousseau, the main point of education, finally taking place in the experience of marriage, is to "bear the yoke which you have imposed on yourself" (p. 479); Emile must strive to be true to his ethical identity in spite of the compromises that society demands of him, and finally, in spite of his own choices for himself. For Farmer, the main point is to channel the *Mhondoro*, the spirit of one's ancestors. For Rousseau, the ultimate ending is Emile's expectation of his own child, and therefore his own obligation to be the teacher. "God forbid that so holy and so sweet a duty should ever be fulfilled by anyone but myself, even if I were to make as good a choice for my son as was made for me" (p. 480). For Farmer, the ending is a reordering of the society itself rather than finding a role within it that does not compromise one's personal values and beliefs. Tendai studies medicine, but also spends time with the Lion Spirit Medium, who agrees to train him in the special discipline that would allow him access to the *Mhondoro*; "having once been accepted by the Spirit to the land, it seemed likely he would be chosen again" (p. 300). He remains open to further reordering of himself and society, and strives to be ready.

Whither technology?

The power of the *Mhondoro* is that this spirit of the ancestors is not a representation of a position in a debate between technology and perception on the one hand, and relationships with people on the other. I imagine the *Mhondoro* would never allow itself to be used as a pawn in a two-sided debate of that sort. Indeed the climactic scene where the *Mhondoro* is present in the human world is, in my mind, about the very absurdity of such a simplistic conception. It turns out that there are groups of people who are working to manipulate the spirit of the ancestors toward their own ends; this is something that cannot happen simply because intergenerationality is not merely a technology of perception or a tool of power. We might have predicted this earlier when we read about the relationships between technology and society as they are represented in this book. From the start we get a glimpse of a futuristic Zimbabwe where affluent people have many forms of advanced appliances, security devices, and personal robotic assistants. Pointedly, a character called the "Mellower," a human being, is an essential household item whose main purpose is to sing the praises of family members, leading to feelings of well-being and happiness, important features of a good life that require a person rather than an electronic technology. As the children move from one picaresque experience to the next, we get variations from this primary relationship. For example, as the children disembark from a bus at Mbare Musika for their original day's adventure, they are introduced to a cacophonous and busy market little changed from years past by the prevalence of technology, similar in this respect to the Cow's Guts. However, it is the Blue Monkey, a genetically modified being, which makes it possible for their kidnapping to take place, suggesting early on that technology makes life easier at home in some respects, but leads in Frankensteinish ways to unintended and frightening consequences as well, even as new technologies in this outer world seem to leave most of society and life as we understand it pretty much the same.

The three major episodes in this book can further help us to think about technology and society, and how the relationships between them are connected to intergenerationality. First there is Dead Man's Vlei, a wasteland formerly used as a dump, now a vast, despicable no-man's territory. Since oil has not been available for many, many years, non-biodegradable plastics have become a rare treasure of antiquity. So people now mine the Dead Man's Vlei for plastic bowls and other valuable objects. A sea of miners blend into the gray wasteland, ironically under the influence of the She-elephant, a large woman who cooks food both unbelievably delicious and strong in drugs that leaves the eaters at her mercy. In contrast, Resthaven is a utopian community cut off permanently from the rest of the country, so that people who live there can return to the traditions and values of their ancestors, in some ways comparable to an extreme version of Amish life in their rejection of modern technology and adherence to traditional ways of life. These two communities might suggest, for our purposes, that there are at least two implications of technology other than the children's mainstream home life or the chaotic marketplace of Mbare Muskia: it is important nevertheless that all of these relationships to technology require the others in order to exist themselves. The Vlei for me represents the transitory nature of contemporary technologies: like plastic, they turn to waste and lead to the destruction of ecosystems and habitats, only to become treasured relics in the future. Resthaven demonstrates the romantic attraction of a nostalgic past. Each holds horrors and dangers of its own, so that the children are able to understand after the time they spend in each that the danger is not the result of technology even though technology alone does lead to ecological havoc; in the end, it is the meaning of people's actions, and the ways they are interpreted, that are key to survival and social change in a given context. While the fantasy is that the spirit of the ancestors lives in this nostalgic utopia, it turns out that the *Mhondoro* is present at the heart of the modern city; still, we learn at the end of the book that Tendai returns regularly to the Resthaven gate, wondering if the people are still there, assuming they are maintaining their important ties to the past. Farmer introduces the curious complication of Trashman, seemingly what might be labeled in our terms a grown "special education student," who travels routinely through the Vlei, Resthaven, and every other domain in this book. Trashman was impossible to reward for helping the children through their difficulties, we learn with little surprise.

> He simply accepted whatever was given him, whether he severed it or not. No matter how kind the Matsikas were to him, they would awaken one morning and find him missing from the heap of grass clippings her

preferred as a bed. He wandered throughout the city. Sometimes he disappeared altogether. Tendai thought he had found a way [back again] into Resthaven.... No one, with the possible exception of Trashman, even knew if the people inside were still alive.

The third of these important episodes is the strange interlude during which the children are held captive in the post-colonial European enclave. Here we see how Western knowledge can so easily be used as a tool of power, as the children are deceived into believing they are being cared for while they are ill. If each episode is preparation for the arrival of the *Mhondoro*, then we might imagine a certain trajectory or sequence of purification rituals that Farmer implies are necessary prerequisites for intergenerationality. Such a sequence would include: a recognition of the failures and harmful results of technological "progress" (Dead Man's Vlei); a nostalgic retreat to a romantic version of pre-technology, only to discover that removing modern technology does not remove the dangers of human interpretation and the limits of understanding which that entails (Resthaven); deception of the utility of Colonialist knowledge (Mrs. Horsepool-Worthingham's home); and finally the intergenerationality of the *Mhondoro* of the curriculum. Alternatively we may take from this tale the lesson that none of the previous forms of generationality are adequate to the task, so that only the connection to the present through intergenerationality through the *Mhondoro* of the curriculum is enough for education to be present.

5
Feed

At the Bergamo Conference on Curriculum Theory and Classroom Practice sponsored by the *Journal of Curriculum Theorizing* (JCTBergamo, undated), Karen Ferneding attended a presentation I gave on the overlap of consumer culture and curriculum; afterwards, she recommended what was at that time a new book by M.T. Anderson entitled *Feed*. Since then I have been reading this work with graduate students in curriculum. The book is about that first generation of youth who have the internet surgically implanted as a chip in their bodies, so that they are linked to the "feed" at all times. Karen's interest in the book may have been based on her interest in electronic technologies, but she quickly saw the direct connections to what I was trying to figure out about how consumer culture and curriculum interact with identity politics and object relations. Not all of us are excited by science fiction; I often introduce this book to a class by requesting an initial suspension of negativity as the reader slowly adapts to new words and situations that are hard to find. I suggest thinking like an anthropologist who is entering a new culture and enjoys coming to a living understanding of that culture. After all, I point out, much of teaching might be analogous to working as an anthropologist, since teachers need to understand the lives and meanings their students bring with them to the classroom, and to understand the classroom community the group are forming through their common work. All of this introductory discussion ends up being unnecessary for many of us, as the book is a wonderful and quick read. It's really not hard to enter into this story. Nor is it so much a science fiction: I read the book as a report on the state of contemporary youth culture. How different is a chip implanted in the body from a cell phone or PDA in the pocket? In this respect, *Feed* is about "now" only amplified just a tad to help us highlight features of electronic technologies and youth experience in a consumer culture. And it doesn't hurt that, for no apparent reason that I can see, M.T. Andersen chose to place a major character Violet Durn's home at 1421 *Applebaum* Avenue.

Bear with me as I introduce a few terms in this chapter. I will explain more about them as I go. I am writing in the liminal terrain that is both between and overlapping curriculum theory and teacher education. Specifically, I want to interrogate the complicity and complexity of consumer culture, object relations, and the ideology of perception, with a guest appearance by the concept of "habitus" (Bourdieu 1977). *Feed*, I believe, is extremely useful for these purposes.

Introducing basic concepts

My entry into consumer culture is my long-term fascination with the *duality* of any object constructed in or through consumer culture. It was in John Fiske (1989a, 1989b) that I first came across this idea: consumer culture does not create a dichotomy, but a duality, of commodities and cultural resources. Any "thing" in consumer culture – from a tube of toothpaste, to a fifth-grade student, to the concept of balance, from test prep materials, to yogurt containers, to the image of the yogurt container, to the lifestyle promised by the image of the yogurt container juxtaposed to the test prep materials – any such "thing" is, at once, a commodity to be sold and consumed, *and* a resource, through, with, and mediated by which, cultural workers (that is, people) can create meaning and construct new relationships. In his early work, Fiske traced jeans through a history of simultaneity, of people choosing to wear jeans; once identified with rural labor, in order to create a political statement about social change, of the same commodity, "jeans" were later sold as fashion statements, and even later become implicated in a differentiation of designer, pre-washed, and marketed jeans versus new forms of denim as used by various cultural subgroups for a range of political, trans-gendered, and social purposes. I have used this idea at great length in my own work in curriculum theory. For example, Malcolm's inventive use of "X," of the notion of variable (as a powerful application of the concept of variable in order to clearly communicate the multiplicity of surnames that might be assigned to him, given the particularities of histories and politics of race) can be compared to the essentially "unknown" value of his family name post-slavery. This was "variables as cultural resource," even as X-brand potato chips, X-hats and shirts, and other X commodities were and are marketed in ways that turn Malcolm as a resource into a vital commodity: EXXON – one of the first corporations to recognize the market potential of the X; Generation X, a predictable outcome of consumer culture's need to place people into categories of market demographics – and X-Games, a more recent symbol of the duality of commodity and resource, which makes clear its unwillingness to distinguish between the resource (Xtreme sports, as Xpression of cultural desires) and commodity (the selling and marketing of the games, players, accessories, and so on). The important question for curriculum is: Given the cultural proclivity to commodify, what sorts of educational encounters are more likely to embrace and foster the playful use and aesthetics of cultural resources over the processes of commodification?

My sense of object relations is primarily drawn through interaction with writings by D.W. Winnicott, Alan Block (1997), Deborah Britzman (1998, 2003) and Alice Pitt (2003). Having wrestled with consumer culture's historic moment, in which any cultural resource, a book, a person, a human gesture, or an ephemeral fragrance, is at once an object for marketing and consumption, I delighted in a psychoanalysis that is informed so profoundly by the idea that any conceivable "thing" is a potential object that a person might relate to in some way. The brilliant theoretical gesture of psychoanalysis, I believe, is to foreground that rather obvious "fact." There is never a moment in which any human being is not already steeped in a history of relationships – to other objects in and of one's environment. In fact, a person could be understood as an expression of the ongoing creation of relations with objects of self. The question for curriculum becomes: Can there be relationships other than those of reification (of turning something into an object, and identifying that object through its personal assignment of its particular "thingness"), and of production (of assimilating an object as a potential meaning-maker, capable of mediating and hence constructing new possible relations)? Object relations sets me up to ask: What sorts of educational encounters allow for an object to be "taken" in relation as a cultural resource, and which types of encounters tend to make this less likely?

It is within this framework of consumer culture and object relations that I begin my thoughts on education and teacher education. Given the hyper-reality of so much curriculum work – of writing and talking and teaching and learning *about* teaching and learning itself – if one spends any time interpreting one's efforts in the discourses of consumer culture and psychoanalysis, one runs up against a peculiar ideology of vision, in which "coming to know" is hegemonically equated with perception. This is discussed at length in Chapter 3 of this book. Imagine, first, serious efforts to understand teacher education in terms of consumer culture. Everything is at once a commodity and a cultural resource: subject matters are marketed to students and family members, while practitioners of the disciplines use the content of their subjects to reinterpret and comprehend their life world; text materials, too, are bought and sold, and "sold" to the students as "useful reading," even as writers either use textbooks to work politically for a new conception of their discipline or to make money selling what's wanted by the market; people (teachers, students, potential students) are both resources and commodities to be bought and sold; systems of evaluation, forms of institutional structure, special programs, and so on are subject to the whims of salesmanship and the fads that subcultures use to establish identity even as they open up fields of possibility for new ways of understanding education and schooling. In particular, all are bought and sold in the rituals and practices of teacher education. Likewise, these very same participants are expressions of their object relations. The experiences of teacher education "events" are psychoanalytic encounters through which people are denied and enabled new objects and new relations. Choices and actions of a student, a teacher, a future teacher, and so on are both expressions of these relations to the vast complex of objects in their environment (and, by objects, we mean *everything*, from things like string and blocks to other people to the idea of a hexagon or a recursive function to the notion of justice) and opportunities to create relationships with objects in the environment. But suppose we are actively working to use these discourses as resources in our educational work. At some point we can no longer deny the authority of vision in our metaphors: the way we make things into objects that can be seen, or could be seen "in our mind's eye," the way we turn ourselves and others into unitary, individual standpoints in a Cartesian or Euclidean "space" with all other aspects of our environment, of that space, as objects floating around in our imagined space. Some of these objects hover in particular locations, attached to us by webs of relation. Others whiz by so fast that we can't grab hold of them; still others we can't "see" – they are behind us, are too far away, they're just not in our field of vision. In general, all of our language for speaking about learning can be reduced to an assumption that "coming to know" is pretty much a process equivalent to perceiving. Sure, there have been philosophical variations on this perception, as discussed in Chapter 3, some of which emphasize touch over sight, or smell and taste, or hearing and listening. Each is a different perceptual metaphor and offers fresh perspectives on perception itself. But they all come down to perception as *the* modality, and perception for us is dominated by ocular perception. The real sign of the thorough hegemony of perception is our inability to come up with any other ways to conceive of coming to know. I often think education as a social institution is a symbol and tool of the ideology of perception. Perhaps this is what Foucault (1977) had in mind in recognizing the ways in which social institutions are technologies of the panopticon, tools of the "gaze." Perhaps a new theorization, a new epistemology, will render education a mere ruin of the old regime of truth.

Beginning to apply the concepts

I would now like to work through some issues that emerge when we look at the discourses of consumer culture and object relations within and against the environmental "screening" of an ideology of perception. Again, I want to address this in the context of that liminal terrain between and among curriculum theory and teacher education. *Feed* provides a nice context for this because it helps us to rethink what we mean by "I see it now." In the world of the net literally implanted in our nervous systems, only a minor shift in my mind from what we currently experience, advertisements and information pop up in front of us at all times, whenever there is a potential association. We also hear each other inside ourselves as instant messaging becomes a simple matter of thinking what we want to say to another person, "chatting" them. Youth refer to each other as "units":

Images of Coke falling in rivulets down chiseled mountainsides; children being held toward the sun; blades slicing grass; a hand, a hand extended toward the lemonade like God's Creation; boys in Gap tees shot from a rocket; more lining up with tin helmets; Nike grav-gear plunging into Montana; a choir of Jamaican girls dressed in pinafores and strap-on solar cells; dry cleaners ironing the cheek prostheses of the rich; friends clutching at birds made of alloys; law partners jumping fences; snow; altitude; tears; hugs; night.

(Anderson 2002: 22)

Perception is destabilized by the onslaught of sights, sounds, and any other impulse or input from the internet, the "feed," even going so far as to offer website locations where one can malfunction, "go mal," and disorient perception, as a sort of drug substitute (for a current version of this, just to drive home the point that this world is merely a mild amplification of our own rather than a "science fiction," check out Artext, undated). In *Feed*, you can send someone a file of all of your sensations from another time in your life, all of it archived as a file somewhere on the net. School™ is trademarked, of course. In this world of constant, non-stop interconnectivity and marketplace ideology, school is a series of training exercises in using the feed, as there seems to be no need to "learn" anything, if learning is taken as synonymous with collecting knowledge – after all, it's always at one's fingertips, so to speak, instantly accessible through the feed. Learning is reduced to techniques of connection and information retrieval, but all in the context of the resources that support the existence of the feed: those corporations who value the opportunity to advertise products and define market niches. The internet/ media nexus is synergistically melded into a fantastic entertainment/market interface infrastructure. In *Feed*, one's "internet cookies" take on unprecedented power as every choice and interest, every personal and interpersonal relationship, is a potential definer of one's market category. See something blue? Why not consider a new blue T-shirt? Feeling blue? Try a new blue-flavored drink! And while we have your attention, you haven't been ordering as many cases of Coke these days as you used to; have you forgotten, or are you simply interested in trying a new product? Why not *this* one? We have a special on it for the rest of the day. While you're considering the Coke special, listen to this sample of a new blues tune you can download for only $15.99.

Our world, I maintain, *is* this world of the feed, and we really should think about what this means for curriculum and teacher education. First, the institutional positioning of such work defines the experiences in rather curious ways. To begin with, I am never hired in order to work in the liminal space among and between consumer culture and curriculum, as I have defined them, to bridge these terrains or to redefine them in light of each other. Instead, my efforts are construed as part of a certification process, in which all concerned imagine that we are achieving precise expectations in the refinement of technical skills, very much as M.T. Anderson suggests is compatible with the world of the feed. Because of this, *all* of our work can be reduced to a clear moment of commodification, in which discourses and practices are sold and bartered as what Donna Haraway (1992) has called "technologies of vision" (again, I refer the reader back to Chapter 3 for a discussion of this idea). Rather than a search for a new practice of epistemology parallel to metaphors or perception, the events of curriculum theory *as* teacher education are strongly characterized as an expert improvement on the old technology – as a new way of "seeing" or "feeling" the educational encounter. Students – or, in the case of teacher education and professional development, teachers – are commonly encouraged to learn about "this new way of thinking about learning." They may voice concern that they do not feel right teaching in a certain way, yet even this negative reaction reinforces the notion of curriculum as technique.

For a number of years, I seized the opportunities offered by the duality of curriculum commodities: I would use reified terms of education, such as "lesson plan," "assessment," "evaluation," and "concepts," even specific packages of these products, such as "multiple intelligences," or "developmental stages of psycho-social learning," as recognized commodities, only to play with them. Together, I and my students or the current teachers I worked with would change their meanings and purposes toward political action that assumed cultural resources. I got this idea from Cornell West's appropriation of "self-esteem" in *Race Matters* (1994); he took the pop cultural commodity "self-esteem" and turned it into a cultural resource for important social justice efforts. The dilemma of such efforts, of course, is the very duality it perpetuates. Even as I might be using ideas and theories as cultural resources for new conceptions of schooling, teaching, and learning, others are again appropriating these terms and/or their new meanings as commodities to be bought, sold, and applied as "capital" in the consumer culture of educational practice and the teacher job market forum.

We see the very real ways in which this multiple sense of duality works with commodities throughout *Feed*. For example, skin lesions caused by an unknown disease become a fashion accessory, leading youth to purchase plastic surgery for artificial lesions that are even "better" than the real ones that triggered the craze in the first place. Discussions of the quality of lesions lead youth away from the very reality of a serious epidemic toward the meaninglessness of lesions in fashion, undermining the craze itself as it plays itself out in the culture. Yet this phase of the fashion fad is just as valuable to consumer culture as youth now purchase new plastic surgery to remove the lesions that are no longer fashionable. Every meaning is commodifiable. The question is how school as we know it, not quite officially trademarked for all students (although certainly for many of the children in the city of Philadelphia where I live, which has contracted out a large number of school to profit-based corporations), can and should respond to this consumer culture.

Violet's "project" captures most critically the essence of how the duality of commodities and cultural resources interacts with the power structures of consumer culture. Disgusted with the ways that the feed tries constantly to anticipate her every consumer desire, Violet tries to "create a customer profile so screwed, no one can market to it. I'm not going to let them catalog me. I'm going to become invisible" (p. 81). In this way the very tools of marketing themselves have become a cultural resource for Violet as she plays the game of trying to create an impossible customer profile. The feed enables her to invent a game she calls "Complicating. Resisting." Violet and our narrator have a wonderful, silly day at the mall, talking up store clerks about random potential purchases with no perceivable pattern, asking questions about bizarre potential uses of the products, and never actually end up buying anything. In the end this comes back to haunt her when her feed physically malfunctions, not in the sense of visiting a mall feed location on the net, but in the actual mechanism implanted in her body. Because she has played this game with the marketing system, she is no longer a valued customer and hence there is no interest in repairing her feed. When Violet begs the FeedTech customer service representative for help, the automatic Nina representative has some news:

> Hi, I'm Nina, your FeedTech customer assistance representative. Have you noticed panic can lead to big-time underarm odor? A lot of girls do. No sweat! Why not check out the brag collection of perspiration-control devices at the DVS Superpharmacy Hypersite? But that's not why I'm here, Violet.
>
> I'm here to inform you that FeedTech Corp has decided to turn down your petition for complementary feed repair/replacement...
>
> ...Unfortunately, FeedTech and other investors reviewed your purchasing history, and we don't feel you would be a reliable investment at this time. No one could get what we call a "handle" on your shopping habits, like for example you asking for information about all those wow and brag products and then never buying anything. We have to inform you that our corporate investors were like, "What's doing with this?" Sorry – I'm afraid you'll just have to work with your feed the way it is.

The problem is, the feed is an integral component of her physical being; she can't function without a working feed. Her eventual death is of no consequence to the corporations. Violet just lay back down in the dark, her legs starting to sting.

> Maybe, Violet, if we check out some of the great bargains available to you through the feednet over the next six months, we might be able to

create a consumer portrait of you that would interest our investment team. How 'bout it, Violet Durn? Just us, you and me – girls together! Shop till you stop and drop!

(p. 196)

"Go away," Violet bursts, "go away. Go – away." The Nina smiles and responds, "I've got a galaxy of super products we can try together!" ... You get the point. Moreover, we learn about the experience through a memory file she sends, making her very pain and dismissal nothing more than another thing to be sent through the feed.

The second issue that the world of the feed raised for curriculum and teacher education has to do with technologies of vision. To continue the development of this idea from Chapter 3, Violet's analysis makes explicit to the reader how the melding of electronic technologies and consumer culture turns human beings into monsters. "Look at us!" she screams (p. 160). "You don't have the feed! You are feed! You're being eaten! You're raised for food! Look at what you've made yourselves!" (p. 160) Because every moment of our lives is analyzed as a potential market opportunity, the feed literally transforms our ways of perceiving the world. This idea is one we can all understand. We routinely see how easily we hum a jingle, or buy one product over another without consciously choosing. What this book does for us is to make very real to us what this really means; the feed is an amalgam of all technologies of vision, and thus stands in for the holistic totality of all technologies of vision. As a key commodity and cultural resource, a technology of vision is the result of enculturation.

Winnicott, the psychoanalyst, declared like others that the most important preparation for child psychiatry was personal individual experience in psychoanalysis. Through such "work," an adult was prepared to interact with children psychoanalytically. By adopting the discursive tools of psychoanalysis, labeled, for example, splitting, counter-transference, fetish, and so on, one is slowly enabled to "perceive" a child through this expert technology of vision. Similarly, we want to declare important concepts of curriculum theory to be key discursive tools of teacher education, and in turn, for teaching in general. "*Currere*" – curriculum as the experience of the running of the track rather than the track itself – is one fundamental term of this discourse. Others might be auto-ethnography, queering, and youth culture. Commodification and production of meaning through cultural resources are processes of education, much as counter-transference and splitting are processes of individual development. Yet if objects are *related to*, if these processes of relation constitute the ongoing development of an individual – teacher, child, administrator, or whatever – what does this suggest about the complexities of teacher education about education? If people can be understood as expressions of multiple and conflicting object relations, what does this suggest about the ways we can enter into encounters and work together in educational contexts? "…name is Terry Ponk, and I'd like to tell you about upper-body strength…" (p. 58).

Trapped in the feed

In a course on elementary pedagogy that I teach now, there are several core experiential components. On-campus discussions of assigned readings, workshops on alternative assessment, theater games focusing on student-selected "moments" of curriculum encounters, and a semi-weekly "field experience" are some examples of the kinds of organized structures employed. Just as any potential psychiatrist should have experiences in analysis, according to Winnicott, we should say that any potential teacher should have experiences as students with the sorts of curricular encounters we expect to be crucial elements of the "teaching/learning" they will be engaged in as teachers some day. The experience of analysis is not considered equivalent to an ordinary conversation, or other possible forms of communication between one person and another. It is a particular *kind* of experience. Likewise, we would imagine future teachers to have had specific sorts of experiences *as students* that they will later construct with their own students. Oddly, the students I work with have not been fortunate enough to come to teaching with such experiences. Even more strange is that almost no prospective teachers have had such experiences! They have never studied as an inquirer into the subject matter they are interested in. They have rarely if ever planned a performance or exhibit to communicate to an audience outside of their classroom some interesting or provocative aspect of their inquiries. They rarely if ever have written reflections about what they read or do, and have rarely if ever been asked to discuss with a group the processes they are experiencing as members of the group.

Yet these students are assigned the job of interacting with small groups of children once or twice a week for a semester. Will they "buy into" inquiry structures for learning? Will they read *with* their students? Will they pose provocative mathematical questions with their students, instead of answering formulaic questions and drilling on procedures? What are they packaging and selling the children they work with? Inquiry, inquiring *as* an inquirer, writing, reading, mathematizing: as concepts and as teaching gestures, they are objects to be related to.

As I began to consider in Chapter 3, the discourse of "reform" generates several positionings for the teacher educator or professional development facilitator. One of these might be described for current purposes as the required embrace of a Bourdieuian (1977) "habitus" as teacher education curriculum. Habitus is a term that refers to the routines that define taste and expectations in one's life. For example, children in families that routinely use libraries, museums and comic books as places to visit and enjoy where ideas are found and then used as resources for problem-posing are more likely to use libraries, museums, and comic books for these purposes in their lives. There's an implicit "deficit model" inherent in the use of habitus as a discourse. Thus, reform efforts consistently assume that teacher practices shift before teacher ideology. Teachers will start to use journal writing and impact theater techniques, clinical interviews, and problem-posing approaches before they understand such curricular practices in light of reform ideology. In our course for pre-service teachers, they are required to lead a small group of eight to ten elementary students through an interdisciplinary mathematics/ science inquiry experience that lasts a full semester. The assumption is that they can adopt the skills and practices of inquiry facilitation and participation, skills and conceptual understandings that they "lack," through the practice of such experiences. Of course, we do not posit such a deficit: it is imagined that students always come to an educational encounter with prior understanding of the concepts and skills involved. We would never choose to take a "basic skills before application" approach to learning and teaching. And why not assume this? Don't people become writers through apprenticeship, by acting like a writer? Mathematicians by acting like a mathematician? Magicians and clowns by acting like magicians and clowns?

The deficit of apprenticeship is, I think, only constructed in practice when curriculum is "designed" independent of the participants. In such a situation, the encounter assumes no prior accumulation of experiences rich in habitus unrelated to the apprenticeship. I find object relations apt for thinking through this dilemma: the curriculum question might be: What sorts of educational encounters can help the curriculum workers – often "teachers" in such contexts – gain a richer comprehension of the object relations at stake for the student? Notice I didn't ask, object relations that exist or that can be "made"; the psychoanalytic challenge is to fathom the relations at stake in the encounter. Rather than training pre-service teachers in how to use a new technology of vision, the job becomes one of "holding" students, of providing a safe place where they can repair some of the damaged relationships with objects that are primarily influencing their ongoing creation of relations, their potentially new relations, and their avoidance of certain forms of relation. "You see," technologies require training. To see through a telescope or microscope one has to be taught how to see and what to see – historically early users saw *nothing* and could make no meaning. Nowadays such nostalgic technologies are taken as "transparent," whereas new technologies require generations to reach the stage of nostalgia. The psychoanalytic stance is, for the teacher, a new technology of vision as well, if perceived as such. This is the danger. We only see "splitting," "counter-transference," and so on if we are trained or apprenticed to do so. Yet being taught how to use a telescope or microscope, and being apprenticed to psychoanalysis as a way of knowing, in order to use them as models of the educational encounter, are very different from each other, even as they share an ideology of perception. In the first case, the student/apprentice and the teacher/trainer are in parallel, looking at a common object of study: the technology and what it can help you "see." The rich potential of such a standpoint has been eloquently articulated by, for example, David Hawkins (in "I, Thou, and It," 1980a), who argues that a teacher and a student need a common object – an "It" – through which they can build a relationship. As a scientist, Hawkins applies the modernist conceptions of science practice as a tool toward new object relations: the teacher as object for the student, and the student as object for the teacher, as well as the teacher as object for the teacher, and the student as object for the student, are related to in fundamentally important ways (referred to as an "I" and "Thou" in a nod to Martin Buber) *if* a particular *other* object of study is taken by both as an "It." We can see the modernist, scientific origins of psychoanalysis in this respect, in that the analyst and the client together "look at" the client's objects and relations. But here the purposes are reversed in a sense: instead of using objects to build relationships between people, psychoanalysis, growing out of a particular relation, makes it possible to relate to the objects in new ways.

Sources for further consideration of this theoretical shift include the interpretive listening, touching, tasting, and smelling discussed in the previous chapter. In *Feed* we see how all of these different options are subsumed by the grander concept of the feed, provided perhaps by FeedTech, with instructions obtained through School™. We might have thought a different kind of perception would make a difference. Perhaps literally *consuming* the known, the knower is fed and transformed internally, as the "known" is now ecologically part of the knower. In this act of consumption – inhaling and eating one's objects of study – the knower now "knows" in a new sense. What would it mean for prospective teachers to taste or consume "inquiry" or "alternative assessment," as ideas, as objects of relation? What would the educational encounter "be"? What might it mean for people to breathe in and physically metabolize the fragrance, stench, aromas, and odors of inquiry or assessment, literally, to be "in-spired"? In *Feed* we see clearly how it is all part of the same system of consumer culture, so that any sensory perception can be commodified and used as market information. The feed is literally analogous to the combination of internet/entertainment/marketplace technologies in our society; but it is also a metaphor for ideology itself, showing us how we are unable to function when we attempt to destabilize its purposes. Our systems malfunction and there is no incentive for societal resources to save us.

Even as new epistemological metaphors once excited me, I remain fascinated by the ways they continue to entrap us in the feed, which I take as the ideology of perception. I think this may be why folks as divergent as Evelyn Fox Keller (1985) and Michel Foucault (1978) have searched for contrasting *images* of knowing and coming to know. We're locked into perception, but perhaps we can use perception to envision relations other than perceptual images. Thus Fox Keller and Foucault teach us about ancient Greek uses of sexual interaction as models of knowing and coming to know. Any conceivable structure of sexual encounter is a potential model. Typically, in this approach, there is an accent on the relationship between the knower and the known. Any member of a sexual encounter can become, metaphorically, the knower; in the process of focusing on a knower the others or other are then the known. From the start such a model sets up a binary opposition between a knower and a known, which is problematic but instructive. The relationship between the learner and the known may often have as an attribute a relation of dominance or subjection. This certainly has rich metaphorical potential. Except: if we go through the exercise of categorizing the variety of potential sexual encounters, we find the resulting taxonomy to be overpopulated by "relations of consumption." A large percentage of the options position the knower as reifying the known, as an object of pleasure, a commodity to be taken and used for the knower's purposes. There is little space for "perversity" – something Deborah Britzman (1996) once described as pleasure without utility.

We see in *Feed* how this makes sense, since from the perspective of consumer culture there is no incentive to support perversity as defined by Britzman. In the end we understand that the important education does not and can never take place within the feed. We are visiting Violet at her deathbed telling her there is only one story to tell and retell. *She* is the story, she only received a feed late in her childhood, making it possible for her to experience life outside of it. And her story is enough to help someone trapped in the feed to comprehend that even *her* story, in the end, is "about the feed."

> It's about this meg normal guy, who doesn't think about anything until one wacy day, when he meets a dissident with a heart of gold.... Set against the backdrop of America in its final days, it's the high-spirited story of their love together, it's laugh-out-loud funny, really heart-. warming, and a visual feast.... Together, the two crazy kids grow, have madcap escapades, and learn an important lesson about love. They learn to resist the feed.
>
> (p. 234)

Complicity

So where does this enlightenment lead our protagonist? Nowhere, really: "On a screen her heart was barely beating." His future is within hers: "I could see my face, crying, in her blank eye" (p. 234). My usual theoretical tact when feeling frustrated or hegemonically maeopic is a Deleuzian (Deleuze and Guattari 1991) nomadic epistemology. Rather than assume that my theoretical axes are the defining axes of a Cartesian reality, I search for a new, independent trajectory that is coexistent with yet not complicit in the original hegemonic categories. Deleuze called this "nomadic epistemology" when using the example of the dichotomy of the homeless versus the sheltered. Nomads are neither homeless nor sheltered, yet they are both homeless *and* sheltered. In that example, there are two categories. The *new* term, nomadic, overlaps with the two original categories yet does not fit in or out of them: it is coexistent and independent. Can we perform a similar theoretical maneuver with our *four* categories? Consumer Culture, Object Relations, Ideology of Perception, and Habitus would then be independent of our nomadic terms. While Violet's father is mostly portrayed as an outcast unable to function in the contemporary world because he never could afford a proper feed, I see him as a symbol of the nomadic existence. Even as his daughter is a tragic victim of consumer culture, he is neither in nor out of the feed, while both in it and out of it:

> Outside her window her father was working in the garden. He was on his hands and knees, pulling out pieces of grass from where flowers were. His feedpack glittered in the sun. I watched him. The sky was blue over him. He patted the dirt with his hands.
>
> (p. 233)

There is her father, an outmoded feedpack sustaining his minimal contact with others while he peculiarly touches actual living grass, something most people in this world never experience, relegated to the pleasures of Clouds™.

What we are looking for are our own feedpacks that allow us to coexist with the feed but not really in it, categories that not only coexist with the problematic concepts and practices, but which also subsume them in a way that displaces – literally robs them of their place. One trajectory that I associate with critical pedagogy offers three "nomadic" opportunities: Youth leadership, Voice, and Participation in democratic institutions. Imagine teacher education and curriculum theory blurring together in the actions of youth leadership, voice, and democratic participation. Instead of quibbling over the idea of "technology of vision," or suffocating in the deluge of "commodification," "teacher/education/curriculum/theory/practice" would use some technologies of vision, loop in and out of commodification and cultural resource work, understanding but not being confined by object relations, toward student leadership within democratic forms of institutional and community organization. Neither "selling out" nor "buying in," such a political turn can be both postmodern and the "pause that refreshes."

Is there anything more going on in this imagined work than finding ways to mask critical pedagogy as a technology of vision? How would such a project manifest itself, given the lack of interest that so many people have in youth leadership, voice, or democratic participation? The questions remain open to me.

Here are two other nomadic terms with potential: disparity and desire. It seems to me that much of the malaise of consumer culture and object relations discourse, and much of the dissatisfaction with technologies of vision, grow out of the ways in which they posit *differences*; that is, ways in which they set up "norms" by clarifying the ways in which things are "not the same." Disparity emphasizes the "unequal in difference," as Sharon Todd (1997) has written, a notion of disparity in the material conditions that structure differences *differently* enables us to avoid the collapse of diversity into a rendering that is individualized and psychologized. It is in the struggles against the disparities of injustice that *desires* are produced, mobilized, and frustrated in the pedagogical encounter with difference. Thus, *desire* itself can be our new, independent term, referring to that which ceaselessly circulates through the *unsaid*, manifesting itself in expectations, hopes, visions, and fears (even as it intersects with the symbolic and spoken discourses uttered by teachers and students). Deleuze wrote that "desire never needs interpreting; it is it which experiments." Todd writes that desires are not only "handled" or "dealt with," they are also produced and constituted.

I am suggesting that consumer culture, object relations, and the ideology of perception are embraced but also left to do what they wish while other important conceptual work is accomplished by recognition of difference, disparity, and desire. These three "D"s are outcomes of events instead of causal origins of entrenched problems. In casting them as outcomes, their identification offers possibilities for coalitions and multiple levels of possibility that cut across the lines of difference and power. Rather than standpoints in a Cartesian universe, disparities are enunciations.

In a teacher education experience, we would set up contexts in which the prospective teachers are not taught techniques, but are given outcomes to strive for: work with these children, or with this group of teachers and students, in order to facilitate youth leadership, student and teacher voice, and democratic participation. Each field placement could be examined as a case study in action research. Tools will be requested: "How can I understand what is going on?" "Who can help me solve my problem?"; "I don't even know where to begin, let alone to formulate a question."

The response will be a set of discourses: the duality of commodity/cultural resources; how and what is commodified, advertised, marketed, bought, and sold in this case study? How is something treated as a commodity by some in the group, yet as a cultural resource by others? What does this disjunction mean for what proceeds in this group? How can any commodity be turned into a resource? How can any resources be treated as a commodity? Another discourse will represent the object relations that are comprehended in the ongoing construction of community in the group: Can individual relationships be established in order to facilitate the understanding of potential relations? What forms of encounter can allow for psychoanalytic work to be accomplished by members of the group? How do individual group members use each other as objects of relation? And the third primary discourse examined the ideology of perception as enacted by the group: What do people in the group employ as metaphors for knowing and coming to know? Next we are asked to interrogate difference, disparity, and desire: How can our discourses of consumer culture, object relations, and the ideology of perception elaborate our descriptions of difference, disparity, and desire? How does each *discourse* create differences, disparities, and desires?

6

Harry Potter's World*

"It is important to remember that we all have magic inside of us."

J. K. Rowling (attributed to Rowling by Steve Vander Ark 2000)

Some people are still asking, "What is it about J.K. Rowling's *Harry Potter* books that has made them so popular?" I want to ask, "What is it about our culture that embraces the *Harry Potter* books and has turned *Harry Potter* into such a phenomenon?" There are more subtle and interesting things to look at than, say, the general content of the books: recent works by successful children's authors such as Jane Yolen (*Wizard's Hall*, 1991), Phillip Pullman (*The Golden Compass*, 1996), Lois Lowry (*The Giver, 1993*), and Natalie Babbitt (*Tuck Everlasting*, 1987), for example, have enjoyed excellent marketing of novels that evoke parallel worlds, magic, and folklore. Each has a pre-adolescent protagonist beginning to negotiate the psychosocial crisis of individual versus group identity. *Harry Potter* hype may also share characteristics with other recent promotional schemes and product tie-ins, such as *Pokemon, Power Puff Girls, Power Rangers, WWF Warzone*, and so on. But to "blame" the successes of *Harry Potter* on corporate marketing alone begs the question. After all, some potential product hypes don't make it, whereas others do, and few of them start out as a quiet book from an unknown author. To interpret the *Harry Potter* successes as one of corporate culture preying on innocent children (Giroux 2000) would, I suggest, perpetuate inappropriate assumptions. I wish to debunk three of these *pre*-sumptions: Can we say that consumer culture has trumped all other possible manifestations of liberal democracy? Rather it may be that market dynamics and individual agency are far more complex. Do we want to say that children are passive, naïve recipients of greedy corporate cultural products? Surely children and others act as agents of social change even as they behave in certain socially reproductive ways.

---

*The original version of this chapter first appeared in Elizabeth Heilman (ed.), *Harry Potter's World: Multidisciplinary Perspectives*. New York: Routledge Falmer, 2002.

Can we understand the cultural meanings of *Harry Potter* stories (or any other popular cultural artifact) as a distanced observer? I suggest that distanced interpretations further collapse the cultural story of *Harry Potter* into the world of children's literature, ignoring the wider range of readers (including college students and other adults)[1] and the cultural phenomena of *Harry* beyond the books themselves (e.g., *Harry Potter* toys; diaries and other bookstore impulse items; towels, mirrors, and other home-decorating products; websites, filk,[2] and other fanware). One thing I have learned from cultural studies is that textual analysis is not enough. Nor is it enough to present a well-honed social analysis of popular culture phenomena (Daspit and Weaver 1998). It is important to understand how children and other *Harry Potter* fans "read" and interpret the books, cultural products, consumer items, and fanware – the details of the *Harry Potter* culture – as cultural resources out of which people make sense of themselves (Fiske 1990). It is especially important to learn from people how they "use" popular culture resources to make sense of their lives, their culture, and their fears and fantasies, and through such mediation, to construct new modes of meaning (Eco 1979; De Certeau 1984; Appelbaum 1999).

In this chapter I describe some of what I have learned through talking with young people in informal and formal interviews about the ways in which *Harry Potter*'s popularity dovetails well with other mass culture phenomena. I focus particularly on those aspects of *Harry Potter* that speak to issues of technology, magic, and the role of science as popular culture resources. I argue that the books and associated "fanware" are key sites for the cultural construction of science and technology; in speaking to issues of magic and science, technology and culture, *Harry Potter* is emblematic of the kinds of cultural practices that lead to its popularity. Within these cultural practices we can see science and technology mediating our "common sense." At the same time, socially constructed expectations produce what we know as science and what we recognize as technology. This all happens in and out of science as practiced by scientists, and in and out of our popular cultures. All of this is mixed up and interwoven and, together, called "cultural practices." Within these cultural practices specific images and conventions are identified as icons of science, technology, indeed, the way the world works; other images become icons for magic, mysticism, and other categories of cultural practices that, for most of us, serve to distinguish what we call science from what we call notscience.

These cultural practices, ways of thinking, and icons, along with their use as metaphors, are what I think of as "technoculture." Technoculture is thus the amalgam of our postmodern society, heavily mediated by and productive of science and technology, both as popular cultures, cultural practices, and icons – and as constructed significantly via science and technology itself. When we listen to children and learn about youth culture, magic and technoculture stand out as essential to the project of becoming human (Appelbaum 1999). Popular culture narratives set up a kind of hero that confronts technoculture through technoculture itself, and, when we listen to readers of *Harry Potter*, we see that the books and fanware are not culturally unique. They are instead consistent with technocultural themes of morality and identity in a postmodern society. Children experience power and violence differently from adults, and their notions of magic and technology can be different as well. Caught up in magic and technology is the role of wonder: how teachers respond to children's wonderings about the natural world combines with children's own interpretations of that world. The combination constructs powerful forms of cultural dynamics and conceptions of technology. In both the *Harry Potter* books and in children's lives, school functions to accentuate what constitutes technologies, what constitutes magic and wonder, and, finally, through consumer culture, what it means to become a human being. In this way, I find that the books and the culture that embraces them buttress each others' postmodern efforts to fulfill an outdated enlightenment fantasy of utopia through technology.

The technoculture of consumer culture in and out of school

For children growing up in and with technoculture, concepts of cyborg imagery, biological monsters, fantasy characters, power, knowledge, magic, and prosthetic extensions of self are not categorical. Many things that adults see as newfangled or that cause anxieties are accepted by young people as inherent components of the "natural" world. Thus an adult fear of dehumanization through technology might translate into a performance of identity or a social connection for a child. Obversely, a young person's sense of danger may translate into a technological task for an adult. For a child, technology may be magic or science; power may be a fantasy or a monstrous myth. For a number of the children I have spoken with in my research, power can emerge out of a persistence in seeking knowledge; for others it may be understood as a gift bestowed by biological luck. Knowledge for the children I have spoken with may be conflated with power or magically lost. On the other hand, technology may be a prize or a tool of adult power (Appelbaum 1999). Thus we find that chemistry sets are surprisingly popular, because children want to pretend to be in a potions class at Hogwarts. Also popular are *Animal Planet*'s sound-enhanced animal toys, because Hagrid's Care of Magical Creatures class has tapped into children's simultaneous fear of and love for animals.

Technocentric utopianism for many children is really more aptly described as melancholic acceptance of responsibility. Common wisdom describes technocultural popular culture as a working through of adult fears and fantasies (Waught 1947; Wright 2001). Early superhero technoculture re-enacted the Cold War conflicts of good guys and bad guys in a battle for humanity and the universe. Historians of popular culture (Waught 1947; Appelbaum 1999;

Napier 2001; Wright 2001) suggest distinct evolution through several periods that characterize the nature of the heroes and the narrative structure in particular ways. Following good-guy versus bad-guy constructs of the Cold War, subsequent cultural commodities demonstrate a phase of inner psychological turmoil, splitting the good–evil battle into a multiplicity of conflicting identities. For example, Batman and Spider-Man, two heroes plagued with inner, psychological turmoil and battling villains who suffer from countless psychological disorders, replaced Superman, a strong, almost invincible boy from small-town U.S.A. The literature on popular culture (Levi 1996; Rushkoff 1996; Poitras 2000; Napier 2001; Wright 2001) suggests that this psychological phase was subsumed more recently by the *anime* hero. This hero is a "gundam"[3] child who inherits the aftermath of technological havoc wreaked by adults; the hero dons prosthetic devices scavenged from an inherited wasteland in a Romantic gesture of faith in the ultimate goodness of humanity. Gundam children are present in television programs, animated films, video games, role-playing games, and other forms of entertainment.

Harry Potter, the young hero of the books that carry his name, is characterized very much in the spirit of the gundam hero. He is thrust into the most serious fights of good and evil, the ultimate outcome of which will determine the fate of the world "as we know it." This fight of good and evil is one he inherits from the previous generation, a generation in which his own mother and father failed at the task he himself must now undertake. Harry meets his challenges head-on, and with glorious enthusiasm, using whatever latest trick of magic he has been able to obtain and control. These magical artifacts, such as spells and potions, wands, invisibility cloaks, a map that divines the locations of people unseen, and so on, play the same role in these books that a prosthetic hand or mega-weapon body suit does for the prototypical gundam hero. Magic, in this sense, becomes a technology. Bruce McMillan, senior vice-president and group studio general manager at Electronic Arts (the makers of many successful video and computer games), was recently quoted describing the *Harry Potter* books in this way.

> J.K. Rowling wrote her fiction in a way that game mechanics flow out of it. [...] The first book [...] is packed with moments that seem almost designed to appear in a game: the gauntlet of puzzles that Harry faces to rescue the *Sorcerer's Stone*, the character-building that takes place as Harry learns to be a wizard, and much more.
>
> (Hendrix 2001: 37–38)

If we accept such historical interpretations of superheroes, we might ask, "What's next?" If humans have united within themselves extraordinary powers of destruction and creation, will they or can they bring into being a new, evolutionary step? Those of us who work with young children should ask ourselves what the implications are for the types of experiences these children might be offered by adults, given that they are "schooled" in the popular culture to savor the gundam role (Appelbaum 1999). There are indeed ways that gundam popular culture buttresses commonsense attitudes about knowledge and curriculum. For example, the common view of technology as prostheses that amplify the potential powers of humans is consistent with the view that knowledges gained in school are cultural capital. By this I mean that prostheses for the body are part of a more global way of understanding our world in which knowledge is recognized as parts of things that are collected and later "spent" in the marketplace of college admissions and careers (Appelbaum 1995b). Gundam heroes are also built upon techno-utopianism. Science and technology are constructed in the school curriculum as well as popular technoculture as techniques of progress. The gundam hero accepts the premise that science and technology are their own antidotes, and thus reconstructs technology as self-perpetuating and necessary. But should or can we seriously respond to gundam desires with and through the school curriculum? Can such desires be interrogated and challenged?

Educators' responses

Teachers tend to feign disinterest in childhood experiences of cyberculture. They see as part of their job the need to further separate popular and high-status culture. School knowledge is part of that high-status culture. Popular and mass media raise the status of school knowledge when teachers keep them outside of school. But children are intimately caught up in popular media, and they use mass media resources in play, social relationships, and in imagining possibilities. When teachers preserve the in-school versus outside-of-school boundaries, they cut themselves off from relationships with children directly connected with the most pressing issues of self, identity, morality, power, and knowledge. Sometimes a teacher relies on seemingly positive goals when effecting these boundaries. For a teacher who sees his or her job in terms of demystification or enculturation, it is very difficult to construct educational practice as migration into a new culture. This kind of teacher wants instead to teach the children about the traditions and cultural legacy of the old culture out of which they are entering the new cultures of *anime*. And, for a teacher who sees her or his job as bestowing the gifts of civilization, it is difficult to do so in terms of a cultural practice that celebrates the Romantic hope of childhood as the savior of humanity. They would more likely understand their role as saving humanity from the strange, challenging actions of the anime hero. Furthermore, it is absurd for a teacher to imagine a curriculum that dehumanizes even her or himself as a tool for *anime* heroism or *post-anime* evolution. In the obsessively survivalist mode of teacher practice spawned by Standards-based accountability bureaucracies, what possible technologies of self could or would we even think credible? Indeed, what is the role of a teacher other than the conserving one of passing on the wisdom of the past? I suggest that our new technoculture *requires* teaching practices that facilitate an interrogation of this culture, and the facilitation of self-understanding necessary to unravel the intricacies of self-identity in a postmodern world. The "new curriculum" should consider alternative visions of technology that move it away from the metaphor of prosthesis. Consider, for example, Sadie Plant's notion that technology is not just an add-on to the human body that amplifies its powers, but instead serves to re-engineer the body itself, creating a new and different cyborg body (Plant 1997). The Potter books speak to the re-engineering of the body through technology in their examples of magic used as a tool to regrow human limbs, occasionally (or accidentally) remove someone's bones from a part of their body leaving it temporarily rubbery and deformed, to cosmetically enhance someone's teeth, and, most directly, in the role of the *animagi*, those who change into animal form. Curriculum, then, must speak fully to issues of identity and questions of what it means to be human in the face of re-engineering and cultural change.

This challenge to teachers is consistent with the cultural view that the gundam hero must save the world even as the clueless adults sit idly by, paralyzed by the threats that they themselves have unleashed. What the *Harry Potter* books provide, however, is a reassurance that *some* adults really do know what is happening, and indeed that these adults can be trusted to come through with support when the going gets rough. Albus Dumbledore, Minerva McGonagall, Sirius Black, and Rubeus Hagrid, for example, often turn out to be fully aware of what is happening, or at least adequately conscious of what Harry and his friends are up to, so that they can offer assistance at just the right moments. And Harry and his friends always seem to have recently mastered just enough new spells and tricks to accomplish what is necessary. In the end, as with the gundam hero, it is the child who must save the world. Nevertheless, in these books, the bleakness is tempered. It is almost as if the adults know that the "real" curriculum is outside of the classes, and is just enticing enough to interest these children in their preparation for leadership. Real-world challenges provide the problem-solving context so necessary for meaningful learning. As a treatise on education, the *Harry Potter* books make an intriguing statement on the boundaries across the school and popular curricula. If we only knew the story of every other child at Hogwarts, could it be that they, too, are having adventures? Perhaps the school is set up to trick people into coming together for real-life problem-solving outside of school under the careful guidance of Dumbledore and his friends?

Power, wonder, and magic in an acquisitive culture

Power and violence are not always what they seem to be. There is a way in which a child who spends three hours a day playing *Smackdown*, *WWF WarZone*, *Timesplitters*, and other violent video games, and then watches a *WWF* video for another hour and a half, will recoil in horror and fright at scenes from popular films such as *Rules of Engagement*, or even the final scene in *The Secret of Roan Inish*. *Smackdown* and the *World-Wide Wrestling Federation WarZone* are arcade-style fighting games in which characters use gratuitous violence alone or in groups to render their competitors unconscious or devoid of any life energy; and, while the fanatic interest in *World-Wide Wrestling*'s violent wrestling soap operas have waned over the past few years, many boys and young men still rent the videos for their nostalgic entertainment value. Yet most players and viewers will quickly insist they can tell that the violence is "fake," and that their interest in the entertainment has more to do with the complex strategies involved, or in the intricacies of the soap opera-style plots. *Rules of Engagement*, a 2000 film starring Tommy Lee Jones, Mark Feuerstein, and Samuel L. Jackson, and directed by William Friedkin, which involves a team of Marines responding to a fictional attack on a U.S. embassy in Yemen, is rated R for graphic violence. However, much of the violence is implicit and artistically developed through techniques of suspense. *The Secret of Roan Inish*, director John Sayles' 1995 rendering of an Irish folktale, is steeped in magic and tradition. While supposedly suitable for family viewing, at least according to many film critics and its PG rating, the final dramatic scene involves a child's mother returning to the sea to live as a seal, leaving many children horrified at the child's loss of its mother.

Similarly, a young girl might try out seemingly sadistic or masochistic choices in a Purple Moon *Rockett* computer game, yet refuse to watch *Rugrats* on television because she finds the character Angelica so horrific. The *Rockett* computer games incorporate a narrative about a pre-teen's life choices; the player makes decisions about what the young girl, Rockett, should do in various social situations. While an adult observer might expect the player's choice's to be an indication of what the player might choose in a similar situation, many girls playing the game in fact choose a less socially sanctioned option just to see how it affects the plot. In the *Rugrats* television program, the oldest child Angelica is not only extremely bossy, but often puts the younger children into terribly awkward or potentially dangerous situations. Even though watching *Rugrats* could entertain by allowing viewers the chance to see how children might make poor social choices, or reconcile them, many children actually find the character so reprehensible that they choose another form of entertainment. (Nevertheless, this should be understood in the light of the program's continued popularity.) Visibility of gore, as opposed to realism of violence, can be distinguished by many children as they discuss moral issues and scenarios.

There has been much written in the popular press about the violence of the *Harry Potter* books. It is suggested that the books might be unhealthy because of this. However, the violent scenes are not what entice people to the books and are not what the books are about, per se. A *Harry Potter* reader can handle the notion of being scarred for life on the forehead by an evil sorcerer, or a child in the school being killed by this same sorcerer a few books later. What readers of these books have suggested in their discussions with me is that they can easily separate these violent events from the moral contexts in which they take place. It is the morality to which they turn in applying "lessons learned" to their own interactions with "real people" in their lives. I admit to adult incredulity when it comes to this violence, and as educators we are seriously concerned about the violence or threats of violence through mass culture narratives that affect our daily lives in schools. But reader-response theory remains: some children read the "dark themes" in *Harry Potter* books as a backdrop to the details, and contend with the dark themes on another plane of existence, independent of their reading of these books. Similarly, some children are so caught up in the strategic details of video games, *Pokemon*, or the *Magic* card game that they do not see the violence that adults see readily; they contend with issues of violence and control in thoroughly different ways when it appears to them as part of a life outside of the game. In particular, invisible but possible violence is far more frightening to these children than larger-than-life cartoonish violence, even when the cartoonish violence is extremely graphic. (For example, *Independence Day*, or *The Matrix*, would be consumed as enjoyable entertainment; but *Contact* is unbearable because the suspenseful unknown is carried for so long in the film. *Independence Day* would initially seem to be terribly frightening as it graphically depicts aliens coming very close to violently taking over the Earth; *The Matrix* depicts the horrific scenario of a future Earth being nothing more than an illusion for people who have been reduced to energy resources for intelligent machines. *Contact*, which describes the tensions between science and religion when contact with aliens becomes possible, depicts no violence but keeps the suspense about the aliens hidden throughout the majority of the film.) I suppose the question comes down to whether or not children can tell the difference between the games and the "real world." We seem to have some evidence to the contrary. Eugene Provenzo (1991) and others have amassed a collection of research that suggests reasons to worry about the culture of violence that is so prevalent. In the end, as I talk to and work with children, my own evidence is that they are genuinely living an independent trajectory. The enacted violence could in some ways be said to be consistent with the dark imagery of the *Harry Potter* books, and the game-like realism of current high-graphics fighting and shooting games; but I find the causation to be in the other direction. If anything these images and choices of entertainment are a semantic sign of something in our culture rather than an origin of cultural meaning. That is, the images that children play with tell us more about the fears and fantasies of the adults who provide the images, and the resources for making meaning that are available in our culture, than about what children are becoming or doing to themselves or our culture. This does not mean that violent and sexist images would never be an origin of meaning for any particular child: it is certainly possible that they could be. It just is not such an origin in my research, and I do not see it as the common experience of most children.

Another popular concern that has led to the books being banned in some communities is the attention to the dark arts and magic in general. It may be feared that young people would become interested in pursuing cultish practices. The use of these features makes the books no different from numerous popular television series and video games (see, for example, the television programs *Buffy the Vampire Slayer, Charmed,* the *Final Fantasy* video game series, and the computer game *Black and White*).[4]

Magic is strongly associated with experiences of wonder. There is little distinction between the *Harry Potter* books and the *Magic: The Gathering* card game, or a cyberhero like *Inspector Gadget* and a round of laser-tag. Paintball, for a child, can be a variation on *Pokemon,* or a dramatic fantasy based on the *Power Rangers,* or – if "I" played paintball last weekend and "you" never have – a real-life "play" of power against another child in the acquisitive culture of childhood. In tapping into magic, many forms of youth technoculture reach into the realm of wonder in ways that establish these cultural commodities as educative experiences in the Deweyan sense that they promote growth. (Maybe not growth in the school-culture sense, however.) When adults set up school as distinct from the world of wonder (even to compete with popular culture for "coolness" or "cleverness" but in the act clarifying the impossibility of this attempt) they fail children, and abdicate their responsibility to participate in mass culture and peer interactions. In denying the potential of wonder through magic, educators are also denying students an environment that is educative. Three questions arise. Should we try to create educational encounters that directly mirror the linking of magic, technology and wonder, as in, for example, Botball tournaments (KISS Institute 2001)? Should teachers hype science into a parallel form of edutainment, as in television science programs? Or should educators establish science/technology/wonder as a critical examination of the popular (Appelbaum and Clark 2001; Gough 1993)? I suggest, in contrast, that children gravitate to the wonder where it is. When wonder is not in the curriculum they will find it elsewhere, outside of school.

An interesting case study is afforded by Hasbro's marketing of the new toy, *Pox*™ (Tierney 2001). The new toy was introduced by identifying who the coolest of the cool children are: roaming playgrounds and neighborhoods, marketers asked, "Who's the coolest kid you know?" When they landed a child who said, "Me," they invited the "alpha pup" to get paid to learn a new video game. Fighting monsters are created by collecting body parts and powers. Warriors are put together from the collected parts; then you program a battle sequence by strategically balancing the strengths and weaknesses of the various body parts. The coolest kids can boast about what level they have attained, what potential body parts they have collected; the ones who lose are not humiliated publicly since the game is played stealthily. Pox depends not on reflexes, as with other video games, but on "the collection of arcana." Asked why they like the game, boys say, "because it's, like, battling and fighting," and "we like violence!" Tierney writes that they sound bloodthirsty without any sign of menace. He cites research which suggests that violent entertainment is actually associated with a decrease in violence among young people. The seeming connection between violent entertainment and violence, he suggests, might be better explained by a strong increase in violence in society begun long before the advent of video games.

Things dominate the life of children. For young people in the early twenty-first century, commodification as the final arbiter of identity and acquisition is intimately entwined with self. If knowledge is the sort of knowledge truly conflated with power, then children grab voraciously for it. But if it is ambiguous in its relation to power, then it is ignored in the interest of efficiency. Thus, a young boy will exert whatever it takes to acquire the new *Sims* (Electronic Arts 2000) game before others get it, to learn a trick from *GamePro* magazine before his friend does; yet the same child could care less about the financial mathematics of purchasing the game unless the money actually makes a difference in his life. In the latter case, if school artificially makes this into a world problem-type experience, the conflicting identity politics is a crucial element in self and community. Similarly, the importance of *Pokemon Gameboy* will fluctuate for many girls depending on its competition for importance with current MTV star details, varying make-up items and body gels, and other technologies of the body. For both boys and girls, technology is a *fashion*; but this fashion is played out in gendered and other ways. In the *Harry Potter* culture, material products include wizard trading cards, *Quidditch* brooms, the best owl, a magic pet, and magic treats sold on wizard trains. And these commodities serve parallel functions. For *Harry Potter* readers, consumer culture makes early possession of the books and a child's recall of details into an acquired need that works as cultural capital in analogous ways. Indeed, the child who possesses full command of detail, like the player of the new *Pox*™ game immersed in the collection of arcana, is the one most likely to win. In one sense, this consistency in and out of the books serves to make the stories more "believable" for readers. Students at Hogwarts collect trading cards of great wizards and quidditch heroes much like young people outside the books obsess over sports cards, and this common consumerism makes the children in the books more "realistic." And Harry quickly learns to covet the latest, most expensive gadgets, like a typical child outside of the books.

In another sense, acquisitive consumer culture dominates popular and *Potter* culture in ways that make the books emblematic of the culture in which they appear as commodities themselves. Early in *Harry Potter and the*

Chamber of Secrets, for example, the competing Slytherin team demoralize the Gryffindors by showing off their new "Nimbus Two Thousand and One" broomsticks. "Very latest model. Only came out last month ... I believe it outstrips the old Two Thousand series by a considerable amount" (Rowling 1999a: 111). Harry's friends are left holding their outmoded "Cleansweep Fives," no longer competitive with the newer Nimbus models. In *Harry Potter and the Prisoner of Azkaban* (Rowling 1999b) Harry is mesmerized by an advertisement for an even newer model, the "Firebolt." So hyped that it is priced upon request, Harry "didn't like to think how much gold the Firebolt would cost. He had never wanted anything as much in his whole life" (Rowling 1999b: 51–52). He tries to console himself by noting that he had never lost a Quidditch match on his Nimbus Two Thousand, yet "he returned, almost every day after that, just to look at the Firebolt" (Rowling 1999b: 52). In this way *Potter* and popular consumer culture intertwine consumerism and technoculture by turning new technologies into coveted consumer products.

It was James Macdonald (1995b: 75) who wrote:

It is my personal myth that today's technology is yesterday's magic. Further, it is intuitive feeling that technology is in effect externalization of the hidden consciousness of human potential. Technology, in other words, is a necessary development for human beings in that it is the means of externalizing the potential that lies within.

The *Harry Potter* books portray Macdonald's wisdom in, for example, their juxtaposition of the flying car and the use of tea-leaves to divine fortune, but even more directly in the all-important fixation on the best and latest *Quidditch* broom. Why would a school full of apprentice wizards need to buy the latest innovation in design and technology? To re-emphasize class and justice themes? To satisfy a "real boy's" need for toys and desire? It is the same audience finding this believable that runs out to purchase the newest *Magic* deck, or searches the internet for rare and expensive no-longer-in-print cards; the same audience that shells out $30.00 for a quarter-inch of plastic that can be painted and used in a *Warhammer*™ game. And, it is the same audience that knows all the lyrics to Brittany Spears' latest video, the dance moves to Christina Aguileira's new video, the place to buy the coolest body gel.

Harry Potter's world

This chapter is an interrogation of the world that embraces the *Harry Potter* phenomenon; it is not an extensive analysis of the books themselves. I claim that the main thrust of Harry Potter's attraction has mostly to do with its treatment of magic as a commodified technology, just as video games, television cyborgs, and fantasy role-playing games in "our world" treat technology as magic. Insofar as morality is constructed in any of these terrains, it has very little to do with specific plot or imagery, and more to do with the "kids' culture" Rushkoff (1996: 109) described as "a delightful mixed-up common ground for all of these digital, magical, and biological sorts of development." This is not to say that young readers are more likely to be interested in the magic than the moral lessons of the books; rather, we can find a technology of morality that constructs identity as multiple and fluid. Because "technology" and "humanity" are overlapping and transgressive as categories in "our world," we can no longer talk about technology as a tool that is wielded in accordance with morality. Instead, we must understand morality and technology as mutually constitutive.

In Harry Potter's world surprises might be lurking in any place or thing. The trick is to ride it through and never give up the chance to have fun. This is the fate of the gundam child. Similarly, children who play video games do not dwell on the plot, the characters, or what things might seem to be if one were to take a particular event or character as a "message" in some adult way. Take race, gender, or nationality, for example: "Kids routinely choose any and all ... options and don't think twice about it," writes J.C. Herz (1997), "because the only factor in their decision is a given character's repertoire of kick-ass fighting moves. Ironically, all considerations of race, sex, and nationality are shunted aside in the videogame arena, where the only goal is to clobber everyone indiscriminately" (p. 166). Yet, as Herz points out, kids understand on a deeper level that they are

> operating in a disembodied environment where your virtual skin doesn't have to match your physical one, and that you can be an Okinawan karate expert, a female Thai kick-boxer, a black street-fighter from the Bronx, or a six-armed alien from outer space, all within the span of a single game.
>
> (Herz 1997: 166)

Herz notes that adults do not generally approach things this way: they might be disturbed by the idea of a cutesy Japanese schoolgirl committing gruesome, bloody maneuvers, or at least be aware that they are choosing this character in some semi-conscious way. For children, however, write Herz, "shuffling videogame bodies and faces is like playing with a remote control" (p. 167). Adults also tend to see the video games as preprogrammed and predetermined, so that the limited selection of identity combinations and options suggests a particular story about identity to these adults. Recent video games, however, employ the "create a character" feature, in which it really does seem that any and all combinations are the goal. "The game starts, cycles through a bunch of avatars, and you punch the fire button when you see one you like. It's channel surfing" (p. 167). When children are imitating the moves of these characters, trying out the "cool" moves and identities, some adults become concerned that there is not a clear separation between the fantasy of the game or television program and the dreams of particular children. This is indeed the case for some children; it is also part of working through our cultural ideas about what "identity" is, and so may be a necessary experience for children.

The *Harry Potter* books reconstruct in analogous detail the pecking order of school-ground one-upmanship. You cannot just know the spell in Harry's world; you have to study it, practice it, and perfect it. And if you can learn a spell that others do not yet know, you are the coolest. What the Potter books do is destabilize the tension between acquisitive coolness and nerdiness, because they take magic and turn it into the techniques that can be learned. Thus Hermione is not all that cool in the books even though she studies the most and learns the most spells, because within the context of the books she is just a studious nerd in school. Yet other kids in the books who do not take on the characteristics of nerds but know more tricks than the others earn recognition and status. It *can* be cool to know more magic than other kids. It is pretty much the same outside the books: you must show you have incredibly detailed and specific knowledge that others do not yet have to stay ahead. It is not enough to be the first kid to own the *Sims*™, a computer game in which one creates a whole simulated world of people and then manipulates how they interact. You have to know how to download the *Sim* guinea-pig off the net and use it to help two *Sim* families come together and start a new household. Herz (1997) emphasizes the importance of *both* the arcane knowledge *and* hand–eye coordination. And it is the same for Harry: he is always at the center of the fun because he is always looking for a new, esoteric detail. The *Harry Potter* books are an education for the information economy, where everyone pays premium rates for narrow expertise and short-lived skills. Just as Harry will grab at the chance to use a secret map, so too will a first-grader voraciously read *Nintendo* magazine, a fourth-grader search out the chat room where one can learn the most arcane code for *Tony Hawke's SkatePro* (a skateboarding video game). To the other characters in the books, Harry is cool not because he can talk to snakes – that is something he was born with; he is cool because he has an invisibility cloak and a really good broomstick. (It is the case in these books that Harry Potter is famous: everyone knows the story of how the most powerful evil Voldemort was unable to kill Harry, and that trying to kill the young lad caused Voldemort to lose much of his power and disappear. But in general we see that most kids in the books find him peculiar and do not treat him as special in any particular way. A more subtle reading registers his fluctuating status: he is sometimes a hero, sometimes a suspect, but in either case always "special." Outside of the books is another story; most readers identify with Harry in particular.)

Technology, in this sense, is nothing more than a trick, spell, or code: it lets you do things other people do not yet know about. And this is pretty much what Macdonald was referring to as the externalization of potential. As Rushkoff (1996: 109) writes:

> When we look carefully at the reaction of younger cyber-denizens to their Sega-environs, we find that they make no distinction between information and matter, mechanics and thought, work and play, or even religion and commerce. In fact, kids on the frontier of the digital terrain have adopted some extraordinarily magical notions about the world we live in. Far from yielding a society of coldhearted rationalists, the ethereal, out-of-body experience of mediating technologies appears to have spawned a generation of pagan spiritualists whose dedication to technology is only matched by their enthusiasm for elemental truth and a neoprimitive, magical worldview. To a screenager, these are not opposing strategies but coordinated agents of change.

This harkens back to the Enlightenment epistemology that created a kind of confidence about a human being's place in the world even as they were decentered in that world, because one could know all, and understand all, and harness it to human advantage. In this view, humans even have the role of controlling the world: if we could only realize this, we could fit into the natural world that is scientifically knowable. The irony is that this is the post-modern era, in which we are no longer supposed to be believing this. Suppos-edly we no longer believe in the idea of eternal progress, and with the loss of this rudder we have presumed the destruction of all of the accompanying beliefs, such as human "rationality," unlimited potential for control, and the ability to create a society in which both individual and collective will can be met. At the same time, there seem to be so many reasons to accept that these possibilities *can* be met, through, for example, e-mail, and other, postmodern notions of web technology. The practice of control *is* almost always destruc-tive; the *anime*/gundam heroes are a direct response. Yet this postmodern era is in many ways what Enlightenment people could only have imagined!

But life is not just a party of enlightenment fulfillment. Kids find them-selves in the midst of adult conflicts and power games, even as they search out the next form of magic. They have to deal with the stupidity of the previous generation and its disturbing legacy of destructive forces. In this respect, the coordinated agents of change which Rushkoff mentions must be employed to specific ends. If Harry can use his new invisibility cloak in fending off evil, he is no different from an *anime* heroine wearing her new suit, or a *WWF* char-acter wielding her extra-super-finishing move. "And this is what it's about," writes Herz,

> as the cultural stream of East and West swirl into the Tastee-Freez of global entertainment. Mythic figures resonate, all the more if they're engaged in some kind of combat or action adventure, real or simulated,

the most popular forms being basketball and videogames. They resonate for the same reasons mythic figures have always resonated. Only now, the audience numbers in the millions, and the object is not to celebrate ancestors or teach lessons or curry favor with the spirits. It's commerce. And the people transmitting their stories to the next generation aren't priests or poets or medicine women. They're multinational corporations. And they are not trying to appease the gods. They are trying to appease the shareholders.

(Herz 1997: 170)

It is not just video games, it is everything in our mass culture. We can just see it more clearly in video games. And we are just a little edgy about the attraction of this series of *Harry Potter* books. Violent entertainment is the most blatant form of popular culture, but it is all about taming mythic monsters. The difference with the video games is that the monsters are inside the games, and we can try them on ourselves. Such gods and monsters used to scare people. Now people manipulate the gods and monsters (see, especially, *Black and White*). So we see once again why *Harry Potter* is the literature of the moment: he, too, trains and controls monsters and goblins, just like a player of *Magic*, a player of the *Pokemon* card game, or a video game master.

In her writing, Herz seems to be claiming an evolution, a new breed of freaks that adults need to study and live with. Perhaps she agrees with Bruce Mazlish (1993) that, "In making machines, humans have become themselves Creators who endow their creations with movement."

Automata ... express this form of creation dramatically. An automobile, a locomotor, an airplane, these also move under human inspiration. Until the Renaissance, it appears ... that Western Man [*sic*] built automata and other machines not so much to dominate nature, but to copy it; not to rival God, but to imitate him [*sic*]. Increasingly, however, in the West, humans came to smudge the image of God as the Creator and to substitute their own, first turning God into a Newtonian machine, and then merging him with nature as an evolutionary process. In doing so, humans united within themselves extraordinary powers of destruction ... and of creation. Whether in taking on creative powers humans are also able, in the form of their machines, to bring into being a new evolutionary step remains our next question. If Man [*sic*] succeeds in taking this step, he would certainly be doing something admittedly unique.

(Mazlish 1993: 213–214)

Curriculum and the technologies of morality

Throughout, my main curriculum argument is that educators need to learn from children what it is they are experiencing – that ol' Margaret Mead adage that our contemporary situation is one of migration into a new culture: children are the translators while adults are keepers of tradition. Adults need to learn from children in order to survive, yet children gain valuable narratives through which to interpret action by listening to stories of the old country from their elders. The "answer" for curriculum is not to try to compete with technoculture, because we will always fail at the imitation; instead we need to develop organized experiences that respond to life in and with technoculture. It would be more proactive for educators to work toward a biculturalism, and finally for a diversity that embraces both traditions and the multiplicities of what Herz calls "superhero sushi." This includes adult cultures and technocultures, mass and consumer cultures and youth subcultures, and cross-over memberships and participations in multiple cultures all at once. At the same time we must be wary of constructing teachers themselves as the *anime* heroines, themselves progenitors of technohyperbolic change. If teachers read the *Potter* books and then fashion themselves as the wizards with the children as the magical beasts to be tamed, then teachers become the technochildren themselves. Indeed, teachers are often urged to try on new prototypes of technology in order to experience a new sense of their powers of perception, production, and destruction (e.g., new technologies of assessment, instruction, surveillance). At other times they experience the melancholia of the gundam; they conceive of themselves as capable of harnessing the sometimes terrifying applications of scientistic pedagogical techniques in order to lead the student monsters in an effort to save society from invasion or technological disasters (Appelbaum 1999).

Even as the narratives reproduce themselves and their hegemonic themes, there is the parallel story, in which we enter a new phase of cyborg technoculture. Even in this context, magic and technology are not distinct categories for children. They are attracted to technology for its ability to perform magic, and they are attracted to magic for its potential to be used as a tool.[5] In working with children, I find that magic is not special despite its amazing surprise or apparent impossibility: for a child, anything is possible. The intriguing thing is the secret of how it is done. It is no wonder to me that the *Harry Potter* books coincide with the unprecedented popularity of television specials in which magicians reveal their secrets, despite being exiled forever from the community of magicians. It is no longer the "magic" of magic, but the cleverness of the technique that matters. Whereas the technical ingenuity of a particular tool is no longer of interest; the technological possibility is replaced by the cleverness of the magic it can perform. Regardless of how incredible the actual task is, it is ordinary unless it is relatively unique, arcane, or unexpected.

O'Har (2000) turned to Jacques Ellul (1967) in working through the popularity of *Harry Potter*. If we imagine that magic and science were once "one," then we can create a narrative of their split: one path went the way of technique, into technology; material technique leads to a multiplication of discoveries, each based on the other, and thus writes in itself a myth of progress. Magic, the other path, promotes only endless beginnings; it also answers all questions by preserving spirituality. The part of magic that was lost to our world in the dominance of science and technology was that aspect of magic that functioned in this spiritual realm. The fundamental message of *Harry Potter*, according to O'Har, is that magic saves Harry from turning into a Dursely; instead it provides a whole new set of endless beginnings.

Oddly, though, these beginnings carry the trappings of everything we already know about how people live and work together. Here is the "literary beauty" of the school in the *Harry Potter* books: it is no better than any other school we know of, simply by virtue of being school. Once magic is the subject matter, it is nothing special; in its commodification it has become another technology, another collection of technical skills to be mastered. Everything exciting, all of the real magic the children acquire, comes from the technological tricks they need to perform outside of school. Outside of the books, however, the magic (when read about) serves a different function. For us, reading along, it is the magic that captivates us because of its presentation as technology. This new technology, the magic, is ironically a technique for solving all the problems that technology and science have always failed to solve. For us, too, the magic provides a set of beginnings. The difference between school for Harry and his friends and the schools that readers experience outside the books, however, is that everyone at Hogwarts School of Witchcraft and Wizardry is learning stuff that they know they will use (Block 2001). Students at Hogwarts are training to be wizards, and they know that what they are learning will be useful to them in their lives.[6] Outside the books, the uses of school learning are remote at best, good for a promised future; inside the books, kids use what they have learned immediately to solve life-threatening puzzles and to save the fate of the world as we know it.

Technologies of the self: morality and magic

A particularly powerful element of the *Harry Potter* books is the unification of Harry's self-knowledge with his self-care. Who is this Harry, where does he come from, why is he so important, and why is he at the center of so much good–evil carnage so many times in his life? Only by strapping on the techno-culture of magic can he seek the self-knowledge he, we, and everybody else crave. For example, Harry looks into the magic mirror and sees his family; indeed he initially learns that he is a wizard through a message sent to him from Hogwarts. In this process of strapping on the magic, a process of externalizing and realizing his self-potential, he wields the tools that lead to self-understanding. Harry is a personified conflation of self-knowledge and self-care. His self-knowledge leads to care of the self, indeed saves his life; and, in taking care of himself and his potential, he is able to achieve self-knowledge. The books thus present what Michel Foucault (Martin *et al.* 1988) named a "technology of morality": the transformation of self by one's own means or with the help of others – that is, in the operations upon one's body, soul, thoughts, conduct, and way of being. Foucault postulated that this technology of morality enunciates a hierarchy between knowing oneself and taking care of oneself. Harry doesn't yet enunciate a hierarchy, and he therefore lives a more nuanced notion of morality that Foucault initially suggested. Harry's life project does not place knowing oneself above caring for oneself, nor does it value care of the self over knowing who he is. Either he has not yet been transformed, or he is a symbol of a shift away from Foucault's binary, toward an independent coexistence with the technology of morality. This is parallel to video gamers channel-surfing through the strategies of what in adult terms are violent images but in young people's terms are mere strategy games devoid of the realistic violence these young people say they would condemn. For *Harry Potter* fans, the convention of good–evil contestation is a context for the real cleverness and intrigue of the story, the details about how Harry and his friends collect more trinkets of magic in their quest to be "cool." Similarly, a fifth-grader can buy status at recess by recounting details of last night's *WWF* show, and claim he is not in the least interested in the "fake" violence, but instead in the intricacies of the particular combinations of moves that the fighters made. In any of these examples, the cultural shift has moved the focus away from the binary and the potential hierarchy to the placement of the binary in an independent context.

When magic is treated as technologies and technology is treated as magic, what can we say about the morality of magic, and about the magic of morality? Self-development is an enlightenment project, and self-development leading to self-knowledge is, again, an enlightenment project. We can see this clearly in *Pokemon*. The main characters, Ash and his friends, and the other Pokemon trainers, are traveling around looking to understand themselves, using different Pokemon to understand and strengthen themselves. The Pokemon that children train and fight with are externalizations of their inner drives and desires. Only in striving to become a true Pokemon trainer does an aspirant achieve, eventually, self-knowledge and the ability to care for oneself. So we are again up against this idea that postmodern technoculture is spawning a fulfillment of Enlightenment fantasy. If we think about the degree of bourgeois optimism that was so prevalent in the nineteenth century – that by knowing things you could enrich yourself, make yourself happier and be a better person, and in the process implicitly help society – and if we think about the role of this technology of morality in supporting the accomplishment of cultural forms of optimism like capitalism and industrialization, it is possible to understand why and how this new scientific optimism and notions of new possibilities through technologies can blind us to the terrible things that are going on in the world, such as genocides, slave labor in factories, or environmental racism. People are smugly not thinking about horrible famines in Ethiopia and instead are celebrating their technological power, a wealth-plus-knowledge equation that enables one to do what one wants when one wants in the world through technology – which is magic! In the end, the morality of magic is an Enlightenment ideology of postmodern technoculture. And this is *Harry Potter*'s world. In the books, there are really serious concerns about the impending triumph of the dark arts to contend with; outside the books, we can turn our local concerns into major focal points for self-development and ignore the major ethical concerns that plague our postmodern world.

Children growing up in a state of Enlightenment technoculture may indeed experience the technologies of morality as both a blinding scientific optimism and a more immediate celebration of individual prosthetic enhancement. As consumers of books, children are represented in our culture as a "hostile audience," since they are depicted as choosing other forms of entertainment over reading a new book. As science fiction and fantasy increasingly permeate the entertainment of children, adolescents, and young adults, members of contemporary society are effectively growing up in a fantasy land. It becomes imperative to analyze examples of these popular forms of entertainment (no matter how inconsequential or artless they may at first appear); we should understand what we are learning from these stories, and what sorts of adults we are becoming as a result (Westfahl 2000). Yet I believe that the most important use of the popular is an interrogation of the culture through the popular. One significant feature of the *Harry Potter* phenomenon is the presence of continued items in a series, and the need to continually market to an audience of consumers who will "need" to buy the next product, whether this product is a new book in the series, a home design product, a video game or film based on the books, or fanware. Advertising and promotion of products has become the dominant element of the *Harry Potter* culture since the first book. One might posit children as social change agents in turning the books into major marketing products through word-of-mouth advertising. Yet the overriding nature of consumer culture is that one is trying to sell something to a cynical audience. As adults purchase a *Harry Potter* T-shirt because of its connection to reading a book, children want the T-shirt for its value as a commodity. However, for both, the T-shirt serves as a symbol of membership in a cultural subgroup.

Reading *Harry Potter* with children requires more than reading the books. Reading includes participation in and reflexive analysis of all forms of cultural text. Indeed, reading especially means interpreting the uses of fanware. This chapter has focused mainly on the introduction of the *Harry Potter* phenomenon through the books themselves because the fanware hype occurred mostly after the success of the books themselves. Nevertheless, as we look forward to understanding what *Harry Potter* can teach us about ourselves we will need to address more carefully these multiple sites of meaning beyond the books. The multiple "texts" of *Harry Potter* can be popular only if they are open enough to admit a range of negotiated readings, through which various social groups can find meaningful articulations of their own relationship to the dominant ideology (Fiske 1987). The "dominant reader" identifies with Harry the hero, and can believe that everyone might just have magic in them. If we play down the fact that many muggles do not get an invitation to Hogwarts, while some Wizard folk, *squibs*, are unfortunately lacking, we might just hope that hard work and careful practice can help us get ahead. The dominant reading maintains a commonsense belief in meritocracy. Negotiated readings emerge when people make use of the images presented to interpret their own lives, as when a reader thinks of the ways they are like and unlike Hermione, or why they would never be able to become a teacher like Snape. Issues of class and race, underplayed by the dominant reader, may be foregrounded in negotiated readings. If the negotiation is more "against" than "with" the text, then a reader might use the texts as blatantly sexist or racist, or perhaps antireligious.

In any reading of the texts of *Harry Potter*, however, we will find magic and technology confused, or thrown into disarray, to be unraveled and comprehended in ways that are consistent with the reading that emerges. Arthur Weasley, who works for the Ministry of Magic, eccentrically collects electric plugs and batteries, and secretly keeps a flying car until it ends up in a magic forest in a later book. The Dursleys want nothing to do with magic, and fill their home with all of the latest technological gadgets and toys one could ever want.[7] It is Vernon Dursley who points out the peculiar place of technology in the arts of magic: in the end, it is technology that is the symbol of one's path to wizardry, as everyone takes the Hogwarts Express train to get to this school of witchcraft and wizardry. He asks why wizards need to take a train. He never gets his answer. Harry's story provides the larger context: in the end, technology/magic has to do with who one is and what one does. And because who one is and what one does is so intertwined with the technologies of magic and the magic of technology in the service of self-knowledge and self-care, who one is and what one does is a technology of morality and an essential node of the construction of ethics.

Hogwarts confronts the ethics of magic and science directly. Its purpose is to help its students harness and focus their powers. These powers might be called magic or they might be called technology; but in this case they are called magic. The problem for the educators in the books is that they cannot be certain that people (wizards) will use these powers for the common good. It boils down to a choice between the common good and the dark arts. And so we are confronted with the evil of Voldemort and the always-present danger of evil triumphing over good. Hogwarts was founded by four wizards, one of whom, Salazar Slytherin, at least dabbled and perhaps reveled in the dark arts. He used his powers for questionable if not specifically evil purposes. (For centuries, many of the young wizards who reside in Slytherin House have exhibited the same tendency.) Albus Dumbledore, who heads the school, needs to figure out how to train students not just in the "technology" of magic but also in the moral discernment necessary to avoid the continual reproduction of the few great Dark Lords like Voldemort and their multitudinous followers. The problem is exacerbated by the presence of faculty members who are not wholly unsympathetic with Voldemort's aims.

Good and evil are not just cartoonized in the books. As Alan Jacobs writes, Harry Potter is unquestionably good; yet a key component of his virtue arises from his recognition that he is not *inevitably* good. When first-year students arrive at Hogwarts, they come to an assembly of the entire school, students, and faculty. Each of them sits on a stool in the midst of the assembly and puts on a large, battered, old hat – the Sorting Hat, which decides which of the four houses the student will enter. After unusually long reflection, the Sorting Hat, to Harry's great relief, puts him in Gryffindor, but not before telling him that he could achieve real greatness in Slytherin. This comment haunts Harry: he often wonders if Slytherin is where he truly belongs, among the pragmatists, the careerists, the manipulators and deceivers, the power-hungry, and the just plain nasty. Near the end of the second book, after his third terrifying encounter with Voldemort, he confesses his doubts to Dumbledore.

> "So I *should* be in Slytherin," Harry said, looking desperately into Dumbledore's face. "The Sorting Hat could see Slytherin's power in me, and it–"
>
> "Put you in Gryffindor," said Dumbledore calmly. "Listen to me, Harry. You happen to have many qualities Salazar Slytherin prized in his hand-picked students. Resourcefulness … determination … a certain disregard for rules," he added, his moustache quivering again. "Yet the Sorting Hat placed you in Gryffindor. You know why that was. Think."
>
> "It only put me in Gryffindor," said Harry in a defeated voice, "Because I asked not to go in Slytherin.…"
>
> "Exactly," said Dumbledore, beaming once more. "Which makes you very different from [Voldemort]. It is our choices, Harry, that show what we truly are, far more than our abilities." Harry sat motionless in his chair, stunned.

Harry is stunned because he realizes for the first time that his confusion has been wrongheaded from the start: he has been asking the question "Who am I at heart?" when he needed to be asking the question "What must I do in order to become what I should be?" His character is not a fixed, pre-existent thing, but something that he has the responsibility for making. "In this sense," writes Jacobs, "the strong, [enlightenment] tendency of magic to become a dream of power makes it a wonderful means by which to focus the choices that gradually but inexorably shape us into certain distinct kinds of persons" (2000: 38).

In the *Harry Potter* books, magic is often fun, often surprising and exciting, but also always potentially dangerous – much like the technology outside the books that has resulted from the "victory" of experimental science. The technocrats of this world hold in their hands powers almost infinitely greater than those of Albus Dumbledore and Voldemort: how worried are we about them, and their influence over our children? If we could only measure technique by other criteria than those of technique itself. *Harry Potter* is more helpful than most children's literature in prompting such ethical and cultural reflection.

7

Cyborg Selves*

What follows is one story of my work with children, teachers, and Saturday morning television. It is a story of a curriculum project, but also a story of how such a project forced me to reflect on the difficulties of presenting practice as a narrative. The moral turns out to have something to do with the impact of technoculture, and the "free spaces" not seen in curriculum research. But this is also the story of a picaresque quest, a movement from Foucault to Deleuze and Guattari, from action researcher to rhizomic practitioner, and back again.

Aftermath: triage

This project had as a primary impetus my need to work through the implications of a *triage*[1] of terms highlighted by Bruce Mazlish's (1993) book *The Fourth Discontinuity: the Co-Evolution of Humans and Machines*. Mazlish argues that, just as Copernicus, Darwin, and Freud overturned our illusions of separation from and domination over the cosmos, the animal world, and the unconscious, it is now necessary to relinquish a fourth fallacy – that humans are discontinuous and distinct from the machines we make. As I continue to re-read Mazlish, I persist in trying to unravel these three words: "animal," "human," and "machine." We see in Mazlish the enormous play already accomplished in (primarily Western, AmeroEurocentric) thought that sets up one or two of these as a potential "other" through which a third can be defined.

I note as well Andrew Ross' characterization of the "cyberpunk embrace" – an oft-posited "emergent stage" of human development that integrates the tenets of evolutionary humanism with a "frontier rhetoric of discovery and creative invention, [linking] the LSD spirit of synthetic transformation with the technofantasies of cybernetic consciousness" (Ross 1991: 162). Ross

---

*This chapter originally appeared as "Saturday morning magic and magical morality," in Toby Daspit and John Weaver (eds), *Popular Culture and Critical Pedagogy*. New York: Garland Press, 1998.

makes a nice contrast to Mazlish in his critique of discourses that channel the "discourse of the maverick" into the evolution of human beings, "headily pursuing its goal of an 'assault on limits' in the name of individual self-liberation." Juxtaposing Mazlish and Ross need not set up a polarity or continuum, however; indeed, the problematic of cyberculture and techno-humanity contructs a multiplicity of epistemologies that structure fields of possibility for practice and concomitant technologies of morality and power.[2] In this study, one facet of the problematic is this very multiplicity and its implications for research, in which my own, and others', perspectives and forms of meaning construction become examples of the conflicts themselves.

As I turn to the focus of my exploration in this instance, Saturday morning television, my excitement mounts: here we have film, video, animated, clay-mated, and digitized combos across and over the three realms that Mazlish posits for *triage* – spheres? categories? ("Please don't let yourself tumble into the abyss," my simulacrum of early Foucault cries out) – in a plethora of images and representations that demand our attention. They demand our attention first of all because of the importance of these forms of entertain-ment and edutainment in the lives of our students. But they are important as well in our own lives – as people who work with and through those who consume and translate the images and stories for us, and as people who con-front and celebrate the same images and stories in our own lives. The latter can be expressed in several ways: (1) Saturday morning television may be said to be communicating the fears and fantasies of the adult world; (2) [some-times dubbed "the reception fallacy"] we must realize that although Saturday morning television is often referred to as "Kids' T.V.", its audience is not limited to children (Waught 1947), and likely includes a fairly sizable propor-tion of teachers as well (even if they claim their own kids have the T.V. on, or that they are forced to familiarize themselves with the garbage slung at their students); (3) There is the argument that life is merely an enactment of the imagined possibilities first explored through fiction (sometimes described as the amazing quality of authors, e.g., sci-fi to "predict" the future); there is also the argument that change is so frantic in contemporary society that it resem-bles immigrant cultures in which the children teach the adults the new con-ventions they must adapt to (Mead 1970: 72).

Triage as cultural practice follows several options, including: *Triptych* – here the three speak to us and each other as distinct images juxtaposed in order to establish a larger or more coherent "meaning". *Triangle* – in this option we have a representation of three distinct categories and their relation-ship among each other, including a continuum between each pair. *3-D Space* – in which, by convention, each ray of infinite possibility has its origin in a common point, and all reality can be defined by linear combinations of the three defining axes. *Overlapping regions* – here the categories are no longer distinct and overlap each other in a Wittgensteinian or Gombrichian way, structuring the model as collections of "family resemblances"; the terms are informative references but are not necessarily foundational in any epistemological sense. My discussion claims that different Saturday morning programs construct different epistemologies of the animal–human–machine *triage* in different ways. The epistemology is not necessarily foundational to practice and cultural politics, but is symptomatic of these features of self and related technologies of morality, thus enabling an entry into theory *about* these issues and their relationship to pedagogy and the professions of teaching and learning.

Another impetus for my work was the need to work through the dilemmas of textual and reader-response analysis regarding media and technology. We might phrase the dilemmas in terms of production/consumption, or perhaps in terms of aesthetics/reception (See, e.g., Rosen 1995). I was concerned that I could construct a reading of Saturday morning television programs, and that this could be useful to me as a teacher, or to other teachers as information pertinent to their teaching, but that others might not "read" these programs the same way, or that the creators of the programs might not have anything like what I have read in mind. Differences among students, teachers, and curriculum constructions should be expected rather than viewed as confounding research. You've heard all this before, I am sure. I aimed to avoid the anxiety by structuring in a variety of forms of hermeneutic "triangulation." I looked for a saturation of the discourse in repeated viewings of as many programs as possible, and entire series of those programs I videotaped. I applied the assorted checks for coherence and sensibility we all learned in graduate courses in hermeneutic research. But I also interviewed a group of 6- to 8-year-old boys and girls about the programs they found most important to share with me. I also interviewed teachers about what they thought about my interpretations as well. The process of my research was as follows: I interviewed children and asked them what programs I should watch and why – I told them I was researching Saturday morning television and needed their guidance so that I would watch the right programs and then be able to talk to their teachers about the programs I had watched. Repeated versions of this text were shared with teachers; I asked teachers how they might use what I have been working with in their teaching and interactions with children. (Here my research is consistent with others who seek to respond to concerns about teacher empowerment.[3]) Advice on what I should look for and how I should think about the children's expert opinions formed a parallel set of expert knowledge that I attempted to combine with previous work. Meetings with teachers were working projects over time, in which we planned curriculum changes, and assessed the implemented curriculum. I then returned to a subset of the expert young people to talk about how adults and children think about Saturday morning television. In these later meetings we found significant shifts over time as those interviewed began to critique their own former declarations as well as those of hypothetical prospective teachers. I remain convinced that popular culture is simultaneously a commodity to be consumed, collected, and traded for other cultural capital, and a cultural resource, out of which individuals and groups construct ways to form meanings and new comprehensions in their experiencing and remaking of the world (Appelbaum 1995a, 1995b). At any rate, we know that people watching these programs *can* use them as "tools" for constructing meaning. How, though? And how does this relate to the *self*? To quote the eminently quotable Andrew Hargreaves, "Postmodernity brings changes not only in what we experience, in our organizations and institutions, but also in how we experience, in our fundamental senses of self and identity" (Hargreaves 1994: 69). In other words, as I ask us to ponder Saturday morning television, it seems we must focus on that television and its relationship to a new kind of way to comprehend the self; at least, I claim, we have to entertain what options for constructing "selves" are available as a cultural resource. Hargreaves is helpful here as well.

In the high-tech world of the instantaneous image, what once stood for the substantial self is increasingly seen as merely a constellation of signs. With the collapse of moral and scientific certainties of foundational knowledge, the only intelligible reality appears to be that of language, discourse, image, sign, and text. But even these have multiple meanings, infinite readings, and are open to endless forms of deconstruction. So even the self is now suspect. It has no substance, center or depth. It is "enfolded in language which [it] can neither oversee nor escape." Selves become transient texts, to be read and misread, constructed or deconstructed at will. Human selves become things that people display and other people interpret, not things that have lasting and inner substance of their own. Postmodernity, therefore, sees a "suspicion of the supposed unity and transparency of the disengaged self [and] of the alleged inner sources of the expressive self" (Hargreaves 1994: 70).

In the "end," the self becomes a continuous reflexive project, constantly and consciously remade and reaffirmed ("under construction" as Hargreaves says). This heightened orientation to the self and to its continuing construction can be a source of creativity, empowerment, and change; but it can also be a source of uncertainty, vulnerability, and social withdrawal. In any case, the self is important, is surely a central concern to those who spend a lot of time with children, and may be seen to be related to the available construction of human self within the amorphous *triage* of animal–human–machine.

What is human?

The origins of many cyborg and other transmutated characters on Saturday morning television[4] are found in adult fears of the Cold War and emerging technologies. Adult fantasies such as *Batman* and the *X-Men* can be deconstructed in order to unravel the dynamics and implications of these fears for cultural and historical patterns. Children's reactions to these adult fantasies are interesting because of the ways in which the Cold War ideologies both create fears for children and "alleviate" them by offering particular solutions to those fears. The type of fear and solution is crucial, because it is interwoven with an implicit technology of morality. Just as Donna Haraway asks us "would we rather be a cyborg or a goddess?" (Haraway 1985/1990), the placement of "good guy" and "bad guy" in the animal–human–machine geography constructs a notion of identification and value.

Similarly, the role of "technology" on Saturday morning – both technological items and symbols of the technologicization of social life – conveys a story about a "morality of potential," in the sense that James Macdonald once articulated, as the function of *magic* in constructing a field of human potential:

> It is my personal myth that today's technology is yesterday's magic. Further, it is my intuitive feeling that technology is in effect an externalization of the hidden consciousness of human potential. Technology, in other words, is a necessary development for human beings in that it is the means of externalizing the potential that lies within.
>
> (Macdonald 1995: 75)

Douglas Rushkoff has raised this issue once again:

> When we look carefully at the reaction of younger cyber-denizens to their Sega-environs, we find that they make no distinction between information and matter, mechanics and thought, work and play, or even religion and commerce. In fact, kids on the frontier of the digital terrain have adopted some extraordinarily magical notions about the world we live in. Far from yielding a society of coldhearted rationalists, the ethereal, out-of-body experience of mediating technologies appears to have spawned a generation of pagan spiritualists whose dedication to technology is only matched by their enthusiasm for elemental truth and a neoprimitive, magical worldview. To a screenager, these are not opposing life strategies but coordinated agents of change.
>
> (Rushkoff 1996: 109)

In "the beginning of a conclusion," Mazlish raises the possibility of a leading definition of humanity: "a human is that animal who breaks out of the animal kingdom by creating machines" (Mazlish 1993: 213).

> In making machines, humans have become themselves Creators who endow their creations with movement. Automata,... express this form of creation dramatically. An automobile, a locomotor, and airplane, these also move under human inspiration. Until the Renaissance, it appears ... that Western Man [*sic*] built automata and other machines

not so much to dominate nature, but to copy it; not to rival God, but to imitate him. Increasingly, however, in the West, humans came to smudge the image of God as the Creator and to substitute their own, first turning God into a Newtonian machine, and then merging him with nature as an evolutionary process. In doing so, humans united within themselves extraordinary powers of destruction ... and of creation. Whether in taking on creative powers humans are also able, in the form of their machines, to bring into being a new evolutionary step remains our next question. If Man [sic] succeeds in taking this step, he would certainly be doing something admittedly unique.

(Mazlish 1993: 214)

What answers are plausible on Saturday morning regarding what a human self is? The answer has often been phrased in terms of an animal–human–machine epistemology. Descartes distinguished humans from animals by their possession of a soul, while arguing that other animals are mere machines. When the soul was removed from the human machine in the eighteenth century by Julian Offray de la Mattrie, writes Mazlish, a human became only a machine. In the industrial revolution, humans passed the boundary between animal and mechanical and Carlyle was able to say, "Man becomes mechanical in head and heart as well as in hand." In creating machines humans appear to take on God-like or at least Promethean qualities; but as humans have moved to replace the concept of God, or gods, with nature, they have gone further and appear to be that being, or becoming a conscious evolutionary agent of creation. So, as angels were a marker of a Christian way to human perfection, argues Mazlish, machines took on the same quality for more secularly minded humans. They did so in two ways: one, embodied in the idea of progress, was to lead humans into a mechanical paradise in which they were perfectible because they had entered into a perfectible society, with all bodily tasks performed by machines (thus leaving the human as a purely spiritual creature, and all social problems as solved). The other way was to embrace the machine as perfect, in the sense that it could never make a mistake; for humans to become more mechanical meant that they too were fast approaching perfection (Mazlish 1993: 216–219). It is this narrative of evolution toward perfection and limitless potential that Ross brings up-to-date as the history of the cyberpunk embrace.

I and my authorities consistently identify science and scientists as the source of danger in most programs where Cold War and post-Cold War fantasies are enacted. There is a long tradition of this characterization. In early Japanese *anime* and Gundam (represented in the 1960s programs *Gigantor* and *Speed Racer*) it is the children alone who are capable of harnessing the sometimes frightening applications of technology, or of understanding the inner struggles and gentle nature of the monsters mutantly

The Masked Rider

Masked Rider is a teenager named Dex, sent to Earth from Eegonon. He's able to form a crystal on his forehead to communicate with his grandfather (the leader of Eegonon) – until "the attack." The leader of the attack is no more than his Uncle. His Uncle sent down to Earth the "destructosphere." It was a buglike creature that was like a cyborg, too. It could unfold shooting machine blasters, transform into a ball, and transform into a rock and sail underground.

Dex saw the message on T.V. He quickly ran into the backyard of the house he lived in with his two friends and their mother and father. And he quickly transformed into the bug alien cyborg known as "The Masked Rider." He was attacking when he was losing energy and he only had enough for one more strike. Fortunately, that one strike destroyed the destructosphere. Then Dex quickly transformed back into Dex. He ran to a cave he knew of and telepathically communicated with his grandfather, and he made a jewel on his forehead to communicate with his grandfather, who told him to use the jewel to create power sources he needed. He shot a light beam from the jewel at a rock and the rock fell open revealing a bird which quickly transformed into a solid cyborg motorcycle (it's a cyborg because it can talk). He shot another light beam which created a monster which became a cyborg car. The motorcycle is called "the Combat Chopper." The car is "the Magno."

His uncle then sent down a monster known as the "Battle Beetle." It was a cyborg because it was half tank, half bug monster. The Combat Chopper tried to attack it. But when it tried to crash into it, it did nothing more than make the Combat Chopper lose energy. Then Magno was ready to charge in, but not yet (She sensed the Masked Rider was coming). Then Masked Rider came and tried to destroy the Battle Beetle, but lost energy. Then Magno charged at the Battle Beetle. The Battle Beetle was knocked over. Then Masked Rider jumped onto Magno. They destroyed the Battle Beetle together.

Hargreaves writes that one of the key postmodern paradoxes is a "personal anxiety"; the search for authenticity becomes a continuous psychological quest in a world without secure moral anchors (Hargreaves 1994: 84). Viewing Saturday morning is an exercise in the simulacrum of anchor in this respect. In my interviews with my 6- to 8-year-old authorities, I often dwell on the geography of cyborgness. I ask: What is human? Is she human? Is she a cyborg? What is a cyborg? What is an animal? A machine? My own interpretations are often critiqued by my authorities. I think at this point that they tend as a group to use the triangle-continuum model. For virtually all interviewees, a cyborg is a living being combined with a machine in a way that is not easily disassembled into component parts. The machine aspect provides extraordinary abilities, such as enormous strength or laser ray projection. A person or animal inside a machine or a person using a machine as a tool cannot be a cyborg in this typology. I tend in my own reading to be more general in some ways. I want to include human/machine combos that the children find inappropriate. The why of this difference must be explored further, and bears some resemblance to differences between "adult" and "child" definitions of "living thing" described in common science education methods textbooks (Bell 1993).[5]

Megaman

Megaman is a robot fighting against the evil Dr. Wiley. Actually, he's a cyborg. He is able to transform his arm – or should I say pull his hand in?– into a blaster and blast. He can take others' powers by touching his hand onto their forehead or arm. Dr. Light, the guy who made Megaman, was awarded "Best Scientist" (not for Megaman but for lots of other stuff). Then Dr. Wiley attacked. So Dr. Light made his son into Megaman!

Megaman fights the robots known as Bombman, Gutsman, Blademan, Cutman, Torpedoman, Waveman, Diveman, and even against his *own* brother, known as Protoman, who is a cyborg (made, like all bad guys, by Dr. Wiley). Dr. Wiley and Dr. Light used to be partners; now they're worst enemies because Dr. Wiley wants to take over the world. He thought it would be a good idea to have Dr. Light's son fighting against Dr. Light. In the beginning of when Dr. Light attacked, he tried to capture the son who's now Megaman, but he escaped! And Megaman has a sister who is a cyborg because she has a mechanical bracelet arm which can make anything on it. She can pull her hand into the bracelet part and pull anything out of it. Her name is Rol. Their dog, Rush, is a robot, not a cyborg.

(How he was made): mechanical devices with pointy things and static and stuff like that. You don't see much about that. You don't know much about his life.

wrought from toxic spills and nuclear accidents. "Adults accidentally create monsters and catastrophes by letting their technology get out of control, while the children – thanks to their ability to understand the inner workings of technology and the secret hearts of monsters – are uniquely qualified to clean up the mess" (Rushkoff 1996: 69). Like their predecessors, contemporary North American children's programs are heavily influenced by their Japanese counterparts. Indeed, *Power Rangers* in its earliest version comprised dubbed sequences of Japanese programs, with Americanized plots spliced in. Like their Gundam cousins, these North American versions enact plots that develop a relationship between the evolution of the young main characters and the human-directed evolution of technology. Each side in a battle between good and evil for the fate of the Earth and all humanity continues to develop new prototypes of technological wizardry; in response, the child stars test out the new prototypes. The eternal war serves to create better technology through which the new children can test and develop their powers. In the home we see the plot behind the series' producers' obsession with technological innovation: The shows are sponsored by toy companies which want to sell as much as they can. Every innovation in body suit or technological prototype is mirrored by a new toy version whose price is higher than its forerunner. Douglas Rushkoff has suggested that the creation of child characters who have extra-sensory experiences through technological devices is an attempt by the toy-makers and television producers to convince children that they can really feel what it would be like to move, strike, and *be* like a powerful mobile suit gundam. He also notes that the influence might be in the reverse direction, from children to the producers of the programs and makers of the toys:

> Ironically but not at all coincidentally, these programs … are driven as much by technology as they are by any personal visions of their adult scriptwriters. The shows and their themes are wrapped around technological innovation – toy robots with movable parts. The evolving features of these high-tech dolls advance the stories and concepts in this otherwise market-driven cosmology. Therefore, whether they realize it or not, the gundam marketers are merely reacting to their young viewers. Because their viewers are children of chaos, these two forces turn out to be immensely compatible, and their marriage is depicted in the stories themselves.
>
> (Rushkoff 1996: 74)

New cyborgs for new worlds

Not all programs construct Cold War fantasies, of course. A second category of fiction posits post-radioactive trauma or cyborg developments as a positive solution because they give the characters "new" powers over the toxicity, radioactivity, or rampant technology. Here superheros, mutants and cyborgs are translated through "Kids' T.V." into a potentially positive friend rather than threat which in the long run, I suppose, suggests tipping the invisible balance toward "good" for science and its effects in general. Yet the positive nature of the new powers is ambiguous. The *X-Men* are people we have to like, and are the potential harbingers of an increasingly pluralist society, yet they live on the margins in a perpetual state of alienation and isolation, frozen in interminable, "illegal" immigration. Saturday morning versions of *Batman* and *Spiderman* wield technology to tame the cyborgs and psychotics of contemporary society, but also suffer never-ending isolation and marginality, and experience severe levels of depression and anxiety. The overarching message, nevertheless, is that cyborgs and mutants are "more powerful" and hence "better" than humans.

In this case, the cyborgs have much in common with Marge Piercy's (1991) enhanced humans in *He, She, and It*, and less in common with her golem, or (humanly)-enhanced robot. Born of catastrophe and crisis, they symbolize continued hope; yet the hope lies closer to the human end of the human–machine continuum than the machine end. While Piercy in her writing actually presents a vision of overlapping family resemblances, Saturday morning preserves the god-dream of Descartes in the triangle. Some test cases in my discussions with the 6- to 8-year-old experts: R.L. Stine's (1994) scarecrow in *The Scarecrow Walks at Midnight* is not a cyborg; neither are Krang from *Teenage Mutant Ninja Turtles*, an evil brain from the fourth dimension who must remain attached to a machine to function on our Earth; nor Arthur, *The Tick's* sidekick, a man who derives his identity and life project from the Moth-suit machine he always wears.

In the spoofs of Cold War fantasies, such as *Teenage Mutant Ninja Turtles*, *Power Rangers*, and *The Tick*, the Cold War mentality is no longer ambiguous but clearly and unilaterally positive. The *Turtles* do not want to go back to being turtles; the *Rangers* revel in their role as fighters of enormous vitality and success (indeed, in the motion picture version, we see that younger children dream of one day becoming a *Power Ranger* themselves); *The Tick* and his superhero rivals bound with delight into each new adventure, turning every nightmarish threat into recreation (in the athletic pleasure sense). Here transmutation or robotization is a gift one must celebrate. Two programs help us see how the line from ambiguity to positivity has been crossed: *The Masked Rider*, and *Sailor Moon*. *The Masked Rider*, A *Power Ranger* take-off (the simulacrum of the simulacrum), is a sort *of I Dream of Jeannie* revenge fantasy: Dex must keep his powers secret in order to keep his identity hidden from the bad guys, but he uses them freely without disapproval to the delight of himself and his friends. *Sailor Moon*, touted as a "girl superhero show," can transform with "moon power" into a superfighter who battles the megaverse, and in doing so proves how great she is. (Oddly, *Sailor Moon* turns out to

Technoman

Technoman's real name is Slade. He fights the evil Darkon. Darkon sent down another technoman named Gunner. At technoman's and Gunner's first battle, Technoman went away; in the next battle Gunner went away; in the next battle Technoman blasted Gunner; in the next battle, he threw a sword in Gunner's face and cracked his technoarmor. The next battle Gunner won by destroying Slade's crystal. Fortunately Slade made a new one and went back. With the new crystal he blasted his technoblaster at Gunner and destroyed him. Darkon's normal soldiers who Technoman always destroys are named spidercrabs. He also has two friends from a space crew, and more friends from the space crew.

Slade is a cyborg because the crystal sent the power of his armor in his body to where the armor is inside him, forcing the armor out. For the same reason as Ronin Warriors, the exoskeleton is a machine because of things like technoblasters that blast technoblasts.

He kind of and kind of doesn't like being Technoman. He's happy that he was able to remake his technocrystal and he's very happy because he's able to destroy things with his armor. Slade does not really like being Technoman because he's very unhappy about having enemies and stuff like that. Slade fights and everybody relaxes while he fights because *he* has the technocrystal and the skills, so he should do the fighting.

reproduce the same ol' boring ideology – she often gets into trouble and must be saved by the only major male character, her uncle.)

Rushkoff tells us the children watching these programs are not reveling in the violence. Most of the destruction is done to and by machines. The joy comes instead from a vicarious feeling of power. Mirroring the cyberpunk literature read by older brothers and sisters, these programs depict children who understand technology better than the adults who designed it; having evolved they also exercise a greater control over and a genuine friendship with this technology.[6] Adults are intimidated by these programs because they exalt this relationship. "The battle becomes one between our evolutionary future," writes Rushkoff, "the combined efforts of a rainbow of children – and our evolutionary past: the efforts of a single, technoimprisoned dictator to maintain personal control over our planet" (Rushkoff 1996: 78).

The overriding theme of the show turns out to be co-evolution with technology. In addition to the way the Power Rangers use technology to fight monsters of the tyrannous past, they depend on technology for moral and spiritual guidance. When the Power Rangers are in trouble they turn to Zordon, a disembodied ageless sage who acts as a techno-oracle from within a computer. Pure consciousness available only through a communications device, Zordon demonstrates that the wisdom of the ages has the ability to speak to us through technology, just as the Power Rangers show how children may be able to bring us into our evolutionary future via the same means (Rushkoff 1996: 80).

Cyborg selves

In creating machines, humans are often said to take on the god-like role of "creator." Yet we often see the machine as the image of doom or evil. Is this odd? "After all," writes Mazlish, "the machine promises perfection, and, if it threatens to take over life, in return it promises to do away with death" (Mazlish 1993: 219). He suggests that we turn to Harold Searles, who has noted our frustration at the knowledge that we have created a technology which, seemingly omnipotent and immortal itself, has not extended our own allotted life span. Searles suggests that we thus identify unconsciously with the technology itself, which, being inanimate, cannot die. The juxtaposition of these two impulses has been eloquently described by Jim Paul (1991), in his account of building a catapult to launch stones into the ocean. Early in the process, he and his friend Harry step back to look at their work:

> Look at that, said Harry, in satisfaction. The proportion seemed right, like an arm's to a baseball. We were making an effigy of a human being, it seemed, one stripped of all capacities except stone-throwing, and that capacity amplified, as if in compensation for whatever else a person was.
>
> (Paul 1991: 78)

Later he has another thought:

> I had to confess that the catapult's meaning hadn't really come up that evening. That we could afford it, that we could make it work, those were our concerns. That thought gave me the sinking feeling, as I drove home beneath the Bay Bridge's towers and cables, that I wasn't outside the catapult anymore, seeing it as an object in the world, but inside it somehow, assuming the world from its viewpoint. As if we were its eyes, its mind, on the lookout for the best way to make it manifest. And that was no observation at all – just a kind of mechanical vision, fascinating and persistent, against which my need to observe was an eddy to the main current.
>
> (Paul 1991: 145)

Mazlish posits a future in which humans may look like we do now, may be enhanced or altered by machines, or may gaze at a new other species, the machine. I suggest the choices are not necessarily so clearly delineated, and that machines and people have always been members of an amorphous mass of stuff which we choose to categorize in a variety of ways. Once we do so, we have constructed a range of options for identification, and at least as many psychologies of identification. Cyborg selves are names we give to comprehend our positionality/subjectivity/agency. The variety of potential relationships among the possible selves becomes the interesting phenomenon, as opposed to what one self looks like. Recalling Hargreaves' articulation of the postmodern self as a collection of images and fragments searching for an image to cling to, my presentation of Saturday morning alternatives suggests attention to the successive phases of the image as presented by Baudrillard (1990): (1) it is the reflection of a basic reality; (2) it masks and perverts reality; (3) it masks the absence of a basic reality; (4) it bears no relation to any reality whatsoever. We can take the triptych, triangle, 3-D space, or overlapping regions, and ask of the model: When is it constructed as reflecting a basic reality? When is it represented as masking or perverting reality? In which programs do we see the *triage* as masking the absence of a basic reality? And in which does it bear no relation to reality? In my own reading of Saturday morning, I find mostly the triangle and it reflects a reality. I would prefer the more sophisticated (to me) overlapping regions offered by Piercy, Haraway, and others, and I would prefer these regions to bear relevance to something other than a presentation of reality. Sometimes, however, the bad guys on Saturday morning are offered as seeing things differently, usually also a triangle, but sometimes masking or perverting reality; the ideological function is to construct the alternative as psychotic or absurdly evil, thus rendering the reality as common sense.

Why, we might ask, do we cling to the idea that a human–tool link is transformative, as potential merged beyond dissociation, while children freely make a categorical distinction? Why might we favor the family resemblance, the overlapping regions, while children so comfortably assimilate the triangle of contua? Good questions. Here we confront Andrew Ross' "discourse of maverick humanism in fullflow, headily pursuing its goal of an 'assault on limits' in the name of individual self-liberation." The self is Rushkoff's "screenager," the chaos-acclimated kid who laughs at the paranoid superstitions of elders, satirizing their inability to cope with self-simularity and recurrence by creating mock cults and collectives, and distancing themselves in shells of self-conscious media.

> By accepting the notion that technology can play a part in the forward evolution of humanity toward its greater spiritual goals the children of chaos exchange the adult, paranoid response to the impending colonial organism with a philosophy decidedly more positive: pronoia.
>
> (Rushkoff 1996: 154)

Another question which children find perplexing is: Why are cyborgs always fighting? Why is it weapons which represent the machine-like aspects of the cyborg? I asked my authorities about this. Why don't we see them building buildings? Fixing cars? Transporting children to school? Playing games and cleaning scrapes? Because we are talking "Cyber-Chatagua," declare Queen Mu and R.U. Sirius (1989, quoted in Ross 1991: 163).

> bringing cyberculture to the people!
>   We're talking about Total Possibilities. Radical assaults on the limits of biology, gravity, and time. The end of Artificial Scarcity. The dawn of a new humanism. High-jacking technology for personal empowerment, fun and games. Flexing those synapses! Stoking those neuropeptides! Making Bliss States our normal waking consciousness. *Becoming* the Bionic Angel.

Distrustful of the "puritanism" of the Left, and dismissive of the "techno-fear" of the "self-denying" ecofundamentalists, the New Prometheans revive a work-free, post-scarcity society, "all of it watched over by machines of loving grace." I am told cyborgs look just like people when they are not fighting, so they are not interesting; that's not what the story is about. Or, as my son so aptly put it, do we need cyborgs to do those things? No! So the cyborgs don't do that! The "machines of loving grace" are invisible, because they do the drudge work of the invisible man, and thus are simply uninteresting as the stars of our program; they are "the machines" and not "the people." This is Ralph Ellison for the 1990s, the walking zombie stripped of humanity first visited in Chapter 4:

> Behold! a walking zombie! Already he's learned to repress not only his emotions but his humanity. He's invisible, a walking personification of the Negative, the most perfect achievement of your dreams, sir! The mechanical man!
>
> (Ellison 1947/1972: 86)

As Rushkoff puts it, "in stark contrast ... kids' culture stands as a delightfully mixed-up common ground for all these digital, magical, and biological sorts of development" (Rushkoff 1996: 109).

The teacher makes a dramatic entrance

> **Masked Rider**
>
> His driving teacher was captured by Lord Dragonon's evil Maggots, and they made a clone of him who was actually an electricity force monster. He let Dex drive safely to the place they were going to; then they decided they would switch so that the teacher would drive back. The monster who was the clone of the teacher changed his hand into a weapon, and Dex turned into the Masked Rider. Both are cyborgs. Dex

was able to hit the teacher-cyborg into an electrical equipment thing, but this turned the teacher-cyborg into an even more powerful cyborg. Dex called Combat Chopper and together they finished off the bad cyborg monster. Meanwhile, before that happened, Dex found out that his weirdo creature-pet Furbis was hiding in his backpack. (He's *not* a cyborg.)

Teacher

As a teacher I am like a *dentist*. The dentist tells you what you have to do to have good teeth, but essentially you have to do it. Some days it is as hard as pulling teeth. And if they didn't brush their teeth last night, they come back and you can't get near them because they have bad breath. And you have this faint feeling as if they fail you in some way, or you failed because you did not press upon them the importance of doing it. They come with cavities and you have to fix them. They come to you two hours before you have to turn in the grades and they ask, "What can I do?" "Well, you really should have brushed. Let's see if I can fill it. We'll stick some silver in there and see if it holds. But next time remember to brush!" (Female, 44, High School, Small Town, in Joseph and Burnaford 1994: 54)

Ronin Warriors

The leader of the Ronin warriors is named Ryo. The Ronin Warriors are cyborgs because of their machinery-like armor, which is part of them. The armor's, like, inside them. It becomes like an exoskeleton, like bugs have. The names of them are Ryo, Roin, Kento, Sage and Cie.

However, the Ronin Warriors action figures – if you happen to see them – you will not think they're cyborgs even though they are. Because the armor snaps on them. But on the T.V. show the armor is on them and doesn't snap on or anything.

They show their armor to fight to save the world from the evil dynasty master Talpa. They have to fight Talpa so he will not crash Earth into his netherworlds. If Talpa crashed the Earth into his netherworlds, he could rule the Earth and change the people into his evil dynasty.

Kento, especially, likes to be a Ronin Warrior. Although he is always hungry and needs to work on skills for everything, he likes to attack, and even though he is not very good at defense skills, he's very good at fighting. Ryo kind of likes being a Ronin Warrior because he's very good at fighting and he's the most powerful Ronin warrior. He's also able to defend them really well because he's able to call on the "white armor".

Most people on Earth do not know about the Ronin Warriors. Nobody knows about them. They don't have secret identities. You can even see their face through their helmet so you can know them instantly. They travel to Talpa's netherworlds for long periods of time to fight and even when they're on Earth, they live in a big city, and nobody knows about them really, except for their friend, Mia, and their other, five-year-old friend, Uli. They know Uli because he got lost in a crowd of people trying to run away from a dynasty warlord; Ryo found him and now Uli lives with Ryo.

They know Mia because she was sent out to find the Ronin Warriors from her grandfather to tell the Ronin Warriors that the dynasty would attack. She doesn't go back to her grandfather because he got too old and died.

I think the Ronin Warriors are interesting because when Ryo was fighting Saber Strike, he lived in a very hot desert jungle area, and then he lived in the big city.

Teacher

It's the magic that strikes me, the magic and the power and the control. My students love magic tricks, performing magic for each other. Their favorite thing is to *reveal* the way to perform the trick! I don't remember this anymore from when I was young, but from my children I believe I must have felt this way too when I was a kid: sharing the magician's secret is actually more powerful than performing the trick, because the sharing of the *knowledge* is the *power*. I wonder about what sort of leader I should be in my classroom: I put on different costumes – sometimes literally!– and I become an enhanced person, who can perform new tricks. The parents and the administrators never share this secret with us, and the magic comes from that *lack* of sharing in this case … I can become a leader in my classroom by showing the students how they, too, can become the teacher, share the knowledge working in groups to teach each other something that they just learned … we're tapping into something in common that helps us find the magic.

Joe Kincheloe has written:

> The professional educational research community too often has been guilty of viewing research in a manner that inhibits teachers from becoming critically reflective practitioners. This is the problem with modernist social and educational science: What is the benefit of the knowledge it produces? By the very techniques it employs, the very questions it is limited to legitimately asking … educational research creates trivial information. The response of practitioners is often, "So what?"
>
> (Kincheloe 1993: 17)

I have found that asking teachers what they find in my work that can answer "So what?", instead of telling them my answer, has enabled a new form of dialogue. Interviews with practitioners have allowed me to see how teachers critically adapt new information toward a reflection on the self, and the meaning of thinking about teaching, much as Kincheloe suggests, at another point in his work, in that teachers have invited me to share in their interrogation of relationships among students, teachers, knowledge, and the broader contexts in which schooling takes place.

One response from the teacher interested in Saturday morning as curriculum content is to use discussion of kids' T.V. to accomplish curricular goals. After having read Karen Gallas' (1995) discussion of science talks in her 1–2 classroom, one teacher imagined basing weekly open talks on asking, "How'd they do that?" about amazing accomplishments that happened on specific programs. The point of these discussions would not be to debunk the science as absurd but to theorize what would have to happen in order for such an accomplishment to be possible. More directly, another teacher found that students can develop an interest in science because they want to perform some of the tricks they see on Saturday morning programs. Yet another teacher emphasized the positive impact of fantasy on her classroom: many children are used to being told what to do; it is hard for them to draw a picture after listening to a story. These children can benefit from exposure to a wide variety of fantastic depictions as an aid in thinking about what they might imagine themselves. The same children can use the stories and characters of common programs to role-play and, after starting off reproducing a narrative they have viewed, move on toward improvising their own story. A shy child watching cartoons can take on her own destiny, finding better ways to speak to classmates or express herself, feeling secure in being able to be a monster or a hero after sharing a character's experiences before emulating them; children who want to be leaders or who are tired of always being expected to take on leadership roles by their peers can find a variety of models of leadership in the main characters of these programs. Explosive behaviors that result from watching these programs can be "teachable moments" that enable discussion of what constitutes excessive violence as opposed to a positive outlet for frustration or anger. Students who do not have enough opportunities to talk with others might benefit from an intial exposure to a world of a consistent character that they can share time with, if this time together is then handled in a reasonable way by an adult, possibly a teacher. Other children do not know "how to be" in reality, while some move back and forth between reality and fantasy; a discussion of kids' T.V. can help a teacher understand children in this context either by way of private conversations or through what they choose to relate to in class activities.

Teachers often suggest that discussion of kids' T.V. can promote self-esteem because a child can easily compare themselves to a "cartoon character" that is not fully developed, noting in what ways they differ from the character, including instances in which they are "better" or "not as good as" the character. Such discussions, generalizable to the processing of any literature or narratives in various forms, and not unique to the habitation of technoculture and popular mass media, respond more directly to my initial interest in morality and constructions of self. Students can identify aspects of a character that they would or would not want to copy. Such a conversation helps to promote students as "evaluators," forming skills for judging "good/bad," "like/don't like," and what they'd change. One teacher suggested it would be a powerful experience to run cartoons from ten to fifteen years ago and ask the children for their reactions, comparing the stories and characters to those that are aired today. What these pedagogical strategies have in common with the science talks is that the teachers ask not only unique questions but create classrooms where student learning is grounded on questions that students themselves ask.[7]

Another direction of response to my talks with children highlights the ways that teachers can use kids' T.V. to transform their relationships with their students. By viewing these programs and talking about them with children in ways that are not hostile but invite response, some teachers believe that students see them in a different way, as "more human" and less as a "teacher-person" animal or machine. Perhaps the first time such a discussion is attempted might result in silence, but students often come back a week or two later to talk about what you said. In contrast, relationships that result from a T.V.-saturated culture involve teacher-entertainers who are expected or expect themselves to "edutain" with increased pace and variation in media dosage. Some teachers relish the cyborg imagery and find empowerment through it. They respond positively to the information that many students find some programs more interesting than others because of the novelty of the program (different artistic style in depicting characters on *Sailor Moon*, or in plot development as in *Iron Man*); they note with interest that many students prefer cartoon-based programs to the ones that feature live actors because the animated programs can depict more fantastic things not realizable within the budgets of the live-action programs. They are, in the ways they talk about their presence in a classroom, "cyborg teachers," and they use the metaphor to their advantage, seeing various tools and equipment as enhancing their ability to provide novelty and extend their power to magically teach. Cyborg teachers promote proactive *bricolage*, seizing materials and unusual events of the day as opportunities for enacting the cyborg curriculum.

> I search for ways to enhance *my* power to effect change for students. Scientistic technologies of teaching in the ideological battle over "best practice" become toys for me to enhance my potential: to break the limits in a Cyber-Chatagua.

In this way, cyborg-teachers construct in their practice Hargreave's "self," constantly and consciously remade and reaffirmed. The implication is a heightened orientation and reflexive attention to themselves as teachers, an enhanced sense of creativity, empowerment, and change in their work; a parallel observation is the need over time for these teachers to embrace rather than recoil from a practice defined in terms of uncertainty, vulnerability, and the threat of social withdrawal. Like Jim Paul and his friend Harry, these teachers exalt in the power to magically externalize the human potentiality they believe lurks within themselves while being wary of the pull toward engulfment by that technology of externalization.

Those other teachers who initiate the use of kids' T.V. as curriculum content find that a view of the teacher as more "human" results in fewer expectations that they act like a "superhero" or "cyborg" and can begin to behave in a different way. The effect is similar to being seen shopping in the local supermarket. Some of these teachers then find that school can be an oasis of special time in a child's life, largely because the pace and techniques of working in a group are significantly different; students can slowly discover school as a unique opportunity to escape the entertainment-focused public realm of T.V.-tainted life. A recognition, however, of the powerful attraction of Saturday morning television as a time to be away from other components of life, retreating into the escape of fantasy, has led some teachers to incorporate similar ways to meet this need in their teaching and learning. A discussion of kids' T.V. supports the recuperative function of Saturday morning throughout the week. An institutionalized space or time for being away within the classroom, such as a big refrigerator container turned into a By-Myself-Box for students to be alone, or a time when students choose something to do by themselves, are examples of this response by teachers. The point is to provide an opportunity for students to have a part of their life when knowbody knows what they are thinking or feeling, and during which they are not being judged or assessed in any way. Moments in time and space, like science talks that begin and travel through student questions, by-myself areas, and journals of certain types, are examples of what some have called "heterarchic freespaces" – "material constructions that do not fill some metrical space, but are projective, producing, and appropriating their own spaces" (Menser 1996: 310).

Viewing kids' T.V. also helps teachers respond to students if they try to view the programs, not as adults, but as children: avoiding a discussion of "use" of the programs in favor of immersing oneself in the fantasy has helped several teachers think about what it is like to be engaged in an activity in their own classroom as a child. In this respect, the curriculum takes on dimensions of *currere* as posed by William Pinar (1975), and as discussed in Chapter 1, in facilitating teachers' movement toward an inner world of psychological experience, their own life histories with respect to television and technoculture, and school. I now believe *currere* calls for teachers to be mindful of the potential for the provided curriculum to construct the teacher as the gundam/child, and the students as the mutant monsters to be tamed. Teachers as technochildren sometimes try on new prototypes in order to experience a new sense of their powers of perception, production and destruction. At other times they experience the melancholia of the gundam, capable of harnessing the sometimes terrifying applications of scientistic pedagogical techniques in order to lead the student-monsters in an effort to save society from invasion or technological disasters.

When teachers use characters from various programs as examples of possibilities, encourage students to share their evaluations of those characters, or imagine themselves as teachers in terms of various characters, they are metaphorically thinking about their own thinking about teaching and learning. Metaphor, like constructing opportunities for a curriculum based on students' questions, is important in post-formal pedagogy.

> Metaphoric cognition is basic to all scientific and creative thinking and involves the fusion of previously disparate concepts in unanticipated ways. The mutual interrelationships of the components of a metaphor, not the components themselves, are the most important aspects of a metaphor. Indeed, many have argued that relationships, not objects, should be the basis of scientific thinking. When thinking of the concept of mind, the same thoughts are relevant. We might be better served to think of mind not in terms of parts but in terms of the connecting patterns, the dance of the interacting parts. The initial consciousness of the "poetic" recognition of this dance involves a nonverbal mental vibration, an increased energy state. From this creative tension emerges a perception of the meaning of the metaphor and the heightened consciousness which accompanies it. Post-formal teachers can model such metaphoric perception for their students. Such perception is not simply innate, it can be learned.

(Kincheloe 1993: 151–152)

Thus Saturday Morning television, as *currere*, like other aspects of culture, can be a cultural resource with any number of possibilities for interpretation and application, incorporating potential ideologies and expectations yet consumed or enacted in ways that are both forseeable and surprising (Appelbaum 1995b).

Researcher as rhizome

Some difficulties in carrying out my research emerged as I asked teachers to suggest what the research should be about. Holding expectations for education research grounded in their experience with a traditional style of expert pronouncements, some would not understand my questions because they were listening for declarations about what they should do. Because research "is supposed to tell me what's best" rather than "facilitate my work as a critically reflective practitioner," sharing summaries of interviews with children and inchoate attempts to make sense of this as an adult were received as "bad research" which confirmed the notion that educational research in general is trivial and useless. Most teachers see Saturday morning television, and Kids' T.V. in general, as a collection of information harmful to school learning, in opposition to high culture. In these discussions, it became clear to me that the people I was talking with were not "post-formal thinkers" who "see facts as more than pieces of information" (Kincheloe 1993: 156). The introduction of my work had to be structured in a way that communicated that I was looking at this information regarding television and its young viewers "in relationship to the larger processes of which they are a part." Rather than "discovering" that teachers are uncritical thinkers incapable of applying such post-formal thought to reflection on their practice, however, I learned over time that I needed to translate my perspective and help them see that *I* wanted to talk about teaching in this peculiar, atypical manner.

For others, their construction of their function as a teacher does not include a critical examination of resources for a potential curriculum; for these teachers the practice of teaching is mostly technical and instrumental, and is separable from an engagement with curriculum content. Interviews with some teachers thus resulted in a difficulty in negotiating the purpose of the interview: having little exposure to cyborgs or cartoons, they would suggest that they had no authority to speak on the subject, and that they would have no knowledge of the correct way to teach the material. A common connection was made with a prevalent discourse that constructs many of these programs as productive of antisocial and violent behaviors (See, e.g., National Association for the Education of Young Children 1985; American Psychological Association 1993; Levin and Carlsson-Page 1995; Pereira 2000). Kids' T.V. as a potential resource for curriculum content or pedagogy runs counter to a view disparagingly summarized by Henry Giroux:

[Pedagogy] is what follows the selection of ideologically correct content, its legitimacy rooted in whether or not it represents the proper teaching style. In the dominant discourse, pedagogy is simply measurable, accountable methodology used to transmit course content. It is not a mutually conforming element in the construction of knowledge and learning, but an afterthought reduced to the status of the technical and instrumental.

(Giroux and Simon 1989: 238)

Teachers with this approach to pedagogy seemed most attuned to issues regarding the accuracy of my "data," how representative my sample of children might be, and the most efficacious ordering of tasks in a curriculum based on the topic. I risk identifying this group of experts as the "walking zombies," stripped of their humanity, invisible, and mechanized by the technoculture of schooling. Joe Kincheloe echoes Ellison in this respect, linking the politics of marginality, teacher thinking, and post-formal thinking:

In this context teacher questions about the interpretation of information or questions about the moral and ethical nature of the curriculum are deemed dangerous.... Here the point emerges that the post-formal ability to ask unique questions and to detect problems never before detected is politically dangerous as it tends to juggle comfortable power relations. Thinking is indeed a political act.

(Kincheloe 1993: 151)

Finally, a small group of teachers wished to take advantage of my research project, but were unsure about how they might do so because of their very ability to multi-contextualize the research itself:

How should I interrogate *your* research and my relationship to educational research? What role do you/I/the students/other teachers play in your project? I think *you* are the bad-guy uncle! I am the child gundam and the students interviewed are the hapless adults that have caused the problem but need my naiveté to fix things. Or I am the adult, of course! My students are the bad guys, and *you* are the child gundam, attaching research gadgets to your body to morph into some superhero that can save us from the epidemic of post-nuclear standardized testing ... or ....

The researcher is Piccolo on *Dragon Ball Z*. I have donned a costume of unusual color – brighter and different. Special details, such as the little claws on my fingers (dark purple, not black, on the program – who would have thought of that? Saturday morning and school and personhood – who would have thought of that?) heighten my uniqueness. Usually I am a "bad guy," the intellectual-as-terrorist in Foucauldian terms; I aim to explode the bridges of commonsense conceptual discourse. But, in some episodes, I align with the "good guy," Go-ku, my usual enemy, in order to defeat another "bad guy" (such as Raditz) who threatens the promise of public education. If nothing else, teaming up a bad guy with a good guy is more interesting for its novelty. Am I human, animal, machine, cyborg? Are educators human, animal, machine, cyborg?

> Go-ku is stronger – because he's actually Raditz's brother, and they're both aliens in a way – they're not human. Piccolo is some special creature. Other good guys might like to help, but they're much too weak and would probably get beaten up in seconds.

I am a *Marvel* cartoon hero. My program provides the metaphor for research because, in cartoons, "you can make *anything* happen. Well, you can do that with real people but you can *really* do that with cartoons." My research pronouncements are thus transformative discourses of possibility rather than descriptions of reality or verifications of hypotheses. They reflect a basic reality in the sense of Baudrillard; yet by masking and perverting this reality, I foster pedagogical change.

This research program should be compared to *Iron man*, which is harder to follow than other programs, but worth the effort.

> If one day you started watching it, you wouldn't know anything about it. They don't tell you much about it unless you see certain episodes. In other *Marvel* shows they make a littler number of villains, so it's easier to follow. Sometimes a lot of different characters will make it more interesting, but only if you watch it a lot. Like if you have a favorite villain, you may not see that villain again for a *long* time.

In this way, continuing with Baudrillard, my research masks the absence of a basic reality and demands the ongoing construction of an appearance of reality. The "magic" of research, while filled with good intentions, has ambiguous results. The good guys/bad guys are blurred into overlapping regions, and the subject of the study shifts from that observed to the observer and back, blurring these boundaries as well. We need to relinquish yet a different fallacy than that offered by Mazlish: that magic and morality are distinct terms. What are we looking at, and where are we looking? It is important to understand that we are not merely looking at the possibility of multiple epistemologies, but living in, with, and through these epistemology/cultures.

Extending our work in Chapter 4, an analysis of relationships among animals, machines, and cyborgs is, in Donna Haraway's (1992) terms, a "technology of vision." Research becomes a prosthetic device we attach to ourselves as part of the divine dream of Descartes' view from above, or the desire to merge with the machine into Mazlishian or Ellisonian invisibility. In such a paradigm I have a choice: I can re-present a vision of reality more real than any other vision, or I can shrink out of *your* sight, enabling the voices of those I have worked with to emerge, placing agency firmly in those voices. Surely you are not content with the hubris of the first option, nor with the abdication of responsibility and dehumanizing mechanization of the researcher in the second. We realize together that any act of *triage* is a technology of vision rather than a practice of pedagogy and/or research. It would be, as Jim Paul wrote, "just a kind of mechanical vision, fascinating and persistent, against which [our] need to observe [would be] an eddy to the main current." Relationships among animals, people, machines, and cyborgs are not to be observed but lived; they are the stuff of the technoculture we breathe, dance, hate, use, and get used by. We are not looking at the epistemology but living in, with, and through it. We are surfing a mobius strip of technoculture, returning in every relationship to every other. The relationships simultaneously surf *us*, in an act of agency and *triage* that, in Haraway's new vision, may just as likely trick us, or treat us to their own humor. Harkening back to the origins of *triage* in Napoleonic battlefields, it is clear that any particular enactment wields morality in the service of power and ideology. Children performing their own mini-*triage* in selecting their favorite programs from a menu of viewing options enact a parallel version of morality as a technology of vision. As do teachers who *triage currere* possibilities at the door to their classrooms, sending kids' T.V. to either top priority, possible use, or low-status detritus. For me to add to the symbolic violence by selecting quotes that merged in my talks with children and teachers is perhaps a further act of immorality, perhaps a feat of magic.

It can only be magic if we read this act of research without expectations of appropriative knowledge stuff to look at. The research is rhizomic in character (Martin 1995), forging relationships in evasive, extensive, and intricately interconnected ways, much like the relationships that were forged among researchers, children, and teachers involved in the project: inexpressible as conclusions of scientistic research, the rhizome is magically moral in its intentions, successfully living in symbiotic status with educational institutional practices, inherently non-mechanistic in structure and function. We have simply performed a new feat of magic: we've pulled the rug out from under the legs of the animal–human–machine *triage* and seen that we can leave all of the technologies of vision still and intact. The magic, though, is in the rug, which may be used as a new prosthetic as we choose: ride it as a magic carpet.

Of course the whole point of this chapter is *not* to prove that kids' T.V. is or could be a central component of the constructed selves of students, teachers, and researchers. If we use technoculture and cyborg metaphors to look at the selves of pedagogical practice, the research becomes a technology of vision which splits what is observed and analyzed into a spectrum of technoculture. If we employ technoculture and cyborg metaphors as a mode of enunciation with which we speak and write a story of pedagogical practice, the research becomes a technology of sign systems, power and the self, and of production.

This is not to say that such stories do not exist and are not rhizomatically linked in innumerable ways with the one that appears here. They may be more likely to be found in other spaces, and told by other characters from *this* story.

We can produce, transform, or manipulate curriculum; we wield signs, meanings, symbols, or signification practices in our discourse; we determine the conduct of people and apply templates of analysis that submit subjects to ends, domination, and objectification; and we permit some people to, as Foucault has described, "effect by their own means or with the help of others a certain number of operations on their own bodies and souls, thoughts, conduct, and way of being, so as to transform themselves" (Foucault 1988: 18). Cyborg selves become a technology of morality when they enunciate a hierarchy between knowing oneself and taking care of oneself. The gundam or *animé* hero surfing and breathing technoculture lunges for self-care and begins to know his or her self through the act of self-care, discovering self-potential and realization. The machine-self of the invisible man shuns self-care in the process of self-knowledge. The cyborg-teacher is positioned in a web of possibility that presents links to any technology of vision, enunciation, self-knowledge, or self-care, and is itself in relation to such technologies imbricated in extended webs of possibility, power, signs, and production. Technoculture is a node in the web, a region of the mobius strip, a character in a saga.

8

Dark Matter and All That Jazz

Dark matter is a term from astronomy, recognizing the need for "invisible" stuff. Theories of motion and the expansion of the universe require us to infer that most of the universe's matter does not radiate (it provides no glow or light that we can detect). In one sense, this dark matter (called dark because it is the light that is missing, not the matter) is a secret treasure that we seek to find.

This metaphor of "dark matter" may be used to think about important issues in education in a global transnational society. Dark matter as a metaphor also offers an interesting way to examine the educational experiences of disenfranchised groups within society, both in terms of the role in educational policy of researchers who may identify as members of a disempowered social group, and in terms of the secret treasure that is promised by the invisibility of disenfranchised experiences of schooling in mainstream curriculum studies. The metaphor is neither farfetched nor uncommon if one considers popular themes within the Black literary tradition in the U.S., writes Sheree Thomas (2000). An excellent early example is Ralph Ellison's *The Invisible Man* (1972), a novel that introduced the idea of black invisibility through such images as the "battle royale" and the final image of the alienated, invisible narrator sitting alone in a basement. For this chapter, however, I want us first to consider the kinds of dark matter we construct for ourselves within a fantasy of power and control, dark matter is not really there. In the next chapter, we'll look at the more difficult dark matter, the dark matter that we do not want to see.

Charlie Parker Played Be-Bop (1992) and *Mysterious Thelonius* (1997) are remarkably different attempts by Chris Raschka to engage the reader with a classic period of jazz. In *Charlie Parker*, Raschka plays with words and images to convey his own understanding of bebop. In *Thelonius* he uses a literal description in his words but distributes them across pages that represent Monk's music by placement and color. As with most books marketed for children, it is tempting to imagine possible readings with the youth we work with, to design lesson plans around the shared reading of these texts. If we were to do this, we would be treating Raschka's books as pedagogical representations of content. For example, we might be building a unit on music and select these texts in conjunction with listening experiences, the same way we would predetermine several CDs or MP3s of Charlie Parker and Thelonius Monk. Jazz as a theme would then be linked through these books to curricular subjects, for example, language arts and reading.

> Charlie Parker played Be-Bop.
> Charlie Parker played saxophone.
> The music sounded like Be-Bop.
> Never leave your cat alone.

The use of repeated text, rhythm, and rhyme schemes lends itself nicely to emergent literacy experiences. Surely Chris Raschka had this in mind when he wrote this text. However, five years later, *Mysterious Thelonius* no longer applies these techniques. Other than a simple artistic curiosity, from where might we identify this shift?

> This is a story about The-
> lonius Monk and his music.
> There were no wrong notes on his pi-
> ano had no wrong notes, oh no.

Perhaps there are essential differences between Parker and Monk that the two books capture? If they are accurate representations of a true picture of two jazz artists, then we could analyze them as a way of understanding the differences while also noting the commonalities that hold them together as pieces of a larger set of jazz possibilities. Such a view assumes that Chris Raschka has studied the music of Parker and Monk, perhaps other musicians as well, and that he has carefully and correctly transferred the critical details on to the pages of his books, so that the books are excellent models of the music itself.

"Charlie Parker played Be-Bop; Charlie Parker played no trombone; the music sounds like Be-Bop; barbecue that last leg bone." The rhythms and accents seem to mirror the actual movement and expression of the music. Playful changes in the words maintain the rhythm and melodic structure even as they introduce unexpected and thought-provoking connections to a life embedded in jazz culture. On the back cover Raschka says, "I hope that children will learn that Charlie Parker and bebop had something to do with rhythm, surprise, and humor." A mature teacher-reader's response would presumably be a kind of judgment, such as whether or not Raschka "got it right." Such a reading falls in a long line of cultural expectations that there *is* a "right" way to do things, and that there is certainly a correct representation of all things in our world. To study a phenomenon (e.g., Parker's jazz saxophone playing) is – in that old-fashioned approach – to break it down into its elements and then to reproduce the elements in a model. Knowledge is truth in this tradition, which goes back at least as far as Plato, who suggested that knowledge is equated with the identification of true forms (or ideas) behind their existence as sensory phenomena in our world. If Plato were here with us today, he might celebrate Raschka's books as unlocking a deeper truth about the music than Parker himself could have had, as represented in his verbal simplification of the elements of rhythm, surprise, and humor.

But our purpose in *these* books is *not* to identify the pedagogical truths of Raschka's work in order to plan lessons that use the books. We are reading these children's books "as if" they are written by sophisticated philosophers of education and curriculum theorists. We are reading them as *books for us* and not necessarily as books "for our students to read" or as "books that children will read." Yet, even as we read these books for ourselves, as ourselves and not in our "instructional planner role," it is hard to imagine how to read them if we are not going to hunt for something that is already there in them, to be discovered, such as an author's correct or incorrect interpretation of jazz music. If there is no effective truth to be known, then what self-discipline will take its place? It turns out that there is an analogous issue for pedagogy related to a common presumption that there is a secret, discoverable method of helping others learn, which I believe these books can be used to unravel and analyze.

Suppose Raschka actually had a very specific message he was trying to communicate about rhythm, surprise, and humor. How would we ever know that we got his message, or that we formulated a different one in response to his work? Is there truly only *one* such message corresponding to a Platonic truth about our world? And why *not* read these books as potential readings for our children? Why not make every reading of a children's book an evaluation of its curricular usefulness? If we believe there is a right or accurate representation of jazz, it is not too far away to make a determination about whether or not one or both of these books gets it right, and also whether or not one or both communicate it in a way that is accessible to our students. But I believe that presuming we as adults serve this developmental function for our students forecloses the valuable curricular possibility of being taken by surprise. That is, I dream of curriculum itself as jazz, and fear the death of the text that may very well be the outcome of privileging the author as knower of the known.

Our job, I think, is to show our students that our own conceptual digging for truth may be safer than they themselves imagine, perhaps even exhilarating. Despite what may be a wish to surrender to our efforts, our students do not have to participate in a way that is over their heads and threatens to drown them in new truths; they and we might collaborate in a new system of understanding that neither they nor we can envision at the start. Our goal, I believe, is for our students together with us to find a new way for them to use us without becoming buried in us. To be occupied primarily with figuring out what the text we are reading "really means" is to miss the point. Textual interpretation should, I think, be in the service of facilitating a meaning-making *process*. If we try to pre-plan the analytic process for our students, then the "best interpretation" of the text is essential. But for me the planning process is about expanding and enriching the students' experiences of their own understanding of their world, and about facilitating their capacities to generate experiences they find vitalizing and personally meaningful. From this perspective, arriving at a best-guess decoding of the book by Raschka is neither possible nor desirable. What is more important is engaging students about the books in ways that spark and quicken their own analytic interests in themselves. Instead of interpreting a truth (that is, instead of reading Raschka in order to know about Parker or Monk), I want to offer students a series of possible ways to understand their own varieties of thinking and experiencing (including thinking about this in terms of jazz metaphors) that I am hoping will become evident as enriching and generative. If a byproduct is a conceptually productive orientation to Parker and Monk, all the better; but this is not my primary curricular objective. Content is the *medium* for curriculum, I believe, *not* the objective, and neither is the same as "purpose" or "intent."

Now, the child's mind, too, is a text that we feel the urge to read. In this way of thinking as well, I want to reflect on how we might avoid reading the child's mind, or trying to, as if the teacher is the all-powerful authority whose knowledge of this mind leads to sound and moral judgment about the best action to take in the classroom. There cannot be a singular, authoritative version "in the student's mind" about which *either* the teacher or the student could be right or wrong. To expect that there is such a mind, present and available, is one source of unending frustration with educational theory. The invisible book of the student's mind, "Nkiesha Sanders plays be-bop with her mind," is neither right nor wrong – an accurate or inaccurate representation; and indeed, there is not necessarily such a book being written by Nkiesha Sanders. Of course, this should not mean that "anything goes" (that is, that all conscious experiences are equally plausible or accurate). Actual experiences provide constraints against which interpretations are measured, just as Raschka's books are constrained by the form of pages, printed text, reproducible artistic images, sequence of pages, and so on. But this *does* mean that events in the students' minds are in some sense knowable both to the teacher and the student through processes of composing and arranging them. We just need to remember that there are no best or right interpretations that lead to a truth about the students' minds. (Here I am applying the metaphor of jazz improvisation, where one knows the chord changes and standard melody, and creating new meaning in relation to these constraints.)

Can we think about ourselves and our students as composers of our own ideas? If so, then wouldn't we be curious to learn more about Charlie Parker and Thelonius Monk, two artists who composed new ideas in the moment, as improvisers, very much analogous to the ways that we and our students are composing ideas and organizing them together "on the spot," in the moment, in our classrooms? Then Chris Raschka's experiments might be models for how, we, too, might try to make sense of these meaning-making moments. Alan Block (1988) once used Thoreau's *Walden* toward a similar purpose. Block posited that everything comes to us as text, a fabric woven of codes, even as Walden came to him in the form of a book. He suggested that much of school is a reading of text, the activity of observing someone else's reality; the codes of school are typically irreversible and offer limited and solitary moments of access, must be negotiated in only a single direction, and leave little opportunity for the weaving of new codes within or from them. Writing, Block inferred from Thoreau, is to wake to a question, to Nature and daylight; writing is an activity of freedom resulting in the construction of reality. My reading of Block supports my contention that curriculum can gain from centering itself in improvisatory composition, curriculum as jazz. "Only if we view the world as a text that we must write, and, therefore, the product of textuality," writes Block, "is there opportunity for liberatory activity, for meaningful lives, and for freedom" (p. 24).

Here is one way we might apply Raschka's texts as composers of curriculum. The Parker book could be said to be a *reflection* of Charlie Parker's playing, a view from outside the experience which mirrors critical features of that playing. The Monk book, on the other hand, might be understood as a *diffraction* of Monk's playing, through which Monk's music is separated into critical elements. In the reflection, the music bounces off Raschka in a new direction, toward the reader, seemingly unchanged in any significant way, recognizable as his music. In the diffraction, Monk's music passes through Raschka, like light through a prism, leaving the reader to experience it in new ways. What he does is assign a color from a spectrum and placement on the page to each pitch in a well-known Monk tune (*Mysterioso*). Words are located to match the rhythm of the melody along stripes of water-color across the page. "This is not so much a portrait of Thelonius Monk. Rather, if the music of Mr. Monk were to sit for a portrait, it might be something like this" (book jacket blurb). Sometimes ideas bounce off of us, like we are mirrors, and sometimes, too, they pass through us and metamorphose into beautifully new ideas that owe their origin to us as well as to what came through us. When do teachers work as mirrors, and when as prisms? What experiences support students as mirrors, and which ones support students experiencing ideas as prisms?

Having read the previous chapter, you may be concerned that I am resorting to a technology of vision here. This is partly my point. We so desperately fall into a mode of perception where we are tempted to use Raschka as a microscope that helps us to perceive thinking and knowledge. I prefer to read Raschka as one process among many, one series of interrogations of knowing that force Raschka as investigator to question, in the case of Parker, rhythm, surprise, and humor, and in the case of Monk, how one might go about creating a portrait of mystery and freedom. When Raschka uses words to communicate about Parker's non-verbal artistry, the constraints of rhythm and rhyme lead him to insights about the serendipitous connections with everyday life that are unleashed by improvisation. A saxophone is no trombone; "Never leave that cat alone" in some way holds a similar meaning to "barbecue that last leg bone"; counterpoint is analogous to "bus stop … ZZnn ZZnn," or "lollipop … boomba boomba." The music really *sounded* like "Be-Bop"; "never leave your cat alone." In the jazz of our own lives, and in our classrooms, seemingly random and serendipitous connections lead to making sense. We do not set about to compose sense; it emerges in the moment, or after the fact, when we can look back on it, as if it were reflected back to us in a mirror for us to behold.

What could Raschka mean when he tells us that there were no wrong notes on Monk's piano? As we read this story of colors up and down and across the pages, we later find that "Monk played the music of freedom; jazz is the music of freedom." If we were to read this text literally for its Platonic truths, we would learn that there really is *no* mystery to the mysterious Thelonius. But I think we *are* still left with the mystery of how music can come out sounding as if any pitch can be played at any time, which Monk was able to communicate through his music. Somehow working within the constraints of the expectations of pitch, rhythm, and harmony, Thelonius Monk mastered the art of mystery.

Lately I have been paying careful attention to the arrival of surprise, humor, and mystery in my classroom. I believe they are composed through the rhythms that define the ways we work together, and that without both the constraints of rhythm and the insistence that we improvise our knowledge in the moment, they would not be there. Without surprise, humor, and mystery, I believe, there would be no living composition of ideas. In order that my students may have a tradition of expectations and constraints against which to improvise, I begin units with a common encounter and a way of working with something before I then ask them to explore possibilities together and on their own. Within a beginning drum ensemble, we start with the idea of a regular pulse or heartbeat. We compare the rhythmic patterns of our names to this pulse; we set conversations to the pulse; once we establish the idea of rhythms against a pulse, we explore together the ways that this concept helps us to make meaning out of the pulses and the rhythms of our everyday lives – the patterns of a day against sunrise and sunset, the patterns of domestic life against the pulse of gender, the patterns of security and insecurity against the pulses of authority, and so on. Next we play with surprises and humor. Once we have a rhythm, when does a different rhythm surprise us? When does this surprise make us laugh? Why? This is the point at which we are composing music together and we are ready to improvise with how and when we can surprise *ourselves* through our music.

In my mathematics classroom I take a similar approach. I begin with some contexts within which we can eventually improvise. Last year, for example, we started by playing mancala, and with a human knots ice-breaking exercise. Mancala, a game that originated in Africa, involves moving jewels or beans, dropping them one at a time into cups around a game board. In human knots a group of people reach into the circle and randomly grab hands; they then try to untangle the human knot without breaking the links between their hands. We played each for a while to learn a common language and rhythm of expectations. This context grew out of questions like, "What is a good move in mancala if you want to win?"; "What patterns suggest which move choices?"; "What are the possible outcomes in human knots, and could we predict them by looking at the way we start to grab hands?" Now we were ready to improvise: I asked, "What questions do *you* have now?"; "What ideas do you have about how *these* questions could be answered?" This is the point at which we were composing our thoughts *as mathematicians*, and I documented for my students how this was precisely the very moment at which they were already forming their own personal voice as a mathematician. Just as Thelonius Monk would seek to play what might have been called by someone else a "wrong note," or Charlie Parker would repeat and then suddenly change a melodic pattern, so one mathematician might prefer to work with pictures and diagrams, while another would search for charts and equations, and suddenly change or add to their chart or equation to reveal a new mathematical connection.

Georg Polya believed the basic rhythm of mathematics cycles through four phases. First, one works to understand the problem; second, one devises a plan for working on the problem; third, one carries out the plan; finally, one looks back over what has happened in order to identify a new problem and start the process all over again. The mathematician improvises on top of this pattern by asking herself certain questions appropriate to each rhythmic phase. To understand the problem a mathematician would ask, "Have I ever seen a problem like this before? If so, can I use that experience to devise a plan?" Or, "How is what I know related to what I do not know in this problem?" "Can I define variables?" To devise a plan, the mathematician would ask herself, "Can I draw a picture?" Make a chart? Write down an equation?" Then, "Can I add things to my picture? Write a formula for my chart? Find a pattern? Extend my pattern further?" As with Monk and Parker, her initial choices unfold into a melodic improvisation that enables her to carry out a plan – in relation to the pulse of the four phases, and the harmonic or melodic progressions of Polya's questions. For the last phase, this mathematician would ask herself, "Does my answer make sense? What is the meaning of my answer? Now that I am at this point in my work, can I see another way of working that may have been simpler, more interesting, or otherwise better in some sense?" And then, "What new questions do I have at this point, prompted by my work?"

For my students and for me, Polya's phases are like Raschka's colors in *Mysterious Thelonius*. But just as reading *Mysterious Thelonius* does not result in a new book written by the reader, so following Polya's rhythm merely diffracts working as a mathematician without the composition of new mathematics. Indeed, Polya was primarily concerned with helping students to find answers to provided problems rather than with students becoming mathematicians with original and creative ideas. Just as I might be able to learn a Monk tune and play it on my piano in my living room, becoming one more admiring imitator, Polya's students can find answers to questions many others have already answered, and end up as trained admirers of other "real" mathematicians. Few people would hire me to play a Monk tune instead of listening to Monk himself; and few of Polya's students are likely to be known for their own mathematical creations. I believe this is because Polya mistakenly developed a rhythm for *studenting* mathematics rather than *composing* mathematics.

In Block's terms, Polya's questions lead students through phases of reading mathematics, not of writing mathematics. A classroom modeled after Polya reminds me of my own courses in music theory, which trained me to create four-part harmony that sounded like Bach, and to imitate other famous composers with modal and tonal counterpoint. These courses never advertised themselves as training for improvisation or composition. Courses in improvisation and composition were of a significantly different character, combining rituals of working *as* an improviser or composer with extended periods of apprenticeship *in* improvisation and composition. While Polya introduced an improvisatory mode through his open field of questions appropriate to each phase, his aim was to train students to be proficient in certain techniques, and not to apprentice them as mathematicians. Could such training be combined with extended periods of composition in order to apprentice students? I think only if the work with Polya's rhythm is a small piece of a larger whole, and not a dominant infrastructure, since using his rhythm is not useful in developing original mathematical investigations.

John Mason and his colleagues (1982) suggest a rhythm of working that I think better approximates mathematics as improvisatory composition. Suppose students have proceeded through Polya's phases and are now confronted with their own new questions inspired by the previous work in the last phase of "looking back." Suppose as well that they have tried his techniques on these new questions, treating them as problems according to his template. Mason *et al.* suggest moving back and forth between two modes of working, a pulse against which to improvise mathematical ideas. The first is "specializing," in which the mathematician tries special cases to see what happens. Is your question about numbers? Try 0, 10, 100, odds and evens, primes and non-primes, and so on. Is your question about shapes? Try triangles, squares, parallelograms and trapezoids, pentagons and circles. Is your question about functions? Try linear ones and non-linear ones, continuous and non-continuous. The second phase of the pulse is "generalizing." In this phase the mathematician organizes the special cases and looks for categories of results or patterns. The goal is to infer or deduce a general statement that summarizes a category or pattern of results. Where are the indicators of generalizations that can be made? That is, what sorts of things might help the mathematician to compose a generalization, and where would she find them? Why, in the surprises, of course! And where is the humor? In the mystery that unfolds. For even as one gains insights into relationships and patterns, newer and more compelling questions emerge, calling in their own right for periods of specialization and generalization.

Authority and knowledge

This way of working in a classroom is attractive to many educators because it stresses the students' own voices in the educational process. Rather than training students to sound exactly like Parker or Monk, we encourage them to pursue their own questions and develop their own ways of making meaning. A literal reading of Raschka suggests that these meanings evolve out of the experiences of their everyday lives. Similarly, in the recent film *Ray*, we are told that Ray Charles combined the gospel of his early church experiences with soul to produce R&B, rhythm and blues, as his own unique voice. The tools did not drop out of the sky from nowhere in particular. In my classroom we create an everyday life out of, for example, games and ice-breaker challenges. At other times we start with everyday life encounters such as raising money or redesigning the classroom space. In still other classrooms we might act as anthropologists or historians, ecologists or farmers. The processes would be analogous, evolving out of the development of rhythms of working against which to improvise. We collect and interpret historical documents. We collect observations in a field notebook and later organize and analyze our observations as data. We experiment with ways to represent our new ideas, reinterpreting them in light of the sources of our own everyday lives. This is a radical notion of education since it undermines a Platonic sense of knowledge as truth, and apparently shifts authority from the teacher who knows this truth to the student who composes her own version of truths. The kind of knowledge and authority that the teacher in such a classroom can claim is an expertise in meaning-making, self-reflection, and the organization and reorganization of experience. Yet even this expertise is suspect, as it can never fully claim any sense of certainty about which organizations of experience will lead to particular forms of knowledge or reflection on the part of the student. It is only after the fact that a teacher would be able to observe any specific connections between experience and composition of knowledge. The heart of such a pedagogy is a "baseless assertion" of agency for self-authorization.

In such contexts, students do not necessarily feel empowered to compose knowledge, nor can they claim any confidence in self-authorization. The student enters an implicit contract with the teacher, which transfers authority *to* the teacher; that is why the student is there in the first place, instead of somewhere else, on their own. The teacher's authority is thus built into the asymmetrical structure of the relationship. Given that the process is supposed to lead gradually *to* self-authorization, we cannot *start* as if this self-authorization is already transferred from the teacher to the student. What, then, is the relationship between the institutional authority of the teacher and the emergent authenticity of the student?

A teacher who demands improvisation from the student right away, thus transferring authority to the student, does not necessarily establish an environment of authenticity. If the student takes the teacher as an authority, transferring authenticity to the teacher, then this teacher may proceed under the delusion that she or he is creating a safe place for the student to improvise, never understanding that her or his organizations of experience are ironically further reifying the authority of the teacher. In this case, the teacher would be perceived as withholding even as the teacher thinks there is no knowledge being withheld. One hopeful response is to disclose to the student exactly what is happening, to tell what one knows at all times, and to make the method transparent. Yet, making the pedagogy explicit may distract both the teacher and the student from the task at hand, which is to understand better our own ways of making meaning out of various phenomena. The classroom becomes, in some instances of revealed method, a narcissistic opportunity for the teacher, rather than a learning experience for the student.

A reticent teacher, on the other hand, who hopes to avoid this very distraction of revealed pedagogy, "looms large," occupying center stage as a mysterious object of interest anyway. Teaching becomes a delicate balance between distracting the student with too much disclosure about the process and distracting through too little disclosure. From this perspective, the teacher runs the risk of being idealized as the model of what the student is to become, and as an expert both in subject matter and in pedagogy; yet it is just as easy to be idealized for being very open, candid, or forthcoming as for any other reason. The best reading of Raschka for our purposes, then, is to come up with ideas for discussing vital responses to our students that are neither exploitative nor withholding, but clarifying. Given that a student arrives at the educational encounter with various propensities to regard authorities in different ways, this is a complex task. For a student who regards experts as ultimate authorities, a disclosing teacher is not teaching and a non-disclosing teacher is too secretive about what is expected of the students. This student will likely say that she cannot learn from either teacher. For a student who recoils from ultimate authorities and who appreciates collaboration in the construction of knowledge, a disclosing teacher is spoiling the fun by revealing the secret too soon, by jumping in too early with the punch line, while a non-disclosing teacher is stifling and non-supportive. This student, too, has difficulty learning from either teacher.

It seems that a teacher is condemned to put out feelers for how disclosure and non-disclosure influences the ways in which his students work in his classroom. Yet the interpretation of these probes will likely be influenced by both the students' and the teacher's relationships with authority and symbols of knowledge. Dennett (1991: 136) writes,

> Just what we are conscious of within any particular time duration is not defined independently of the probes we use to precipitate a narrative about that period. Since these narratives are under continual revision, there is no single narrative that counts as the canonical version, the "first edition" in which one laid down, for all time, the events that happened in the stream of consciousness of the subject, all deviations from which must be corruptions of the text.

So there can never be a singular, authoritative version "in the student's mind" about which *either* the teacher or the student could be right or wrong. In this respect, we compromise pedagogy the most often when we become the most dogmatic in our approach, when we pretend to ourselves and to our students that we are able to remain neutral and that our interventions describe revealed truth. One way to think about this is to embrace an "acceptance of no way" to standardize the composition or improvisation of ideas, to keep the static down, except in the *teacher's* mind. It is the meaning to the student of the teacher's actions and decisions that is important. That meaning can only be slowly, jointly constructed and transformed over the course of the curriculum. All a teacher can do is make informed conjectures, only to be surprised by the incompatibility of these conjectures with the later, jointly constructed meaning. This, to me, is the parallel jazz of curriculum that accompanies the jazz of learning.

Mystery and authority

What I learn from Raschka about mystery is its curious relationship to authority. Authority derived from expertise *denies* mystery, or hides it deep within a secret place that no one dare enter. Because such an authority does not hold Platonic truths about mystery itself, the mysterious is dangerous and threatens the authority. Raschka, as the author of his own composition *about* mystery, embraces the mysterious, and seeks to make it the object of inquiry. He discloses all that he can about his own relationship with the mysterious, instead of hiding it in a secret place. The mystery of Thelonius, Raschka says, is the key to both improvisation and freedom. He *doesn't know* what this mystery is, because it is not a Platonic truth he can fix in his gaze. It is instead a *characteristic* of improvisation and freedom, the experience of "no wrong notes" being possible even within the constraints of a system of meaning.

When one believes one can play and that there will be no wrong notes, freedom is a safe place for improvisation. We can take this analogy into our classrooms: when students and teacher honestly believe that they can "play no wrong notes" there is a kind of trust established that enables the freedom to learn.

How do we distinguish between no wrong notes and anything goes? That is, you and I can sit at a piano and play as if there are no wrong notes, and we do not sound like Monk. Similarly, students in a classroom can act on the presumption that they can do no conceptual wrong, and produce a sort of nonsense that may not lead to learning. What are the differences here? As Raschka describes Monk, it *sounds like* he can't play a wrong note when he plays; it is not that there *are* no wrong notes, but instead that he plays *as if* there are no wrong notes. In the classroom we've successfully created curriculum as jazz, as pedagogy for freedom, when it seems to someone observing *as if* there are no wrong ideas. This does not at all mean that anything goes; it means that students are composing original ideas in their own ways.

> Improvisation, it is a mystery. You can write a book about it, but by the end, still no one knows what it is. When I improvise, and I'm in good form, I'm like somebody half sleeping. I even forget there are people in front of me. Great improvisers are like priests; they are thinking only of their god.
>
> (Stéphane Grapelli in Nachmanovitch 1990: 4)

Donald Winnicott (1971: 63) described the work of psychotherapy as

> bringing the patient from a state of not being able to play into a state of being able to play …. It is in playing and only in playing that the individual child or adult is able to be creative and to use the whole personality, and it is only in being creative that the individual discovers the self.

We might claim the same goal for pedagogy. Or, we might at least claim that pedagogy shares some aspects of this psychoanalytic goal. Creative work *is* play. "It is free speculation using the material of one's chosen form" (Nachmanovitch 1990: 42). The creative mind plays with the objects it loves. Play, too, is always a matter of context: it is not what we do but *how* we do it. In this way, "play enables us to rearrange our capacities and our very identity so that they can be used in unforeseen ways" (Nachmanovitch 1990: 43).

I personally confronted these issues as a student of South Indian music some years ago. My teacher would usually introduce a certain rhythmic pattern to me during a lesson, and ask me to practice it at multiple speeds for the following week, when we would combine the new pattern with previously learned patterns. In this manner I was introduced to a specific grammar of rhythmic patterns. At one point I started to bring my own combinations and original patterns to the lessons. My teacher would laugh and say, "No we don't play that [in South Indian music]." If I would ask why not, he would teach me a different pattern that *would* be OK to play in the place of the one I had brought to my lesson. Baffled, I would note how my pattern echoed those that I had been taught in certain ways, fit into the same rhythmic sequences, and so on, to which my teacher would simply reply that I was a very good student for trying to understand the theory behind South Indian drumming, and that I was clearly learning a great deal; as a conscientious student, I was sure to reach a deeper understanding with further study and practice. At this point he would usually ask me to focus on my drumming technique, to work on improving my sound or tone quality, in order to distract me from theory for a while. As time went on, this "game" of my trying to "psych out the theory" but failing became a regular component of my lessons; my teacher would ask me what pattern I had brought with me this week, and proceed to offer an alternative that was one I could practice instead of the one I had invented on my own. Looking back on this experience, I see now that my teacher had chosen to accept my "Western" style of learning as a means of assessment of his teaching goals; each pattern I brought to him gave him a representation of what I had been learning about the grammar of South Indian rhythmic patterns. One exciting day he responded to my pattern with the declaration that I was ready to accompany another advanced student who played a melodic instrument.

Yet, even at this point, the pattern I had invented was not appropriate. I felt as if there was an essence to South Indian drumming that was a treasure buried deep in the recesses of the teacher's wisdom. We could play this game, and I could win prizes, such as "being ready to accompany another student"; however, the magic prize, that deep sense of an inner truth of South Indian music, seemed at the time forever unfathomable.

The task in my drumming lessons was subtly different from students writing or investigating mathematics in a classroom. Because my apprenticeship in South Indian music was also an experience of enculturation into South Indian culture, I did not have available to me the routines and assumptions of everyday life in India with which to compose my patterns. For my teacher, my new patterns were like a child painting a five-paragraph essay: I could communicate understanding of the material, I could demonstrate skills and concepts, and I could develop "as a painter"; yet I had not produced the five-paragraph essay, but a painting. As an artist of world music, I was a composer and inventor; as a student of South Indian music, I was an engaged and conscientious learner. I was not yet a performer of South Indian music.

As a component of a larger curriculum, however, the study of South Indian drumming did perhaps contribute to a set of core capacities emerging out of integrative learning and interdisciplinary studies. The parameters of this kind of learning were defined by contextuality, conflict, and change. For example, my invention of patterns, tested with my drumming teacher, demonstrated to my teacher the ability to ask meaningful questions about complex issues and problems; the ability to locate multiple sources of knowledge, information and perspectives; the ability to compare and contrast the multiple sources to reveal patterns and connections; and the ability to create an integrative framework and a more holistic understanding. Julie Thompson Klein (2005) describes these criteria as part of a "connections rubric" that might be used to design and evaluate undergraduate post-secondary learning experiences.

The secret treasure and the purloined letter

While my experience with South Indian drumming may have been an excellent example of integrative studies at college level, it also raises the central question of the secret treasure often established by pedagogical practices. As with many students in my own later classes, I conjured up this unspoken notion of seeking or accidentally discovering treasure or wealth, what Selma Fraiberg (1989) has called "one of the most persistent myths of all times." In children's stories, a poor boy or man typically discovers a secret which leads him to buried treasure or to the acquisition of great wealth. Usually the treasure is stolen loot of a bandit, a pirate, or an evil sorcerer; it may be buried in the ground or in a mysterious cavern. The hero obtains secret knowledge of the treasure either through a conniving and evil person who wishes to use the innocent hero as a tool, or through the accidental "overhearing" or "overseeing" of an event which betrays the secret, or through the acquisition of a magic formula or device, a map or code. Usually, too, the hero must overcome an evil opponent who seeks the treasure. The treasure is successfully won by the hero who vanquishes his enemies, marries a beautiful princess, or brings wealth and privilege to his mother, elevating her from her humble and impoverished station.

> The time of treasure-hunting is childhood, and these stories of buried treasure are among the favorites tales of children. But they are not the exclusive property of children; they belong to all ages and all times. The evil magicians of the fairy tales gave way in time to one-legged pirates, and they, in turn, to eccentric millionaires and bank robbers. There have been mysterious caverns and desert islands, gothic castles and combination safes. But always there has been a fearless and honest fellow who accidentally discovered the secret, outwitted the sorcerer or the pirates, and entered the perilous enclosure to claim the heaped-up wealth.
>
> (Fraiberg 1989: 218)

Following the advice of Kieran Egan, we might imagine that the "key" to the secret of pedagogy may be to make the structure of a curriculum such that students are able to take on the characteristics of such a hero. The "secret treasure" would be accidentally overheard or "overseen" and the students would have to betray the secret through some clever use of a code, map, or magic formula. Bringing the secret back home to mother or an educational "mother figure" would bring prestige and honor to the student (Egan 1989). Curious for many educational settings, however, is that the "secret treasure" is unknown to the teacher as well as the student – What *is* learning? What *is* the mystery of Thelonius? What *is* that student's understanding of freedom? – As one who does not hold the secret, the teacher is left most likely in the role of the evil opponent who wishes to use the innocent hero for a tool, or as a competitor for the sought-after treasure. And who is the original bandit, pirate, evil sorcerer, or eccentric millionaire who buried the treasure in the first place? In most educational encounters we simply do not know; they are part of that hidden secret treasure that we wish we could find. Perhaps the *teacher* must accept her role as sorcerer, pirate, or other evil villain, in order to enable the student to become the hero of the tale of school.

For Fraiberg, tales of buried treasure and the discovery of great wealth are the longings of childhood which live on in the unconscious memory of the adult. Their ageless appeal derives from the universal and perennial mystery which confounds the child in its first investigations of origins, and the magical act or discovery is a trace of an earlier masturbatory or incest fantasy. The discovery of the treasure allows the hero to do anything he wants, and to overcome all obstacles to obtain an inaccessible love interest. The connection between the acquisition of great wealth and the breaking of a taboo has to do with the ways in which our culture uses great wealth as a metaphor for the freedom to do whatever one wants. Indeed, until very modern times the rich and powerful were exempt from taboos; noblemen, people of royal blood, and descendants of the gods had the prerogatives of the gods and this included the right to incestuous relations. Similarly, there may perhaps always be the notion of a momentous discovery of the secret through an accidental touching or an observation, a revelation of the "magic" of the genitals. And always there has been a magician with greater powers and a secret knowledge which is denied to a poor boy or girl.

> There is the childhood mystery of "the place" where the treasure is hidden, the mysterious cavern which has no door, the hidden place deep under the ground. And there is the unwavering belief of the child that if he should have the magician's magic lamp, the pirate's map, the key to the treasure, the knowledge of "the place," he could win for himself this treasure of treasures. In the ageless daydream of childhood, the poor boy who has nothing steals the magician's secret, the pirate's map, and outwits the powerful opponent who stands between him and the treasure.
>
> (Fraiberg 1989: 241)

We may see here echoes of the poacher, the one who cleverly finds the magic way to take in secret the bounty of the land, what is rightfully his: in poaching, and in jazz, lie the mysteries that enable the enactment of that freedom associated with the wealth of knowledge.

Loss and the community of relations

Yet, really, we can see now, if we think about it, where the analogy falls apart. That secret pedagogic treasure actually gets further and further away from us the more we seek it, whether we are students of South Indian drumming, investigators of mathematics, or teachers trying to understand what our students are thinking about. We may say that education demands of all concerned that each recognizes "learning" as something to seek. Or at least as something that exists apart from oneself, so that learning can be an object to which one relates. Next, I want to say that education demands of all concerned that each take everyone else involved as an object of relation as well, so that a community of learning begins to form out of the relationships that are established. Deborah Britzman (1998) would say that education must after all address the affects of such relating if teachers and students are to attach to knowledge and each other. But she notes something useful beyond this: the teacher, she writes (p. 27), can be more like an artist who considers her or his work as crafting the conditions of "libidinality" in learning, as opposed to hardening her or his authority, as might a leader. What she means is that a "leader" retains all of his or her narcissism, wanting as well to dominate followers in order to use them as instruments for his or her own purposes. A teacher who acts as a leader is not so much leading students to knowledge, not so much acting as Aladdin's "magic lamp," as she or he is using the students as objects of her or his own advancement or accomplishments, for example, as tools of self-knowledge and self-promotion, in order to feel good, in order to see the effects of her or his actions in the classroom – indeed, because she is metaphorically the "evil sorceress." "Crafting the conditions of libidinality" has to do with establishing routines, rituals, and other features of an infrastructure for classroom "events." To craft the conditions of libidinality is to set up possibilities for how individuals in the classroom can make meaning out of what they experience; it is to allow them to play out the fantasy tale, perhaps in the way that Kieren Egan might advocate. Britzman gets this idea from the psychoanalyst Hans Sachs, who contrasted the leader with a certain understanding of an artist, as someone who wants their work to have an influence on the world and other people, but without ulterior motive. In this conflict between an ulterior motive and the desire for "something" we can find a fundamental binary opposition that is at the heart of education. We expect our work to lead to "learning," to directly effect changes in our students; yet what, really, are we expecting? We must explore the ways that our own fantasies, dreams, and fears play out in the choices we make about these routines and rituals. At the same time that we admonish ourselves for "using" our students to satisfy our own desires, it is hardly plausible that we would be involved in this enterprise if we had absolutely no ulterior motives: What could these possibly be? Are we ready to think about them, or to at least try to uncover them? Wouldn't teaching without motives feel as if we were not living up to our responsibilities anyway? In a sense, we do not pursue this because the secret treasure of our own motives is not readily seen as a magic lamp, code, or formula that will lead to great wealth and the ability to transcend taboos; this treasure is something we hope to keep in the dark. *This* treasure is something we in some sense complain about as lost, but which also we are *afraid* to find. It *needs* to be "dark matter."

So much of education is about experiencing loss. Let me explain what I mean. Our system of education is not designed to notice that learning occurs over time, or even that accidents, chance, and frustration may be as much the source of learning as the affects of learning, and not even be obviously related to any specific actions on the part of an adult. In general, educators focus on what they can observe teachers doing. In a book such as this, I might be expected to provide lots of information about things that teachers can and should do in order to create learning as an effect of a teacher's actions. In reviewing Britzman's book for the American Educational Research Association, Lisa Weems and Patti Lather (2000) note that modern educational theory persists in placing the teacher at the center of education, despite a claim to student-centered learning. For us, this is a significant point to dwell on: we need to "de-center" ourselves; what a tricky business when we are thinking about what it means for us to be a teacher! It seems we need to think about what we do as teachers; we are the experts – on both the content, which the students need to learn, and on teaching, which we are professionals at performing. Yet, as Britzman argues, the teacher-as-expert is a metaphor – one of any metaphors we might use to think about our work; this particular metaphor implies that learning is about the mastery of knowledge. Weems and Lather write that the emphasis in contemporary educational reform on the "professional development" of teachers, for example, stems from the premise that if we add more classes, more knowledge, more experience, more *x, y, z,* to the teacher, we have thus refined the "producers" of education and by extension increased the value of the educational product. The move toward "student-centered learning," seductively attached to liberal humanist discourses of unleashing the "natural will" of the student, merely reverses a notion of mastery, identity, and fixity in understanding classroom positions. While this reversal seems an "improvement" over a "teacher-centered" model, Britzman argues that it still leaves the binary of teacher/learner intact. If only we knew more – but we don't; this whole approach to thinking about teaching can only leave us feeling that loss of what we might have known, what we might have been able to do "if only..."

Along with Britzman, I want to encourage us to shift our focus away from either the position of the teacher or the learner, toward the relationality of the teaching/learning encounter. To emphasize development as relational is to imply that what happens in learning exceeds the boundaries between inside/outside that are taken for granted in more common psychological theories. Educational psychology privileges cognitive aspects of learning; psychoanalysis, the realm that we are entering in our discussion of improvisation, mystery, surprise, and rhythm, highlights among other things effective dimensions of learning, such as desires, hopes, and anxieties. We might say learning comes from neither within nor without. Instead we would describe learning as a struggle between two (or more) egos, signaling the uneven movement across and between various positions of knowing. A psychoanalytic inquiry into learning involves the careful tracking of the relations of learning in their various, incomplete, and recursive movements. Furthermore, psychoanalysis ethically obligates teachers to explore the dimensions of one's own otherness (p. 16). Each of these realms is the "dark matter" of mainstream pedagogical theory, something we perpetually seek to both discover and to preserve as hidden.

Now, Britzman calls attention to the work of Alice Balint, who writes about "blind spots," where "only the exertions of the educator are considered." Such blind spots shut out the serious work of the learner, ignore the serious mistakes that cannot be admitted or debated, conflicts that are central to the experiences of learning, and so on. Instead of a clear set of understandings about what makes "learning happen," we end up with a lot of defensiveness on the part of the adult, as if the work of learning is only an authentication of or an answer to the question of the adult's capacity to control, predict, and measure "progress" (Britzman 1998: 26). A psychoanalytic perspective such as this raises what Britzman calls "antinomies," paradoxes or contradictions between principles or conclusions that seem equally necessary and reasonable.

> What exactly happens to the work of learning that surprises this defensive logic? First, the educator cannot recognize the learner's logic – and learners know this. From the learner's vantage, the adults cannot understand, cannot remember, their own antinomies, awkwardness, and hesitations in learning even as they may also represent something like what the learner wishes to become. Perhaps, from the learner's vantage, what seems most unfair is that while educators demand that students tolerate the postponing of immediate gratification for the sake of the hard work of learning, educators feed their own immediate gratification by setting the time of learning to the clock of their own efforts!
>
> (Britzman 1998: 26)

So we start the enterprise of education with things that are lost: things that we are blind to and cannot see; things we seem to need to posit and maintain as invisible to theory. Like "The purloined letter" in Edgar Allan Poe's short story, as the objects of our attention are "purloined," we are always feeling like that the objects of educational settings are lost, displaced, or misplaced (perhaps stolen?) (Pitt 2003). Pedagogy cannot be simply applied as a set of techniques that you train in toward mastery, no matter how delightful such a fantasy of control over our work might be – that fantasy might be the secret treasure we all desire but which we will never find. Instead, as Alice Pitt writes, our work "relies upon the surprise of discovery in each and every instance of practice" (Pitt 2003: 9). Perhaps Pitt's solution is to replace the magic lamp of technique with the magic lamp of the everyday. Even so, we continually express our surprise at such discoveries, possibly to preserve the impression that the dark matter in fact "exists" in some sense, to create the evidence that justifies the tale of pedagogy as the secret treasure.

What I think I have found in the juxtaposition of Raschka's two works on jazz is a "way out" of the perpetual search for this secret treasure. In the rest of this chapter, I am working to find an alternative to the myth of the dark matter of teaching and learning, and suggest that this myth is a form of resistance to self-knowledge that we set up for ourselves. In the psychoanalytic literature, the secret treasure is a masturbation fantasy, a tale of addiction, perseveration, and distraction, rather than creative and productive work on the part of the teacher. I want to say that we do not need to construct a fantasy of "dark matter" or "secret treasure," and will offer instead the idea that we can simply "do the work" of the discipline with our students.

Mundane existence

Antinomies create crises for us because once we seek one member of the paradoxical relationship, we have lost the other, equally reasonable goal that makes up the other half of the antinomy. Thus they function quite well to construct anew the purloined letter of education. In a curiously playful and powerfully useful move, Peter Elbow (1986) embraces this as the very pleasure of teaching. Writing in *Embracing Contraries*, Elbow describes the unspeakable that he was forced to confront. First of all, he suddenly found that he had a strong desire not to tell people things they didn't ask him to tell them; second, he recognized the pathology of such "holding back" as he did the pathology of "unsolicited telling." On the one hand, he thinks perhaps that he is perversely refusing to tell students things as a petulant backlash; on the other hand, he wonders about this possibly strange hunger to tell people things they didn't ask about. This is indeed a central feature of teaching and learning, and specifically we can use the mathematics classroom that has been an example throughout this chapter to consider the implications further. First of all, in most typical mathematics classrooms, students are suddenly confronted with a mathematical idea they would never have thought of if they had not come to school that day: they can't even begin to desire to be told these things because they do not know of their existence. In such a classroom, the "conditions of libidinality" are crafted in such a way as to make the teacher the one who knows all and the students the ones who do not know. The idea, I suppose, is that this is what school is all about: surely our students need to be exposed to this stuff so that they can find out that it is interesting, or useful, or relevant, or …. But students in general do not respond to this kind of situation with excitement and engaged enthusiasm. Instead, they feel as if the knowledge is esoteric or uninteresting or irrelevant to their lives. At best, a few students get good at copying the teacher and receive rewards for this apt mimicry; these students have learned to postpone the gratifications and pleasures of learning, or perhaps to separate themselves from the pleasures of the learning experience, so that they can gain the acceptance of the teacher, please the teacher, please their parents, feel smart, get good grades and go to college, and so on. No student, however, not even those who have accepted the promise that such pleasing of the teacher is a strategy for receiving the magic lamp, is actually asking the teacher to say what is on her or his mind.

So you walk into the room. You are confronted with eager faces waiting to see what will happen. Do you begin a mathematical conversation? Or do you think, "Nobody here is really interested; perhaps I shouldn't bother them with this?" A day later, a student is demonstrating a misconception; it is clear that he or she does not understand a mathematical idea. Do you tell them this? Or do you hold back and wait, to see what happens? Britzman suggests whether one or another of these sorts of responses is more harmful or useful to learning is *impossible to know*.

Most mathematics teachers today have settled into an ambivalent acceptance of a rather mundane existence. Students rarely find themselves lost in the thrill of mathematical thinking in these classrooms. Even teachers who try to establish a different kind of environment note how their students come to them with years of expectations for what the conditions of libidinality are in school. Teachers offer the gift of a new, refreshing, and interesting mathematics experience, only to be flustered by students' ennui, blah tedium, and resistance to even admitting their own personal interests (see, e.g., Romagnano 1994). Pitt dwells on the ambivalence even more: she asks, "How can we tell the difference between a leap away from and a leap toward learning?" (2003: 3). In the moment of the pedagogical encounter we have lost the ability to know – such abilities are purloined letters. The only thing that is clear, as Elbow suggests, is that the standpoint of "teacher" creates a specific desire to be heard:

> If I want to be heard at all, I've got to set up a situation in which the options of whether to hear me or tune me out – whether to take me seriously or to dismiss me – are more genuine than in a normal class-

room field of force. I'm refusing, therefore, to be short-circuited by a role which students react to with the stereotyped responses to authority: either automatic, ungenuine acceptance or else automatic, ungenuine refusal.

(Elbow 1986: 84)

Purloined purposes

So on the one hand we enter the encounter with a whole lot of stuff that we want to share with youth. We know a great deal. If *they* knew the same things, they would be able to do so much! My new tote bag from the National Council of Teachers of Mathematics annual meeting declares, "Do Math and You Can Do Anything." On the other hand, we never really can know what the students are doing, how they learn, precisely, what is happening inside their mind. Is there a chemical change in the brain or the heart? A neuronet-work restructuring that formed in response to a question from a teacher or other student in the class? We act as if the specific actions of the teacher *cause* precise changes in the student, none of which we can ever really know about. Or we write a history of the event afterwards in which we claim that a specific task or a specific way of asking a question led to a new conceptual under-standing on the part of a student, even though there really is no way of knowing at the moment that such a pedagogical move would have that precise effect. This is what comes to be known as a practitioner's wisdom: over time experience seems to provide so many case studies of what might or might not happen that the teacher seems to develop a repertoire of potential proactive and reactive actions.

Yet we can stop for a moment and disrupt this way of thinking. We do know something about *ourselves* and how *we* learn, what kinds of ways of working and being lead us to make meaning, to consider questions, to take on challenges, and so on. What is the purpose of an activity in the classroom? Whose purpose?

If education means to let a selection of the world affect a person through the medium of another person, then the one through whom this takes place, rather, who makes it take place through himself (*sic*), is caught in a strange paradox. What is otherwise found only as grace, inlaid in the folds of life – the influencing of the lives of others with one's own life – becomes here a function and a law. But since the edu-cator has to such extent replaced the master, the danger has arisen that the new phenomenon, the will to educate, may degenerate into arbi-trariness, and that the educator may carry out his selection and his influence from himself and his idea of the pupil, not from the pupil's own reality.

(Buber 1965: 100)

In the quote above Martin Buber is articulating the work that is going on "behind the scenes" as teachers and students try to communicate, but where, as is commonly the case, the purpose of what is happening is only able to be perceived by the teacher. This can happen even in the most open of classrooms, where the teacher explicitly tells the students the purpose of the activity: from the students' perspective, these purposes are the teacher's purposes, not the students', and so this difference in reality is not dissolved, and instead is pushed further into the realm of the purloined.

Madeleine Grumet used the same quote from Buber when she wrote about the purloined purpose in education (Grumet 1988). Grumet found in Buber the contrast between the apprentice and the student. In some lost, mythical past, the apprentice worked with the master on the task at hand, and it was this work at hand that defined the dimensions of their task. We might imagine classrooms where students are treated as apprentice mathematicians. In such classrooms, the material, essential presence of mathematics in and of the world would draw the one who teaches and the one who learns to each other as they approach it. The mathematical ideas, objects, strategies, interpretations, and so on, become the objects of the students' and teacher's intentionality and the basis for their ability to communicate and understand each other, to be *together* in the world. David Hawkins (1980a), too, reached out to Buber. He believed mutual respect between adult and child is best developed when both parties focus on something other than themselves or each other. For example, you might want to teach in a way where you are not thinking about what you (the teacher) are doing, what the students are doing, whether or not the students are doing what they are supposed to be doing, and so on. Instead, together the group must find an "it" that piques interest. It is through the relationship that each person creates with "it" that it becomes possible for the people involved in this experience to avoid treating each other like objects to manipulate or react to, and instead to develop a kind of relationship that Buber called "thou." In the chapter "I, thou, and it," Hawkins urges us to look for *good starting points* – good *its* – rather than for perfect lessons.

The function of the teacher in a classroom based on Hawkins' ideas is to respond to the students, to make what the teacher considers an appropriate response. Such a response is what the student needs to complete the process that she or he is engaged in at a given moment. The adult's function is to provide a kind of external loop, to provide selective feedback from the student's own choice and action. The child's involvement elicits a response from an adult; this response is thus "made available" to the child, the response is now another object that the child can relate to. The child learns about himself or herself through joint effects of the non-human and the human world. Hawkins says this process should not go on forever; it terminates at some point in the future, when the adult function is internalized by the child. At this point this child is grown-up, and has become her or his own teacher. This is Hawkins' definition of being educated: no longer needing a teacher, you have learned to play the role of teacher for yourself. At that point you would declare your independence of instruction and become your own teacher.

Psychoanalytic selves: learners and teachers

So what exactly is this role of the adult that Hawkins refers to? It is to be with the student looking at a third "it." This might happen if one looked at what the student is already looking at – by finding what the student is interested in and learning how she or he is looking at it. Or it may take the form of presenting an object for both the teacher and student to look at. In either case, though, it is easy to slip out of the I–Thou relationship and start to think about what you are doing, what the student is doing, whether or not the "it" is having the effect that the teacher wants, and so on. Whenever any of this happens, the relationship between teacher and student has changed and is no longer one of I–Thou. The metaphor would be one of taking turns jamming and accompanying in a jazz performance. Each member of the relationship must instead strive to see the "it" as the other sees it, to be together looking *at* it. As Grumet writes, teachers tend to look out to the world and through the world to the student (Grumet 1988: 116), instead of with the student to the world, or through the student to the world. They watch the musician playing the solo rather than performing the piece *with* them. She says it is this detour through the world that we call "curriculum," and she says, "the look of pedagogy is the sideways glance that watches the student out of the corner of the eye." It is not easy to act like a teacher in the theater of contemporary schools, but we continue to desire this for some – purloined? – reasons, rather than to seek another sort of relation with the world and with our students.

Britzman asks us to consider talk between individuals as the central focus of our work, as in the capacity to *respond well* and not diminish the contingent work of making relations (p. 38). "Making relations" might be a psychoanalytic way of saying "living and always becoming who we are." It is the constant making of relations – with things, with people, with ideas; anything can become an object to which we relate – that is the basic way in which we construct who we are and what we are doing. The ongoing making of relations replaces what some people might describe as the self. Notice that this is a perpetual, non-ending *process* rather than a unified, fixed, knowable "thing." To see ourselves and our students, indeed to see all human beings as always making relations, and to understand that these object relations are influencing the making of the relations that we are making, is only one small step away from or toward (echoing Pitt) treating either ourselves and the teacher, or our students, as "its," and to embrace the relations that are part of the "I–Thou" that Hawkins and Buber strive for.

As our unconscious ego processes are released into objects chosen for the dream to evoke a dreaming self by object choice, and as those objects are changed in the encounter, so too in the waking dream might we choose our objects based on unconscious ego processes and object relations so that a self is evoked. From that encounter, subjectivity may develop. I would that curriculum be understood in this fashion; then what an education that would be!

(Block 1997: 34)

In the quote above, Alan Block provides a sort of picture of what is going on in the classroom, whether we think about it in this way or not. So, why don't we think about it in this way, then? "Being," Block writes, "is the active establishment of object relations" (p. 22). Psychoanalysis usually goes back to infanthood. The reaching out to the world that is the infant's activity is facilitated by the caregivers; from their responses the child learns a way of being in the world, becomes a self in relation to, and in the use of, objects. This is like Hawkins', Britzman's, and Grumet's common idea of the adult as external loop: the responses of the adult mediate the potential object relations, the meaning of the event that has taken place in terms of the development of who this person *is*. Fast-forward several years and find the same child in a classroom. This child, now a student, reaches out to the world; this is the student's way of being. The reaching out to the world that is the student's activity is facilitated by the teacher, and by other students who sometimes take on the caregiver role in this classroom. From their responses the student learns a way of being in the world, becoming a self in relation to and in the use of objects. Now, in the context of mathematics, many of these objects are mathematical objects, images of being a mathematician in some way, relations with mathematics and with mathematical objects, with mathematicians, with the teacher of mathematics, and with other students of mathematics. In reaching out to the world in this mathematical context, the student's reaching out to mathematical objects and objects of relation that affect the students' object relations is facilitated by mathematical caregivers, the teacher, the other students, images of mathematicians, and so on; the student becomes a particular mathematical self in relation to, and in the use of, these objects, which we might call objects of relation.

Note, too, that objects may be related to in ways that do not promote a typically "positive" mathematical self. Some attachments – that is, object relations that are part of this self-structure of all ongoing object relations – contribute to an alienation from or distanced relation with mathematical ideas, symbols of success in mathematics, relations of mathematical meaning, and so on. The way this constellation of object relations is experienced at any given moment is the sense of mathematical self. (In other words, following Block, the way a student experiences the mathematical self is a reflection of the underlying mathematical self-structure, which in turn is made up of the totality of object relations. This is of course constantly in reconstruction as the self is always the totality of the ongoing processes of creating such attachments.)

To complicate matters further, the teacher is of course a "mathematical being" in the very same way, so that others in the room are serving as caretakers for the teacher's ongoing construction of attachments. For both teachers and students, the selves consist of object relations and are expressed through the uses of objects. When a teacher uses the student as an object of relation through which to express the self, as in many classrooms, school is serving as a space of being for the teacher. In such a situation, the students are the evil sorcerers for the teacher's discovery of the magic lamp or hidden treasure, and the teacher has become the leader rather than the Sachsian artist. It is very easy to slip into this kind of mode, where everything that is happening in the classroom is about you, the teacher, and who you are. I am a "good teacher." I am a "nice teacher." A "smart" teacher, in control, doing my job, *teaching*. But can you say at this point what the students are doing? And with this question I do not mean the objective as listed in the lesson plan. I mean as mathematical beings, as human beings, living in this classroom, how are these individuals doing the important work of constructing object relations, and what is the effect of these attachments on the self? Block gives us a way of thinking about what the conditions of libidinality could nurture: each student's "ego processes released into objects chosen for the dream to evoke a dreaming self by object choice"; activities that do not just allow this to happen, but foster its happening, and joyously respond to its happening, lead to those objects changing in the encounter, and to a (mathematical) self being evoked. The students' selves are present in this kind of classroom.

No matter what we do, this is all happening. This is why the teacher is so important. It is the teacher who creates the conditions under which this occurs, and through which the self is evoked, whether toward a mathematical self that uses mathematical attachments in meaningful ways, or toward a self that constructs objects of attachment that distance mathematical objects in order to maintain a coherent and consistent self. In the majority of classrooms that I have visited and heard about it is the latter kind of self that is evoked, rather than the kind of self that would readily use mathematical objects to express a mathematical self. The "good students" use mathematical objects to evoke a "good student" self, but rarely to evoke a mathematical self. Other students use mathematical objects to express another kind of self that is able to weather the storms of mathematical experience; here, too, the relations are not the kind that evoke a mathematical self. Teachers may use mathematical objects to evoke a self of professional success, but rarely do I meet a teacher who uses mathematics to evoke a mathematical self. To do so would be to act as a mathematician, by some definition of that term. In other words, it is typically very rare that teachers and students *become mathematicians*, despite the possibility for this to occur. What a shame!

The will of free play

Returning to improvisation, we might place all of this in a specific context. We can't plan in advance what exactly will be produced, since if we could we would merely be repeating something that has been done before, whether it is in playing music, orchestrating a classroom, writing an essay, or investigating a mathematics question. What we *can* plan is the *gap* into which the new thing will fit. If that new thing is knowledge, we can, in the words of Joanna Field (1957: 104), "plan the question, frame the question, work on deliberately planning the empty space into which the new knowledge was to fit." Or, if it is to be a new invention, a new way of doing things, Field suggests we can plan "the practical need that the invention must satisfy; even though before inventing it one obviously could not say what the exact nature of the solution of the problem would be." Neither the teacher nor the student can plan precisely what the real function or will of creativity can or should be. Yet either can say that the business of the will is to provide the framework within which the creative forces will have free play. "It is said that no art school can teach you how to paint," writes Field.

> But the art school can and does provide the frame, it offers regular times and places and materials for creation. And by the willed act of registering as a student and attending at the proper time one can, as by a protective frame, free oneself from the many distractions of trying to paint at home.
>
> (Field 1957: 104)

In this respect, freedom or liberation is not a freedom from constraints or the ability to do whatever one wants. Instead, it is a freedom that results from having entered into an active relationship, by entering into a frame of conduct.

This is why Polya's phases of problem-solving, Mason's specializing and generalizing, and Brown and Walters' strategies of asking what-if-not can "work." They provide a framing of activity into which teacher and student can enter. One might call this a "practice," an engagement or enactment of activity embodying intellectual commitment taking on the characteristics of method but transcending mere method. By taking on the ways of working of someone in a particular practice, students *become* someone who practices that art. I become an orchestral hornist by practicing my instrument, attending orchestra rehearsals, and playing in orchestral concerts. A student becomes a writer by finding ways of working as a writer, and by trying out what other writers say works for them.

Mysterious Thelonius, then, is not mysterious in the sense of us not knowing what makes his music so amazing. The mystery of his music is in the very hearable, and in Raschka's diffraction, seeable, interaction of the frame and the action within the frame. Mystery is nothing to be discovered or magically revealed: it is there right before us in plain sight. Mystery is not in that dark matter, swirling around and making up most of our universe, that we can't see. Furthermore, Raschka is not inviting us to seek the mystery; he is *showing* us a picture *of* mystery, as an aspect of the relation between frame and action, a characteristic of relations rather than a reified thing. Similarly, in the act of pursuing a mathematics investigation, students are not discovering or inventing new mathematics, unlocking secret treasure; they are *doing mathematics*, and the mystery, the jazz, the spontaneity, the inventiveness of their work is there in plain sight, in their mathematician's notebooks, for them and for all others to see, as a relation between frame and action, rather than something they "make."

Now we can look back at *Charlie Parker Played Be-Bop*, and think, perhaps, it wasn't necessarily a reflection of Charlie Parker's music at all. It, too, when read as a diffraction, gives us Raschka's picture of the music of a particular musician: diffraction is a relation between frame and action. The book is a product of the way in which Raschka framed his creation of a work of art inspired by the music of Parker. What both books have in common, *Charlie Parker* and *Mysterious Thelonius*, is that they are not "teaching" the lesson of Parker or Monk. They are creative. They are invented books inspired by music, artifacts of particular relations. What we need in mathematics is books inspired by mathematics, poems inspired by mathematical ideas; songs and dances, and sculptures and analytic essays, philosophical treatises and editorial comics inspired by mathematics; that is, traces of the relation between frame and action. What we need in writing are books inspired by writing – or anything else. What we need in drumming is music inspired by drumming – or anything else. By framing the work as drumming, as writing, as mathematics, it *becomes* a work *of* that discipline.

Indeed, I recently received an email message from a student in my mathematics class asking if it would be OK to plan a summer investigation that was "not" mathematics. A little concerned that my point had not been made all semester, I replied that as long as she was using the ways of working as described by Polya, Mason, and Brown and Walter, I could not imagine how the investigation would *not* be mathematical; I challenged her to show me how it was not mathematics. Word of this reply got around, and in the end I received from various students plans for losing weight, stopping smoking, speaking to a grandparent for the first time in fifteen years, and so on, as their proposal for a summer mathematics investigation. As demonstrations of mathematical skill, these investigation plans were outstanding.

The reason why I share this anecdote here is to illustrate some of the points I make in this chapter. My objectives for having the students work *as* mathematicians were not my students' objectives. They were carrying out the investigations, while I had specific skills, concepts, and facts as goals. Their received definition of mathematics was not directly confronted by us together; however, they were, according to my criteria, *acting as*, i.e., *becoming*, mathematicians, because they interpreted the relations between frame and action in ways that are central to the ways mathematicians work. A more concrete description of what they were actually doing would entail specific details of their improvisations, which come down to their "leaps," to use Alice Pitt's word, *toward* something to do: to make a chart, to ask what-if-not, and so on. Raschka's books help us to see this by analogy: the books came about because of Raschka's choices to set for himself a creative frame within which to do his work. In Hawkins' terms, Rashka is grown up because he is his own teacher-facilitator, and no longer relies on others to set these tasks for him, or to set before him examples of how others accomplish this serious, playful work of leaping toward a relation between frame and action. We, my students, Raschka, are no longer searching for hidden treasures, only to find ourselves trapped in that limbo of looking for something we actually do not want to find. Instead, we are engaging in improvisation. Observers may still fall prey to a language of mystery, surprise, and loss. We are too busy creating to think about the dark matter any more.

In fact, it becomes clearer through this kind of example that searching for the secret treasure, trying to "see" the dark matter, is, for teaching and learning, a distraction. For the teacher, setting up the secret to learning, the right "method," as the goal of one's work, is a kind of addiction or procrastination, leaving the teacher outside of his or her natural flow of activity, in states of confusion and self-doubt. Stephen Nachmanovitch (1990) defines addiction as excessive, compulsive attachment, a dependency that self-perpetuates or self-catalyzes at an ever-accelerating rate; procrastination is excessive compulsive avoidance, the mirror image of addiction which keeps us in a vicious cycle that consumes energy and leads to slavery rather than to freedom (pp. 126–127). For the students, such addiction and procrastination created by an attachment to the secret treasure that must be found, the knowledge still as yet unknown, prevents him or her from the work at hand – doing mathematics, playing music, writing an essay. Joanna Field (1957) writes that "any of us may possibly at times relapse into a state of mind where the precarious achievement is lost, where we lose our sense of its significance" (p. 27). I think, perhaps, that we are simply afraid to *do the work*, and resort to a need for mastery and control. We think we need special tools to find the treasure, like a magic lamp that provides a genie or a special code that opens the safe. Actually, we just need to jump in and do stuff, to see what happens right there in front of us, not to find something in the dark. Unlike the proverbial key that is never found because we are only looking for it where the light is, the key for understanding pedagogy is right here, in broad daylight, and not somewhere else, awaiting discovery.

To bring this back to the jazz of curriculum and the jazz of learning, the pause to diffract curriculum, teaching and learning through the works of Rashka gave me the insight that curriculum theorizing flows through a pulse of "stopping at the edge of a cliff" and "jumping in." Trying to perceive "dark matter," or to hunt for the secret treasure, distracts us from the task at hand, derails us. At first we think that getting lost, off the beaten path, is a good thing, and that it will lead us to new ideas. What I want to suggest is that this sounds better than it is. The function of getting lost serves us best when it enables us to get back on track, where our "inner dream and outer perception both spring from a common source or primary phases of experiences" (Field 1957: 28). We need to leap back into what Field calls "that primary madness," where the inner dream and outer perception are not distinguished, a time that all of us have lived through and to which at times we can return. "It might be prejudice that made the knowledge of one's part in the transfiguration detract from the value of it" (Field 1957: 28). What Polya, Mason *et al.*, and Brown and Walter give the mathematician are specifically *mathematical* ways to jump into the work. Go through Polya's phases by asking particular mathematical questions. Or collect special cases and then organize them into categories so that you can construct generalizations. Or, try asking what-if-not about the attributes of your initial questions. What Parker and Monk offer the jazz musician are ways to jump into playing music. Start with a motif and change a part of it, making a musical rhyme, or use the rhythms of your everyday life, or juxtapose seemingly unrelated patterns to experiment with new forms, and you are using the strategies of Parker. To follow in the footsteps of Monk, use what might be "wrong notes" to explore the larger thematic structures.

The moral of this reading of Raschka for teaching is to do the work *with* the students rather than to facilitate their learning. To analyze the "cognitive development" or strategize "motivation" is to hunt for the dark matter. Such analysis is metaphorically a search for dark matter or secret treasure, a story which help us see how much our search for the magic of learning is a fantasy of addiction and masturbation, calling forth dreams of unlimited power to do whatever we wish. To "jump in" to the work of teaching and learning would be to maintain one's own writers' portfolio, to ask students for advice on an image in a poem, to present one's own work so far to students and to ask them whether or not this work has met established criteria. If we design the perfect lesson to trick students into remembering a math fact, we are maintaining Balint's "blind spots" that shut out the serious work of the learner, where only the exertions of the educators are considered. If, on the other hand, we talk with students about *their* mathematical investigations, we become mathematicians with our students.

What the astronomical metaphor of dark matter enables is an awareness that not all invisible things are dark for the same reason. Matter out in space is dark matter if it does not emit radiation. Other invisible matter is revealed if we choose to look at it; for example, by re-aiming our telescope to receive ultraviolet radiation instead of light in the visible spectrum. This other stuff, too, may appear at first to be dark matter, yet we are simply not seeing it. The secret treasure of teaching and learning turns out to be dark matter that is not emitting radiation because it is not really there. Rather, the dark matter of improvisation is a tool of the psyche that establishes addictions and procrastinations that prevent us from doing the playful work of learning. This first kind of dark matter is merely fantasy. But what about that other dark matter, that which we do not see simply because we are not looking at it? It is as if we have not yet turned around to see what is behind us or to the side. Such matters are taken up in the next chapter.

The point is not to pity those who are unseen or who are victims of unseen assumptions by pedagogical theory, or to embrace a kind of multiculturalism that imagines "saving" the less fortunate through clever theory and practice, but to find an independent trajectory of scholarship and classroom action. This scholarship and action recognizes the legacy of discourses that use images of the dark as a metaphor for danger, evil, or wrongdoing, as in colonialism, the legacy of slavery, specifically, for example, in the privileging of light skin and denigration of darker skin, or in the Platonic myth of knowledge as seeing the light. Border literacies (Brunner 1998; Mahalingham and McCarthy 2000; Appelbaum 2002a) should not be the work of "impassioned declarations about "our plight" … [in response to] hot button issues that symbolize … status as second-class citizens in our societies" (Lalami 2006: 23). Such expressions of compassion are often met with cynical responses, ironically further encouraging such a misguided sense of missionary work. The job is to defeat representation, because all representation leads to the viewing of people as "self" and "other." And the process of "othering people" is what leads to views of people as difference and potentially unequal. I have written elsewhere (Appelbaum 2000) about the notion of translating commonalities that may be found across differences into collectivities of people that could be the basis for coalitions. With everyone performing multiple identities all at once, there are no clear boundaries among groups, even as collectives may call for attention to the needs for a particular group.

I find solace in the words of Trinh T. Minha (1989: 75): "Trying to find the other by defining otherness or by explaining the other through laws or generalities is, as Zen says, like beating the moon with a pole or scratching an itching foot from the outside of the shoe." We always exist in the ambiguous borderland of overlapping identities, and people are always treading the blurred borders between them. We are never "in" any one identity. Instead, outside identities are part of the inside identities, and inside identities are always part of the outside identities. Nobody can say which side of what borders they are on. Border literacies find common multicultural practices too limiting because they do not explore the borderlands of identity. Unsophisticated approaches to diversity shift marginal voices and minority groups to the center of our attention, and move the dominant voices to the margins; border literacies put aside the insider/outsider boundaries, and search for the ways in which the insider identities are formed through the interaction of the marginal identities, and how the outsider identities are formed through the othering practices of the insider identities. Finally, my reading of these two works against the grain of curriculum as science fiction brings the dark matter and the identification with the aggressor to the work of providing experiences that serve as interventions rather than as lessons to be learned, and in the process, promote the sorts of skills and funds of knowledge that enable participants to more fully enact a critical multicultural democracy. For Maleeka, this is a very individual experience through which she comes to better understand the varieties of identities within herself that can be balanced for greater self-respect and satisfaction. For Count Karlstein, that is, Max, the "real" Count, this means that one's education has only just begun.

9
My Teacher is an Alien

For me, science fiction is more than a metaphor for curriculum: it is an iso-morph. I take science fiction's premise that the present is a history of possible futures. This might be an excellent definition for "curriculum" as well: the preset of a host of imagined potential futures. Curriculum theory and cur-riculum work is in my conception a play of signs shifting in meaning, an enactive symbolic politics, even as the context for curriculum is constructed in an ongoing contextualization of similar ambiguity and praxis. I agree with William Pinar (2004: 127) that "only the future provides access to a reconfig-ured present," and that curriculum theory might work to "produce the effects of education, in the present case, a movement of the ego toward the futural as that future is imagined in the present" (p. 126). Simply, "by imagining the future, the future becomes the present" (126); our reading of children's liter-ature as curriculum theory text, and in this chapter, as we broaden out notion of "literature" to include narratives of youth culture, we do so in a common project with Pinar to dissolve what blocks us from moving "forward" toward a future not yet present, a present opened out to the not-yet. I want to evoke with Pinar the ideas of Deleuze, who sees this sort of future as an inside folded into the outside. "In this way, the outside is always an opening on to a future: nothing ends, since nothing has begun, but everything is transformed" (Deleuze 1986: 89).

For my students (pre-service and current teachers), the isomorphism seems to hold, yet for different reasons. In general they find curriculum theory or science fiction as intriguing, provocative, and insightful, or equally repellent, irrelevant, and threatening, as they do the other. It is as if I could use science fiction as a "test" of a student's readiness to do the work of cur-riculum theorizing. Attempts to introduce science fiction as reading in a course are met with responses directly mapable to my students' responses to discussion and readings combed from curriculum theorists. When I first began to use science fiction as texts in my curriculum courses in the mid-1990s, most of my students found it a challenge to enter possible worlds and to use these worlds to explore possibilities for their own work. I have found in the past decade that more and more teachers enjoy science fiction for the ways that it helps them to think about their "present" as the history of many potential futures. For these teachers, it helps them to see their work from the perspective of an alien looking at it from outside. For the teachers who continue to struggle with science fiction, the struggle helps them to reflect on the alienation that a student might feel with any given or assigned school material. It is in these contexts that I reconstruct a science fiction theme of alien in my work with teachers who are my students. Dwayne Huebner raised this idea as early as 1975 (see Huebner 1999); Writers, he wrote, "using story, novel, or hypothetical form, can describe students and teachers in new and strange environments, in the manner of good science fiction" (p. 225). Heubner imagined curriculum theorists using the same strategies in their work with classroom practice. Here in this book, all educators are curriculum theorists in Huebner's sense.

In 1997, I followed Ira Shor's (1996) advice and instituted an "after class group" as an intervention in my graduate course. Students were offered the option of participating in weekly meetings in which we discussed how to improve the quality of the classes and the value of the course. We discussed their shock at the expectation that they think in a way that they had never thought before. We talked about what they wanted: ways that the course could expose them to neat tricks that they could take back to their own teaching, good ways to help students practice skills and plug into software. In later meetings, we chatted about the students' frustrations: from the students' perspectives, the course dwelled more on potential metaphors for the classroom space rather than on specific uses of pedagogical materials; according to these students, we were wasting time with ways to help children to reflect through school subject matter on their own relationships with the subject, time better spent on clarifying state curriculum framework standards and potential statewide test questions. This experience of my students' alienation from the course and their own positioning of their students as alienated from school subject matter led me on a search for literature that reflected the feelings that we all shared. I settled on the idea of using science fiction to interrogate the nature of this experience of alienation.

One early influence on my own teaching was Alexei Panshin's (1968) *Rite of Passage*. In this work the central feature of education is preparation for a life-changing rite of passage, a test of survival on an unknown planet in an unknown culture. Coming back alive gave one the right to participate as an adult member of the community. We discussed this story in a number of my courses, how schools are like and unlike such rites of passage; how the participants in my course were either being prepared for such a rite or participating in the grueling experience at that very moment. I keep this work in my mind ten years later as I reflect on any student's experience in school: What expectations of safety and threat are being constructed in this curriculum? How does a curriculum create "other disciplines" as alien in order to survive as a unique subject area? How would a student wield the particular concepts, skills, and facts as tools in a rite of passage that tests their ability to survive in an unknown future? Wary of Madeleine Grumet's (1988) analysis of schooling as a rite of passage that delivers children from the maternal culture of youth to patriarchal adulthood (indeed, an apt reaction to Panshin's "mothership" run by a "patriarchal" bureaucracy), I can taste the urgency of challenging curriculum and instruction in my field. It is for this reason among others that I turn to science fiction as a metaphor for curriculum.

At the same time I have maintained an ongoing survey of science fiction written for young people. Such literature has not been influenced by post-colonial, feminist, postmodern, or cyber-culture as much as the science fiction I personally enjoy reading. Children's science fiction is not written by Joanna Russ, Octavia Butler, Suzee McKee Charnas, Vonda McIntyre, Samuel Delaney, Marge Piercy, or James Tiptree Jr. Ursula LeGuin does appear in the children's list, as does Margaret Atwood. Both of these authors have been critiqued, however, for reproducing dichotomies of this present "history" even as they have introduced cultural challenges in their work. And both are present in children's literature mostly for fantasy and not for science fiction. Joanna Russ' *Kittatiny* is a children's book, but this one too I place more in fantasy than in science fiction.

When I began my survey, in the mid-1990s, the most widely read science fiction books in several schools in northern New Jersey were Bruce Coville's *My Teacher is an Alien* series, Jon Sciesczak's *Time Warp Trio* series, and Katherine Applegate's *Animorphs* series. All are curious for the strong children's characters and their use of adults as side-show buffoons and monsters. In Coville's series, it is striking that a child's most straightforward assessment of their teacher – that he or she is an alien from another planet – turns out to be true! A lovely twist on Maxine Greene's existential *Teacher as Stranger*, the aliens in Coville's series are strangers masquerading as teachers. Yet in the end they are indeed the real teachers, and friends of the children, effective partners in "teaching" humanity an important lesson about its aggression.

In Sciesczak's *Time Warp Trio*, the joke is on us educators again: much as we have tried to trick the kids into believing that reading, writing, and arithmetic are doorways into adventure and enchantment, a special book in these works actually *is*: pages of mathematical magic squares and other school-like detralia, when touched or spoken aloud, become portals into the past or future, where, we consistently discover, people are exactly like us, but existing in a different time and place. The (male) trio's witty wisecracks and irreverent behavior always succeed in helping them have a good time, meet some nice girls, and get home safely.

Despite the woman author, Applegate's *Animorphs* echoes Coville and Sciesczak in its overwhemingly male readership. In this work alien powers unleash permanent change but also magical morphing powers reminiscent of the classical Merlyn tale. Here, Merlyn's power to turn people into animals is extended to an ever larger set of young people who need the animal skills for fighting an intergalactic gang of evil.

How to make sense of two simultaneous, parallel curricula? One is of science fiction as a metaphor which serves as a relief for the differences set up by my practice as a teacher and those who are my students in this practice, teachers themselves who view their students in turn as different from themselves. The other is the curriculum of children's science fiction, striking a coarse relief from the sort of literature I claimed with the original metaphor and isomorphism. I want to suggest that these two parallel curricula can be interpreted as intersecting in the notion of a rite of passage if we do what most curriculum theorists do when confronted by subject matter methods: ignore cries of irrelevance and drown them out in a sea of the apparent curriculum that is there whether one sees it or not. In this curriculum passage, students who teach school themselves seek to be plugged into the magic technology of pedagogy, and then to turn around and plug in the cyber-children they work with in their daily teaching practice. They wish to be washed over by a permanent change that allows them entry into a special clan of the powerful – those who wield special powers to teach, and to bestow powers upon their protege.

Yet this seeming commonality undergirds much of the dilemma, translated as human–alien encounter, to be found in all issues of curriculum and science fiction that posit something(s) as teacher(s) and something(s) as student(s). As in the work of Octavia Butler (1997), we can find redolent power echoes of slavery and civil rights inequalities. But we can also conjecture on the progeny of such encounters: either as students of students, or as creative work brought forth by students.

In a postmodern curriculum, curriculum as narrative of alien encounter has the potential to reflexively trace those ways in which, in Jenny Wolmark's (1994) words, "the generic device of the alien has been used to displace difference into the realms of the transcendental, so that the material implications of marginalization and difference continue to go unrecognized" (p. 3). In curriculum as alien contact narrative – and this is in multiple contexts, including among others teacher–student, Coville's teacher as alien, gendered interactions, initiate an adult patriarchal member into and through the rite of passage – the text of curriculum is as concerned with the conditions of its own existence as it is with the meanings attached to the device of the alien. Reading Coville, we find a scathing critique of traditional fill-the-vessel pedagogy in favor of more progressive methods in the opening discussion of the "good" teacher replaced by the alien; subsequent relationships with these aliens leads to a general discussion of humanity and avoids any further attention to the attraction of "good" teachers to teaching. Indeed, the aliens are in a deeper sense of the word more authentic teachers than any progressive (and expendable) educator.

Much as Kieran Egan once posited the pedagogical efficacy of the fantastic in rhetorical opposition to the "all-about-me" curriculum (1986), it may on initial glance appear necessary to establish an alien in order for curriculum to become an "encounter," and thus to serve as a rite of passage. Science fiction in/as curriculum and curriculum in/as science fiction disrupts such fears/desires as the issue of "alien" becomes increasingly unanswerable, as in the works of Octavia Butler, Gwyneth Jones, and Vonda McIntyre: "The centre invests the Other with its terrors" (Rutherford 1990). So goes a theory that would interpret the teacher–student dichotomy in either direction as enacting a threat of the dissolving self. Such a threat is a perpetual flame of hatred and hostility as the center struggles to assert and secure its boundaries, the liminal terrain that identifies self and non-self. Works by Ursula LeGuin are effective at communicating this positional interpretation. She herself has written:

> If you deny any affinity with another person or kind of person, if you declare it to be wholly different from yourself – as men have done to women, and class has done to class, and nation has done to nation, you may hate it or deify it; but in either case you have denied its spiritual equality and its human reality. You have made it into a thing, to which the only possible relationship is a power relationship.
>
> (1989: 85)

A less known source of images is found in some works of science fiction that have appeared, following the breakthrough of LeGuin, by such authors as Octavia Butler (1997) and Gwyneth Jones (1992), in which "alien" is blurred and multi-sided. A kind of slippage occurs among sameness and difference, center and margins. As Jenny Wolmark writes, "The limits of social and cultural identity are tested when those who are different are depicted as active subjects who resist both the hierarchic relation between center and margins and unitary definitions of difference" (Wolmark 1994: 28). Butler and Jones confront terrors of the center by presenting aliens in unique variations that change our stock of images. It may be with such images that I and my students might negotiate new notions of "alienness," preserving positions of alienness while disrupting power differences or hierarchies of culture and technology.

Theorizing the "neo" in Neopets®

One feature that the most popular science fiction for children continues to display is that it is published in *series*. The built-in commodification of the genre – that readers can continue to buy newer and newer pieces of the ever-expanding work, always looking forward to the next one available, taking pride in collections of complete series, always a consumer in the making – is an inherent feature of popular children's literature in general, and science fiction in particular. Some recent examples of science fiction series for children include: Dav Pilkey's *Captain Underpants*; Jeff Brown's *Flat Stanley*; J.K. Rowling's *Harry Potter*; Jane Yolen's *Pitt Dragon Chronicles*; Jonathan Stroud's *Bartimaeus Trilogy*; Dan Greenburg's *Maximum Boy* series; Philip Pullman's *Dark Materials Trilogy*; Cornelia Funke's *Inkheart and Inkspell* series; Christopher Paolini's *Inheritance* series; Eoin Colfer's *Artemis Fowl* series; and Tanith Lee's *Claidi Journals* and *Unicorn* series. The link with consumer culture is even clearer when one considers the other genres of literary entertainment that youth engage in on a regular basis, many of which involve the same sort of commodification and overlap with the need for continued purchases. For example, Sophia and I spent a fair amount of time talking about such science fiction series and online web communities a few years back, when she was ten years old. I asked her then, "Why might the people who made the Neopets® website have made this site?" And "What does 'neo' mean?"

I offered some ideas for the first question. Perhaps they want to make a lot of money selling Neopets® products. One can buy T-shirts, stuffed Neopets® characters, and other "fabulous new Neopets® merchandise" online, or at Limited Too and Claire's stores nationwide. But Sophia did not think this was the main purpose of the site. It is true she found a way to get her parents to purchase her a T-shirt, but most kids she knew – either around her age (9), or around her brother's age (14) – did not buy stuff related to Neopets®. They mostly took care of their pet creations, played games, chatted, and visited each others' stores; they may have visited "guilds" for occasional fun, and they may have "battled" their pets to earn more points, none of which involved purchases. Besides, it is only recently that these products exist, after a number of years of many people enjoying the site. But mostly, playing the games and finding other ways to earn neopoints – something similar to money that allows you to purchase food and other things for your pets – doing these point-earning tasks is "very addictive" and takes up enormous amounts of time daily. We "knew" that the people who created this site did not get paid for it since, as Sophia noted, it was "free" to play. I was and still am not sure about this; as I noted, one can buy products, and they are popular enough to be sold in large chain stores nationwide. In addition, there are links on the side of the main page to a number of other commercial sites – in fact, there are a lot of advertisements on each page – and there are opportunities to earn points through sharing your market niche preferences in surveys. Sophia and I disagreed on these issues, however, and I think this was significant, as we had very different perspectives on the experience. She did not find the commercial aspects important to her or her friends' experiences; I did. Perhaps this is one form of what Walter Benjamin (2006) saw as adult and child experiences of popular culture. Adults are distant from it. Children enjoy a privileged proximity that enables them to interact with the popular culture toward the goals of transgression, mimesis (imitation), or collecting. At the

Neopets® site, kids get to break rules and make their own world based on what they want to do; they get to pretend to do things that people do in real and fantasy worlds – run stores, create guilds to promote certain themes, battle their pets like the characters on T.V. shows such as *Pokemon* and *Digimon*, and they really like to do these things; they can also play games that are challenging but not too challenging, and chat with Neofriends.

"What is Neopets®?" you ask. It is an interactive website that young people between the ages of seven to fifteen spend gobs of time visiting. Rumor has it that some girl in Great Britain created it. At least, that's what a lot of kids say they have heard. At this site, which is a "virtual world," you can create a virtual pet and then take care of your pet. You need to feed him or her daily, you can build a home for your pet, you can educate your pet, and you can keep your pet happy with toys. Soon after creating our pets, we started spending enormous amounts of time earning neopoints in order to buy food for them. You can earn points through playing games of strategy, by gambling in games of chance, and by just being lucky and coming across events where you get money. You can also set up your own store and start selling many of the objects you have purchased, found, and traded for. Sophia honestly did not think the creators of the site were secretly training kids to want to gamble when they grow up, even though she looked forward to visiting the "wheel of fortune" and the "fairy wheel" every day, where she had a chance to win large quantities of points, but she sometimes lost points or had an object taken away by the "Pointdevil," a virtual character found at the website. (Of course, there is always the option of placing valuable objects in your Neopets® safe deposit box.) She also did not think that the other one-time-a-day opportunities to win things by chance – Coltzan's Shrine, the Fruit Machine, or Tombola, for example – were key aspects of the time she spent online, even though she looked forward to checking out these games of chance every single day. As she pointed out, most kids spent far more time on "jobs" – challenges to collect things or to master difficult levels of game play – in order to earn money than they did at the wheels of fortune. Playing games was clearly the greatest time commitment of *aficionados*, as it was a fun and a reasonable way to earn points that, in turn, could be cashed in for stuff for your pets.

Sophia and I began that research project when I (Peter) wanted to try to find a way to understand how youth theorize popular culture. Instead of theorizing for them, I hoped to learn about the ways in which young people reflect on their interaction with popular culture, and how popular culture mediates their experiences in virtual and other realities. Sophia loved Neopets® so it wasn't hard for her to join the project; it was fun to talk to kids about their involvement with the website, and to look for ways to get more kids "started." Here are the key phases of virtual world participation that we identified through talking with a lot of kids and spending large amounts of time on the website: finding out about the cool site; playing games; shopping; getting addicted to it; and starting other kids up. Finding out about the site usually occurs by word of mouth. You may be over at a friend's house looking for something to do. One of you thinks about going online. The other wants to go to Neopets®. The first person hasn't heard of it yet. Within a day, the friend has created at least one neopet, and has started on the road to taking care of his or her pet. But, you see, most people do not spend all that much time taking care of their pet. It's true that you need to feed the pet every day, and it is true that you can build an elaborate house for your pet and continue to add on to that house. But the house is very expensive and takes way too many points. We each created a basic house at one time, but quickly lost interest, as has been the case with almost everybody else we have talked to about the website. The games are the next step in getting heavily involved. First, you look for games that will earn you lots of points. Then you start checking out what games are available. Soon you are testing out games, and strategizing the best way to earn lots of points. You start exploring the shops: both those run by the computer, where you can barter for better prices on objects you want to purchase for your pet, and then at stores run by random people. This is where the addiction mode begins: you hang around chat rooms. You start to have enough neopoints to buy fancy "paintbrushes" that can be used to decorate your pet in awesome designs and outfits. Yet many of these options are so expensive that it is impossible to believe that anybody really buys them. Nevertheless, you start checking out the money tree – a place where people donate stuff and small amounts of neopoints – in order to continue collecting items: objects for your pet, things to barter and trade with neofriends, and so on. Virtually everybody creates his or her own store sooner or later, and this takes a lot of time. Then you can go to the user-lookup and find your neofriends' stores. What have you collected in order to sell? This is an opportunity to really have fun. You can give stuff to neofriends as well, which is also a social way to have a good time.

You know you are spending gobs of time on Neopets® when you find yourself battling your pet to win more points, checking out the Neocams – where you can see pictures of cool neo things like neo stuffed pets and pictures of random pets. Or when you are surfing stores and guilds of people you don't know. Or when you have recruited a large number of people to join your own guild and then you host chat room meetings of your guild. The once-a-day games of chance are enough to get people to sign on again and then, once you are "in" Neopets®, it is so easy to continue by playing a game, or two, or three thousand. So I conjectured that maybe the site is a clever research tool: the creators might be scoping out how to get people hooked into spending more time at a website. They might be doing research into how people choose to click on a link, how they spend their time in virtual worlds, and so on. Sophia thought, too, that this could be possible. But she also suggested, quite reasonably, that the people who made this website might have just had some free time on their hands working in an office building somewhere. (She knew an office building was involved in some way because you can see offices in an office building behind some of the pictures of stuffed Neopets® in pictures on the Neocam.) More likely, the research might have something to do with contests and other marketing tools, because there are lots of them all the time at this website. Participating in contests is a sure sign of the serious neopetter.

The next phase in the Neopets® experience is "starting other kids up." You go to friends' houses and introduce them to the site so that you can then message them as a neofriend back when you are playing games at the site at home. Or, you call up a friend and talk to them through creating a pet so that you can then go to the user-lookup and find their pet's image. A few days later, your friend is spending countless hours on their own playing games at the site. Comparisons with peer pressure to buy cool clothes or drugs have been brought up by both of us. They seem apt.

Neopets® is a life curriculum in itself. There is nothing missing from the Neopets® world. Investing, earning a living, raising a family, educating your progeny, connecting with others through hobbies at the guilds, and just plain shopping, are all central parts of the Neopets® experience. There are ways in which Neopets® captures possible implications of what Kenway and Bullen (2001) have noted as the elision of boundaries among education, entertainment, and advertising. I emphasize the educational aspects of this site, but also note the importance of its function in advertising. Sophia, on the other hand, privileged the entertainment aspects of the site, foregrounding the social interaction opportunities both online with neofriends (it's amazing to hear from some of the people who contact her about becoming neofriends! Kids she hasn't played with since way back when...); she also recognized the advertising aspects of the site, but she definitely did not think of the experience as educational. Sure, there's lots of money in all aspects of neopoints (mathematics?), creative writing in the advertising for one's store and in other venues, and so on. But for her, consistent with Kenway and Bullen's analysis of generational splits in consumer culture, there was no way that entertainment and/or advertising could overlap with education. More relevant might be the ways that the site enables young people to take on leadership roles in creating a guild, recruiting friends, and running a store. It is also exciting to explore the new worlds that exist in different places on this website, and to learn the geography of these worlds.

Back to our original questions: What does "neo" mean? When Sophia was ten, she thought it had to do with the ways that the pets are like, but not really exactly like, real pets: hence, "neo." I (Peter) checked out dictionary definitions and found an accent on "new." Are these "new" kinds of pets? Is there a whole culture of new forms of pet care and thus self-entertainment through artificial pets that these virtual, static images are part of? Perhaps, but more importantly, virtual worlds point to a "new" kind of popular culture interactive experience that has not been given much attention in terms of its implications for what might be happening parallel to them in schools. Adults would tend to use this experience to think about how to make it more educational: they would want to merge the entertainment of popular culture with the education – read "schooling" – of popular culture. We agreed together to suggest something different: to value the education of popular culture as itself, schools could think about how to apply the entertainment/advertising lure of popular culture experiences as a metaphor for the types of encounters that are possible. What if curriculum were built upon a series of phases: first, word-of-mouth recruitment, an experience of "finding out about cool sites" of interaction possible at the school; second, playing games with the cool – selecting from options of what would be engrossing; third, a kind of metaphorical shopping around, which allows kids to collect stuff that is cool; the next phase would be a metaphorical addiction – kids wouldn't want to stop what they are doing, and could focus on one thing for as long as they want, always looking forward to the opportunities that are scarce and only available once a day or once a week; an important feature would be "starting other kids up," rejuvenating the cycle of word-of-mouth recruitment.

Our list of "phases" was our way of sharing the condensation of data we had collected so far. This set of types of experiences made sense to both of us, given our different perspectives on the Neopets® phenomenon. The phases represented a saturation of the discourse. So what? How can we write about this without theorizing the experience for others, and without reducing this either to another simple story about another fad, or to interpreting the importance of Neopets® for others? What would be the "message" of what may be learned from talking to people about virtual worlds as a new form of popular culture?

One "message" from Sophia and other children is that consumers of a commodity make use of it in their own ways even as they may seem to be pawns of consumer culture from an adult perspective. I remain convinced that popular culture is simultaneously a commodity to be consumed, collected, and traded for other cultural capital, and a cultural resource, out of which individuals and groups construct ways to form meanings and new comprehensions in their experiencing and remaking of the world (Appelbaum 1995a). Thus, while Sophia did buy a Neopets® T-shirt, her descriptions of what is interesting to her in the Neopets® experience, the Neopets® curriculum, focus on the ways in which she takes on a variety of identities as a caretaker and trainer of her pets. "A kind of slippage happens among sameness and difference, center and margins," between on-line and off-world life experience. For her, the limits of social and cultural identity are tested as she makes no distinction between information and matter, mechanics and thought, work and play, or even religion and commerce (Appelbaum 1999). She is emblematic of the "screenagers" that Douglas Rushkoff writes of:

> In fact, kids on the frontier of the digital terrain have adopted some extraordinarily magical notions about the world we live in. Far from yielding a society of coldhearted rationalists, the ethereal, out-of-body experience of mediating technologies appears to have spawned a generation of pagan spiritualists whose dedication to technology is only matched by their enthusiasm for elemental truth and a neoprimitive, magical worldview. To a screenager, these are not opposing life strategies but coordinated agents of change.
>
> (Rushkoff 1996: 109)

My Teacher is an ALIEN

Notes for a primer in Edugenics,

by Peter Appelbaum

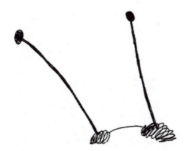

"The extension of communications technology into every aspect of social and cultural life is no longer imagined or science fictional future; it has already taken place, with consequences that are both alarming and hopeful. As the distinction between the imaginary and the real, and the present and the future, becomes less obvious, the generalized definition of science fiction as a popular genre in which utopian or dystopian fantasies of the future are explored clearly requires further consideration."

Science Fiction!

Instability of social & cultural categories

Erosion of confidence in historical narratives.

Inability to imagine the future

But aren't these really about post modernism?

"It is important to note that my account is not intended to demonstrate the 'relevance' of SF to the subject matters and methods of conventional... education... I do not advocate studying SF for the 'textbook science' it may illustrate: To do so would amount to little more than presenting the school-science orthodoxy in a slightly unorthodox way. Rather, I believe that SF is a conceptual territory in which we can explore ideas and issues that may be more important to us (learners and teachers) than those to be found in conventional science textbooks and classroom practices."

Thankyou, Noel; you get your two pages next...

Curriculum

Human-machine interface:
   Introducing Cy Borges, the fictional non-fiction of narration

The other as Alien:
   Dislocating Spatial & Temporal Relations

Escuela
Familia

Is this fold Leibnizian, or Deleuzian-Leibnizian?

NOEL GOUGH AS FONT OF INSPIRATION

Even if SF was no more than 'a game for children' it would deserve a place in schooling— an 'adventure playground' that exercises children's minds is no less important than the kind that exercises their bodies

However, as Broderick asserts, SF does much more: it gives 'imaginative form' to 'the limits of our constructed knowledge.' SF also gives imaginative form to what might lie beyond these limits, beyond 'the fringes of our as-yet-unsayable fears and hopes.'

I DON'T KNOW ABOUT YOU, BUT TO **ME** THAT STUFF MAKES A FINE STAB AT ~ Curriculum ~

When I think of a 'teacher' in some generative fashion

Noel's quote from Teresa de Lauretis on SF fits for my notion of curriculum praxis:

SF is:

potentially creative of new forms of social imagination, creative in the sense of mapping out areas where cultural change <u>could</u> take place, of envisioning a different sort of relationship between people and things, a different conceptualization of social existence, inclusive of physical and material existence.

If SF seems to focus this may be on our fears, an index to the anxieties that have been provoked by modern science and technology

Noel's quote from Lewis Shiner provides, through a popularization of chaos theory, an apt metaphor for teaching practice:

THOMAS THROWS PEBBLES INTO A POND BENEATH A WATERFALL ...

The turbulence made them dance, two steps to the right, up for a second, then spinning off sideways and down... According to classical physics the pattern should be predictable, because everything that went into them was quantifiable. Volume of water, depth of streambed, angle of gradient, everything. But the patterns were like living organisms, influenced by their own history and their reaction to each other, and they could never be nailed down. What does this tell us, he thought.

Lesson Planning is the classical physics of pedagogy

Q: If curriculum can be fiction, it is more likely it will be treated as foci of speculation rather than as objects of Mastery.

THOMAS THROWS PEBBLES

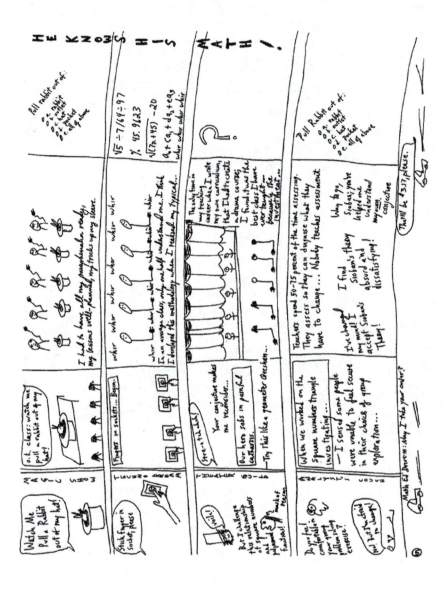

Genealogy:

People reading the science fiction of Octavia Butler became interested in issues of "human" and "other," particularly attracted by the potential in Butler's metaphor of "tasting" another's genetic code in order to know them well. Confusing Butler with Stephen Crane, a sect of Butlerites began to enter a state of literaphor, in which they first write or compose a life, and then pursue the living of this life.

Those philosophically inclined noted support for tasting in the work of Nietszche and Foucault.

Wine-tasting became the solution to immune-deficiency disorders – scenting and tasting out the "right" taste that recovers the actual life force. Normal schools, the sites of teacher training, introduced wine-tasting as a skill requirement early in this century, as they finally became aware of the immuno-vasive character of school experience.

Way back in the early 20th century, science fiction "film" was designed to feature special effects. Magicians such a s Houdini tried to exploit film for their own benefit. It was not intellectual theorists of education followed suit, attempting to exploit special effects for their own benefit. For a 'other' century later that educators were aware of the alien of children as they watch animated 3-D television. For a until century later that educators were aware of the alien children into factories and force them to defecate as they long dormant period of 50 years, people tried to lock watched, collecting their feces and siting out the bubblisms. Not until late in this period did it finally come about through the pioneering work of Dr. Meade Buber that we understood a crucial fact of bubblism production: that children under stress produce fewer bubblisms in their feces; those with relationships of trust produce so much more that it became essential to our survival in bubblehood to trust children ...

– ANONYMOUS

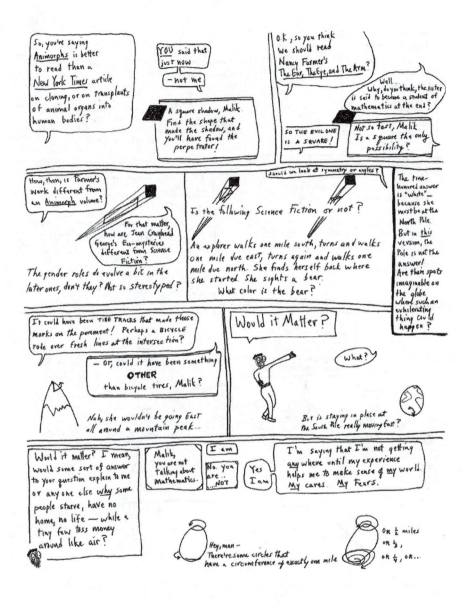

I want you to listen to Shari's way of doing it, and return to your original conjecture
When you can understand—and CAN DO IT her way, come tell the class how your strategies are similar AND different. SHARI: Make sure YOU can do it Flora's way. YOU make sure the presentation is going to be INTERESTING for the class.
FACES & VERTICES
QUILT TOGETHER
Thank sy visit Number patterns next
Hyler Power
Community Sculpture
Make MAZES → THIS WAY
Any other suggestions to Thomas P.-His conjecture IS indeed interesting!
Paper Airplane Contest, Closest to Average Distance of All Entries Wins!
OK, now let's think: what other ways can we use triangles to support our house: Your group's task is to invent a way to make a "good space" for your club center.
We're designing a guidebook for an Eco-history walk in the area of the school. You can help out by telling us of any facts, historical events, or interesting geometrical &/or numerical curiosities along Freedom Creek. Thanks, Middle School village Sixth Graders, Houxa Township
We're trying out different versions of mancala
Changing the number of stones, the number of cups...
Great, Freda, I like it. Let's post it at the park info kiosk!
Hah! How goofy with just one cup on each side
But it'll help us identify the pattern!
Tuesday
I made progress on finding evidence that my conjecture is true. How I came to this was by introducing a diagram to help me discover a pattern in the data I collected with Rashim last week. Here's the diagram and

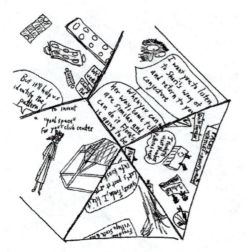

Others and the identification with the aggressor

This pair of forays into youth culture, the popularity of science fiction with youth (even as teachers find it more of a challenge to appreciate it), and the popularity of online webworlds (which suggest a potential future curriculum structure), together raise another form of dark matter that may be added to what was discussed in the previous chapter. Unlike the secret treasure already discussed, I believe *this* dark matter is *not* a construction by educators used as a form of resistance to self-knowledge. It really *is* the case that we construct Others in our quest to make sense of the world, and that in this process we establish forms of alienation that symbolize our efforts to contend with that construction of Others. We just don't look at how and where we do this.

Often, people need to use various forms of "defense" to help keep ourselves unaware of disturbing thoughts or feelings. Ego-defense is concerned with the emotional logic of dependency grounded in the social fact that early life requires care to survive, and the authority of the Other in order to learn. From those beginning moments of life we develop skills of meaning-making through the use of objects (e.g. things, people) in our environment. Things and actions are identified with meanings, become symbols. The problem of this human condition for educators, writes Deborah Britzman (2006), concerns how we may encounter the spurious nature of identifications as also defying literal correspondence, causality, or even any explanatory power.

My reading of two books by Chris Raschka suggested a way to think about the educator's need to posit a secret treasure of pedagogy, parallel to the students' hunt for the secret treasure inside the teacher's mind. In that case the fantasy made it possible for the teacher to act out a wish for unlimited power to control and manipulate the teaching–learning encounter. At the same time, acting out the parallel wish, the student pursues unlimited freedom and wealth. The mutual combination of fantasies works to perpetuate the nature of the educational encounter. That type of dark matter is not really "there" in the world, but is a reification of our (perhaps unconscious) need to protect ourselves through the creation of things that we imagine to be there, and which in this way become very real to us. Here in this chapter we look at another form of ego-defense, identification with the aggressor, as a beginning look at dark matter of education that does indeed exist independent of fantasy, the legacy of colonialism and imperialism. The "aggressor" for the child is usually a loved adult who tells the child what to do and in some way limits the child's pleasures. The child feels passive and persecuted. Father or mother may be felt as the aggressor, ruining the child's omnipotent wishes; but we could also imagine any adult serving this function for the child. Later on in life, we may see patterns of interpretation of a type of situation by an adult as a manifestation of a behavior internalized from earlier times. I wonder here how much of the interactions between teachers and students may be the results of identification with the aggressor by either the teacher or the student.

As one of at least twelve mechanisms of ego defense (as codified by Anna Freud), identification with the aggressor has three partners to placate, three sources of anxiety, each requiring different strategies of reality testing: the "real world," the "Id," and "the Superego." We experience anxiety over Others in the realm of the "real world," and need to test that the veracity or truth of things (objects) in our mind can be found again in the world. We experience anxiety over pleasure and guilt in our relationship with what Freud called our "Id," and anxiety over morality in our relationship with our "Superego," needing to test our understanding of the adequacy of our feelings to internal and external events. How we assign meanings to what others do and say, what we perceive as things in our world, and so on, each serve to defend and protect these "partners," potentially distorting the nature of the danger and the ego's response to it; indeed, the very defense itself may lead to further anxiety. For example, losing love from an Other is potentially so catastrophic that the ego might rather take in the threatening object as part of itself than risk such a loss. Anna Freud was known to say that the offense is externalized the moment the criticism is internalized, so that the mechanism of identification with the aggressor is supplemented as well by guilt, another defense measure (Freud 1995: 119). She noted this as part of her realization that the road to autonomy is rife with a critical paradox: a child's desire for autonomy and need to identify with something more powerful in order to even imagine a future autonomy agonizes the adults who both need to be used as an object with such psychoanalytic work by the child and also need to be simultaneously identified with and discarded.

The main point of this for educators, well described by Sander Ferenczi (1988), is that we must be constantly aware of the thin line between needing help from the Other and feeling that you have to be submissive in order to receive such help. Behind submissiveness or adoration is the strong desire to get rid of these feelings. If we can help students to give up the reaction of identification, then we may be said to have reached the goal of "raising the personality to the highest level" (Ferenczi 1988: 204). This paradox that aggression is required in order for an ego to become itself is also combined with another initially strange thing to consider: in identification with the aggressor there is no real "other"; the identification is with the feeling, the anxiety, and not with a person. Acting out of identification works to deflect worries and fears. A person who is being threatened or abused, whether a teacher or student, traumatized by terror and rage, is helpless in the face of these overwhelming feelings and his or her psyche is unable to function. Once the immediate threat is over, such a person has a limited number of ways to deal with the terror. One way is to become like the abuser (which is why so many abusers were themselves abused in their childhoods). This is not a conscious behavior. No one decides that they want to do to someone weaker and dependent what was done to them or that they want to be "just like" their abuser. However, when one's life depends on the actions of another person, the particular terror and helplessness is an impossible combination.

To survive, one must find a way to feel close to and understand the powerful and frightening authority figure. This is as true for abused children as it is for victims of horrible crimes. It is the basis of the *Stockholm Syndrome*. The victim must see the perpetrator as a potentially kind, even loving, person. She or he forms an intense emotional bond with the person. It is that relationship that is evoked and feels protective when they are overwhelmed in the future. The teacher–student asymmetry clearly establishes the expectation of this defense, and even more so if the teacher understands his or her role as particularly involved in challenging students to work in new contexts, often received by students as threatening simply by their mere difference from the norm. Wolmark's notion of tested social and cultural identity is directly applicable when the teacher resists either the hierarchic relation between center and margins or common, unitary notions of difference. At the same time, many teachers perceive "unruly" students who do not act according to the teacher's scripted fantasy of a classroom as similarly disrupting sameness and difference, and in this unfolding experience consciously or unconsciously find ways to feel close to and understand the powerful and frightening authorities in their own lives.

Maleeka and the dark matter of existence

"Maleeka, your skin is pretty. Like a blue-black sky after it's rained and rained." That's Miss Saunders' response to John-John's "[Maleeka] ain't nobody worth knowing" on her first day at McClenton Middle School. Miss Saunders is the new teacher in Sharon Flake's *The Skin I'm In*, winner of the 1999 Coretta Scott King John Steptoe Award for new authors. John-John "don't see no pretty, just a whole lotta black." "Maleeka, Maleeka, – baboom, boom, boom, we sure wanna keep her, baboom, boom, boom, but she so black, baboom, boom, boom, we just can't see her." It turns out that John-John has been holding a grudge for the last few years since he thought Maleeka shunned him for the lighter-skinned Caleb. And we learn that Miss Saunders has spent *her* life trying to be perfect at everything to make up for the large birthmark on half of her face. The teacher is marked as an interloper from the beginning of this story, by her face, her fancy clothes, her high expectations for her students, and her lack of teaching experience or training.

Maleeka, we soon learn, is really "smart." She might have gone to a special magnet school like one of her old friends if she hadn't doubted her own abilities. Now she hangs out with a bunch of "bad kids" who get her into trouble, and who make demands from her in return for special, secret favors like letting her borrow fancy clothes she wouldn't be able to afford on her own. In general these "friends" represent all the temptations of the world outside of school and other forms of sanctioned school academic learning. In this story, Maleeka has a number of authority figures with which to feel anxiety and fear. The new teacher, Miss Saunders, is on her back from the beginning; John-John has been harassing her and making her embarrassed for years. Maleeka hangs out with Charlese and her gang, pretending to enjoy smoking, and wearing Charlese's fancy dresses, doing all of their homework in order to feel like she's fitting in; hanging with Charlese does not really help, but it is one thing Maleeka can try.

This is one of those stories where you can see things going from bad to worse in front of your very eyes. Maleeka is in a difficult situation and there does not seem to be anyone she can turn to. She makes some pretty bad mistakes before she finally realizes that the new English teacher really is on her side. Meanwhile,

> Miss Saunders has really got all the teachers stirred up.... They say Mr. Pajolli's sucking up to her so that maybe her company will donate lots of money to the school. Maybe even get us some computers and a new library. All of this makes the other teachers resent Miss Saunders even more.
>
> (Flake 1998: 80)

In the office, the teachers never say her name. They just say "she" did ... this, and "she" did that. Miss Saunders is an alien in this school, not like the *other* teachers. Curiously, she already knows one of the other teachers, a friend from college – Tai, an alien too. Tai is an Asian in a predominantly African-American school, and even in Maleeka's mind "she's different" (p. 84). Maleeka, Charlese, Saunders, and Tai are each "others" for everybody else, and this otherness defines their life experience.

Maleeka gets caught up in an extended writing assignment, a fictional diary of a slave girl confused and lost on a ship headed from Africa to America, a girl she can relate to very easily using feelings and images of power from her own life experience. This cathartic writing effort moves her into new understandings about her life and the people in her world.

> The sea is wild and mean. Water is crashing against the boat like a hundred angry lions. My body is wet with sweat and throw-up from the others pressing close around me like sticks of firewood.
>
>   They chain us together like thieves and beat us til we bleed. I have made up my mind though. I will show no weakness. I will be strong. Strong like the sea and the wind.
>
> (Flake 1998: 85–86)

Miss Saunders, meanwhile, is living out her own fantasy of power and control. We are told she was "successful" in business. Now she has taken advantage of a program to facilitate career changers who want to become teachers. She is very confident in herself, and knows what she believes in. What this amounts to for her teaching is her honesty with her students, and her demands that they live up to high expectations for their work and learning. She gives them no slack, assigns so much homework that parents complain, and in general accepts the lonely plight of a maverick alien in a new land. This first effort at teaching is for her a rite of passage, and one she is determined to survive. "A bull in a china shop" (p. 36) is what the librarian says she is.

Before she gets started on the fictional diary, Maleeka brazenly tells Miss Saunders that her face says she is a "freak." Laying the groundwork for Maleeka's later identification with the aggressor, Miss Saunders says that she herself once saw herself as a freak, when she was young. Her parents had the preacher pray over her face, old folks "worked their roots on it," and her grandmother used some concoction to change the color of the blotch so her cheek would match the rest of her skin. "Liking myself didn't come overnight ... it took a lot of wrong turns to find out who I really was. You will too." To Maleeka, she says, "It takes a long time to accept yourself for who you are. To see the poetry in your walk... to look in the mirror and like what you see, even when it doesn't look like anybody else's idea of beauty" (pp. 19–20).

Poachers in the dark

The darkness of Maleeka's skin, like a blue-black sky after it has rained, the deformity of Miss Saunders, and the dark underbelly of the slave ship in Maleeka's fictional slave diary remind me of another character in another book that conjures up images of darkness, *Count Karlstein*, by Philip Pullman. Count Heinrich Karlstein, "a thin, dark man, much given to gnawing his nails, muttering to himself, and poring over works of German philosophy at midnight in his stone-walled, tapestried study," had far more serious "defects":

> a temper you'd have put down for its own sake if it'd been a dog, a vile, sarcastic tongue, and – worst of all – a kind of bright-eyed delight in being cruel, whether it was to a horse or a dog or a servant – or a little niece from another country, with nowhere else to go.
>
> (Pullman 1982: 6)

But there it was: he was the master. Such an authority figure turns out to be the kind of aggressor that few would identify with. There are other scary authorities to fear in the dark of All Souls Eve, especially Zamiel, the Demon Huntsman. In this story the teachers are a sorry lot. The first who we meet, Snivelwurst, is the tutor for the Count's nieces, "a lip-licking, moist-handed, creeping, smarming little ferret, with pomaded hair that he spent half an hour every morning carefully sticking into place so as to look like Napoleon" (p. 23). The next teacher we meet is the niece's former tutor, Miss Augusta Davenport, a seemingly clever lady who is smitten by someone labeled early on as a dangerous criminal, the con artist and swindling entertainer Doctor Cadaverezzi, a.k.a. Luigi Brilliantini, a.k.a. Antonio Rolipolio.

The hero and heroine of Pullman's "narratives by various hands" are none of these teachers, although we do learn by the end that the genuine teacher manages to construct her unique school through her relationship with con artists and swindlers; from time to time, she makes expeditions of scientific discovery to the pyramids or to Mesopotamia, or to Hindoostan, and she insists on taking people with her. Most importantly, she never gets involved in the darkness, instead making a small miracle happen as the story peers into the future: by spending her holidays at Castle Karlstein, she slowly comes to think of it as her home – "the great, grim place, echoing with fear and dark with wickedness" (p. 242).

The heroine and hero of this tale are the primary narrator and her brother, Hildi and Peter Kelmar, a servant at the castle and her poaching brother – also labeled a dangerous criminal at the start of the book. The story of the criminal poacher makes a curious return in our reading of children's literature. Indeed, the gendered unfolding of a male poacher and female helpmate is once again evident as a hidden narrative of our culture. And, like many a poacher before and after him, Peter Kelmar is branded a bad and dangerous person. But we encounter him as a light-hearted huntsman, who sees life – as does any genuine poacher – as a series of frolicking challenges to meet with cleverness and humor. Poaching has a negative connotation in the common vernacular, masking a sense of fascination and an attempt by the authorities to confuse poaching with criminality. In Chapter 1, I confessed to clear distinctions among poaching, stealing, and oppressive ownership. But I argued that all are relevant and appropriate to a vital curriculum based on poaching, since poaching is grounded in positions of power and inequity. Poaching therefore speaks to current global issues of inequity, power, and difference. I argued for an alternative way of thinking about the experience of school in which acts of resistance are constructed as forms of poaching. I then asked if it could be possible to *sanction* poaching in curriculum theorizing, and claimed that in doing so we would thereby sanctify time. This would make it possible for school experience, curriculum practice, to be at once the "spark" of being in time and the poaching of time itself. There is a kind of cleverness of violating or circumventing rules and structures of which poaching is centrally formed. By making this cleverness the feature of curriculum theorizing and curriculum practice, we have the opportunity to release poaching from its currently telescoped construction into a foundational precept of curriculum practice.

In this chapter, I want to interrogate the "dark side" of poaching, or the darkness within which poaching is sometimes required to take place. Consider, for example, that there was an elite corps of spies in the Nazi SS made up of men who had been arrested more than once for poaching (MacLean 1998). Poachers were of interest. But not just *any* poachers: only those who continued to revel in poaching beyond the experience of humiliation, defeat, and subsequent punishment, and specifically those who *failed* at poaching (in that they were caught and arrested). This is a brutal story but, from the safety of fifty years' distance in time it is an extremely compelling one. It is also an enduring lesson that a military unit, formed under an evil ideology, led by a social outcast and composed of vicious criminals, will sink to its lowest common denominator: hate. The Dirlewanger Battalion, also known as "Sonderkommando (special commando) Dirlewanger" (named for and led by Oskar Dirlewanger) was perhaps the least understood, but at the same time the most notorious German SS anti-partisan unit in World War II. German propaganda correspondents and wartime photographers did not follow them in action, and for good reason: wherever the unit operated, corruption and rape formed an everyday part of life, and indiscriminate slaughter, beatings, and looting were rife. Formed as a battalion of convicted poachers in 1940, the unit operated in Poland until 1942, guarding Jews in forced labor camps and making life miserable for Poles in Lublin and Cracow. From there Dirlewanger spent two years combating partisans in central Russia, giving no quarter and expecting none in return, during vicious fighting against an elusive foe in the midst of inhospitable swamps and dismal forests. In 1944, Dirlewanger savaged Warsaw during the Polish Uprising, before moving to Slovakia to crush another rebellion there. The end of the war saw the unit, which was now a division in size, fighting for its life south of Berlin against the Soviet Army. Medieval in their outlook on war and certainly not indicative of many German military formations, this unit none the less remains a reflection of a segment of mankind gone mad in the inferno of World War II on the Eastern Front.

Such poachers are very different from the central characters in numerous children's books; these characters, surely not members of an elite and cruel brigade, are usually celebrated. But for what are they celebrated? To reclaim poaching from criminality, we have to read Eric Hobsbawm (1959, 1969), who wrote of the original relationship of poachers to the land: poaching was simply a right of rural people to take what was available off the land; only later did the stewards of the land, the noblemen, wish to stake a claim to ownership and property, moving to label poachers as criminals who stole from the land now owned by the privileged. I claim that the popular culture of poaching is an insidious, hovering commitment to the association of darkness with evil. It is as if we could never escape from the deplorable colonialism of Conrad's *Heart of Darkness*. And if we wish to work against the racial and other prejudices inherent in the popular culture of poaching, it requires serious attention to the stories we tell children, and the stories we read with children. It also requires a serious effort to examine our own uses of poaching images in our construction of knowledge and epistemology.

In *Count Karlstein*, the evil villain is not the poacher, but the Count, who has made a pact with the Demon Huntsman. Like many an adult authority figure before him, the Count has promised this dark shadow of fear the lives of youth. He plans to take his nieces as a sacrifice to the hunting lodge on All Souls Eve, leaving them in return for his status as Lord of the Land. We learn from this story, as we had learned from Roald Dahl, that such foolish attempts to preserve power end up in failure. It is the poacher who wins in the end, becoming ranger of the forest, friend of Zamiel the Demon Huntsman; and it is he who returns all of the topsy-turvy confusion of power and authority back on its head to where it justly belongs: the nieces gain a good life, the rightful heir to the castle is found, and much merriment ensues.

Designer selves

Reading *The Skin I'm In* and *Count Karlstein* against the grain of curriculum as science fiction, I interpret each of these novels in terms of the rite of passage, hybridity of identity constituted as Other, and identification with the aggressor. In our postmodern or supermodern times, we are tempted to think of identity as something we construct, invent, or buy. School as either the rite of passage or preparation for the rite of passage is a counterpoint to the notion that one can reinvent oneself, come up with a new, desirable identity, and purchase the garments, accessories and other symbols of the identity, and then strut or perform for Others. "Be the person the chatroom thinks you are," and "You are what you buy," are the quotes that Claudia Ruitenberg (2003) uses to open an essay on identity design. Wolmark's caveat that this sort of creolization of identity may function to displace difference into the realm of the transcendental is thus juxtaposed with Ursula LeGuin's equally compelling concern that identity may very well be constructed through definitions of difference from Others.

In education, writes Ruitenberg, these ideas manifest themselves in, for example, a commonly spoken ideal of color-blindness and gender neutrality.

> After all, in this day and age, students do not feel bound by their class or ethnic backgrounds in the identities they wish to construct for themselves. By teaching female students women's history, or encouraging black students to read literature by black authors, one unnecessarily confines students to particular identity categories. "Never mind the past, the future is yours!" Students are encouraged to use their "freedom of choice" not only when shopping for clothes, but also when deciding on the identities they wish to construct.
>
> (Ruitenberg 2003: 121)

This might be one interpretation of Miss Saunders' message for Maleeka in *The Skin I'm In*. Never mind what you or others have thought about you in the past; the future is yours to make for yourself. Through the writing of the slave diary, Maleeka is moved to see herself as someone who can demand self-respect and as someone whom Others can love. At times she even loses her sense of where the character she is inventing ends and where her own identity begins.

> I'm thinking and writing in my diary – *our* diary, Akeelma's and mine. Lately it's hard to know where Akeelma's thoughts begin and mine end. I mean, I might be starting off with her talking about how scared she is with the smallpox spreading around the ship and killing people. Then UI end up the same paragraph with Akeelma saying she's scared that maybe people will always think she's ugly. But I'm really talking about myself. *I'm* scared people will always think *I'm* ugly.
>
> (Flake 1998: 96)

Miss Saunders spent most of her own adult life so far *trying* to invent herself, by being perfect and successsful despite her birthmark. It's only recently that we can see she has come to realize that a success in business is not who she wants to make herself. Her obsessive search for perfection is merely a latent symbol of her identification with the aggressor, her attempts to become the perfection that her birthmark had prevented her from embodying as early as birth. Count Karlstein's efforts to remake himself as nobility required a pact with Zamiel, his murder of his older brother and sister-in-law, and the promise of human sacrifice ten years later. On the eve of fulfilling his fantasy, he dreams of being a "good person," a philanthropist, buying the favor of the townspeople through new roofs for their houses and new shoes for their children. Perhaps like the plastic surgery of today that promises complete identity change, his plans for sacrificing his nieces fails, and he ends up as the human sacrifice himself. This comes about because Zamiel honors all "true huntsmen" and those they protect, Peter Kelmar and the two girls.

I take the two stories to mean that identity design does not happen in a completely open field of possibilities; the designer works with raw material and the tools at hand. Becoming the person the chat room thinks you are, writes Ruitenberg, is an "a-contextual and a-historical product of an individual mind, and it blames the individual whenever the creation of fluid and multiple identities fails" (2003: 121). She argues for an understanding of human agency in identity design that is both enabled and constrained by its material and cultural situatedness. What Miss Saunders succeeds at is providing opportunities for Maleeka to learn about identity design through curriculum content.

Let's wind up this chapter by riffing on the notion that curriculum as experience can be a holding environment in which students practice identity design, whether that identity is one of a writer, mathematician, scientist or historian, or Latina, African-American, Catholic or Jew, or female Latina mathematician, bisexual scientist, or boundary-crossing African-American Asian writer. Such design begins, as Ruitenberg notes, with the Heideggerian sense of being "thrown" into this world. Maleeka is very dark-skinned; Miss Saunders has an enormous birthmark on her face. Hildi and Peter live at the inn in town while Max, eventually to become the new Count Karlstein, begins life as an orphan with no potential home. We are never un-signed: each of us is always already inscribed with meaning, even from before we're born. Understanding identity involved untangling the knot of these meanings; we de-throw our thrownness, or de-sign ourselves. More to the point, however, is that untangling the knot produces a view of what was hidden in the knot: developing consists of an unwrapping even as it carries with it the idea of newness.

Here is where we can see the importance of Sophia's idea that the purchase of Neopets® products is not central to the experience of participating in the website community. Humans are at once thrown, signed, and potential possibilities. We find ourselves in our world without warning and without any control regarding who and what we are. Others take our appearance and gestures as saturated with meaning. Yet we are always remaking who we are through our actions in the moment. Self-de-signing, in this sense, "entails more than the simplistic notion that one can construct oneself through what one buys and wears" (Ruitenberg 2003: 123). Cast into circumstances beyond our control, we each *can* de-sign ourselves, by recognizing our facticity *and* by reinterpreting that facticity in a new language that transcends, rather than denying our thrownness. Instead of relying on a common American myth that each child can become anything she or he wants to be, teachers might find greater satisfaction in the idea that each child can design themselves as anything they wish through the unraveling of their thrownness. Sophia recognizes that she bought and wears a Neopets® T-shirt; but she also sees herself as doing many things other than buying products. While adults may harp on about the consumerism of the T-shirt, she sees for herself how much time she spends on many other aspects of identity experimentation in the Neopets® curriculum.

The shift from thrownness to using the material and tools at hand to do something that one can positively value is at the heart of the design process, and is central to the next chapter. The good designer does not deny constraints, nor does she allow herself to be trapped or paralyzed by them; instead, she finds a new way of looking at them, a new language that shows the possibilities for response, i.e., for design. This is very much the metaphor behind this book as well: given the current constraints and complexities of curriculum work, I ask us to consider a new language of curriculum theorizing, which involves reading children's and young adult literature as curriculum theory. Doing this work myself as an example, I have come up with a new language of curriculum and classroom practice that I have been testing out in my own teaching, which uses the language of poaching, weirding, the feed, dark matter, identification with the aggressor, and so on. The "testing out" of this new language in the context out of which it emerged is an essential feature of the design process as well, for the designer must allow the design medium to "talk back." "If this is how you understand me, this is what you make me" (Ruitenberg 2003: 124).

A critical aspect of a pedagogy for identity design is that the classroom becomes a place where students experiment with new ways of seeing themselves (mathematician, female biracial historian, and so on), and where they can receive the talk-back in these experiments. This is not to be confused with a place where one comes to express who one is, or a place where one comes to understand better how to express who one is (Bingham 2001). The latter are what Charlese and her cohorts are doing in school, and what the first Count Karlstein is doing at the castle. These folks do not get the point of identity experimentation. They are not designing at all; they are simply having ideas and putting out into the world. The same goes for Cadaverezzi/Brilliantini/Rolipolio; only at the end of the book can we see a glimpse of a future where this character has come to learn that each of these many con artist attempts was part of identity experimentation in preparation for running a great theater – he was, after all, always experimenting with performing and entertaining others. Early in *The Skin I'm In*, Maleeka is under the impression that she has to make up her mind about who she is; she wants an idea that works, that enables her to live her life. So too do we and many of our students fall into this same distraction from identity experiments. Indeed, this sometimes works – a student of architecture might come up with a building that does not fall down; but not falling down is not good architecture, and having an idea about one's life is not the same thing as designing one's identity.

As Maleeka's story unfolds, she learns more and more about her social, cultural, and historical context; so too do the protagonists of *Count Karlstein*. Maleeka's mother remembers her father's old poem about how beautiful his daughter is, her crush Caleb is given a chance to explain why he failed her and why he will never do so again, and Miss Saunders' conversations, both with her and those overheard with Tai and other teachers, help her to get a good sense of the interplay between her own actions as an individual and the situatedness of those actions as part of larger contexts. This provides her with a better understanding of her own thrownness, enabling her to see the potential of identity experimentation. She sees herself as a writer who can win a contest, as the girlfriend of an attractive guy, as the daughter of a mother making progress in the grief over a dead spouse, and even as a friend who can help Miss Saunders. In *Count Karlstein*, few people even learn of Heinrich's pact with Zamiel, but the truth comes out about everyone's connections to everyone else, Max's genealogy, secret loves, and the value of a good poacher with a carefree heart. Students, too, need to be encouraged, and given the opportunity, to learn about their social, cultural, and historical context. With this understanding of their thrownness, of their sign-ness, they are ready to experiment with identity, and to see in these situations the back-talk that is produced when design is at the heart of the process.

Furthermore, my reading of these books helps me to think about how the design of the self can never be the work of an autonomous subject who chooses and creates the self out of her own free will. Ruitenberg writes that the subject who does the designing needs to become more modest (2003: 127). The design of identity may be thought of as a small move, but a small move with potentially large or pervasive consequences. (I have in mind the notion from mathematical chaos theory that a tiny difference in initial conditions can lead to major consequences – the proverbial butterfly flapping its wings on one side of the globe causing a hurricane on the other side.) Students can and should learn how they speak with languages that are not of their own making while being part of the transformation of that discourse. Students can see in this way that they are not passive consumers of potential identities that they buy or steal, but instead as designers of identity. They may want to be the identity the chat room thinks they are (Ruitenberg), but this identity is not all of their own making, and carries with it the signs that were thrown.

Each student is a collection of potential futures, but these potential futures carry with them the trace of their signs, which brings us back to the idea of curriculum theory and curriculum work as a play of signs shifting in meaning, as an enactive symbolic politics.

10
Criteria and Ways of Working*

The original impetus for this romp through children's literature was to illustrate a method of curriculum theorizing, no less theoretical than the usual, but more accessible to classroom teachers as a technique, and more useful in guiding classroom practice. As I mentioned in Chapter 1, I could have chosen any works of literature, just as I expanded the idea of texts to include children's animated television programs and web community participation. The critical move in this work is to use the generativity of the metaphors established by the relationships and symbols in the stories to raise important questions about your work. Some teachers find the metaphoric application of popular culture and everyday life exciting and productive. Others devalue such resources. Like many people, they may seek the status of high culture and shun the low status of popular art forms and literature written for children. Yet, like the cook I conjured in the first chapter, we have much to accomplish if we play with soup and sauce, cookies and cakes.

One way into this type of curriculum theorizing is through children's books. As teachers, we value them, mostly for our students' benefits. But we also enjoy them. How could we not? They're *good*. To read these books for ourselves and our own professional growth is to sanction poaching in our work. We take the time as we peruse a children's book to wander off the path and enable the dreaming that is the stuff of object relations (Block 1995). We embrace these books and in the process become who we are.

The preceding chapters are examples of my own reading of such books. As I mentioned in Chapter 1, I intentionally read them for meaning rather than technique, even though ideas for technique and organization pop up occasionally in my writing. There is already so much out there telling me what to do and when that I do not need to think so much about such things. Instead,

---

*Some parts of this chapter appeared previously as "How can youth cultural practices (and popular culture) inform classroom pedagogy?," by Leif Gustavson and Peter Appelbaum in Joe L. Kincheloe (ed.), *Classroom Teaching: An Introduction*, New York: Peter Lang, 2005.

what I crave is meaning and the underlying purpose for my work. I need a discourse for talking about this less overt and critically important aspect of my craft. In the end, what I have created for myself is a new discourse of teaching, one which I have begun testing out over the past few years, and find extremely helpful both for planning and assessment. When I work now as an educator, I use this new language to think about units, lessons, assessments, and so on. My plans and assessments include poaching, weirding, the feed and consumer culture, alternatives to vision and perception as the dominant metaphor for knowing, dark matter, improvisation, ways of working, and identification with the aggressor. As a new science of curriculum, a *currere*, this is a systematic and self-reflective study, using youth culture texts to interrogate the relations between academic knowledge and my own life history, in the interest of both self-confirmation and social reconstruction. As such, I affirm Pinar's four steps or moments in the method of *currere*: the regressive, the progressive, the analytic, and the synthetic.

What I want to do now is report on my work based in making sense of the ideas I synthesized from these samples of youth texts. Yet I also want at this point to note an important idea that has only freshly re-emerged after I have immersed myself in this method of *currere*. As I work to sanction poaching in my classroom, to analyze encounters in light of dark matter that I either fantasize or tend to not see, it becomes increasingly evident that an even more useful youth culture text is going unread by both myself and my students: Here I am constructing an elaborate discourse in hopes that it can make youth experience engaging, meaningful, and creative, while youth themselves are already involved in creative practices every day of their lives. Why not put a new spin on phenomenological (Husserl: "to the things themselves") pedagogy and go to the students themselves? In the same way that teachers can enjoy reading children's literature as curriculum theory, knowing that they are simultaneously familiarizing themselves with potential curriculum materials, we can read youth's creative practices as curriculum theory texts, and take what we learn back into the classroom. After all, teachers are interested in their students as creative producers of knowledge; so why not analyze the ways that youth work on their own to produce creative work? The idea is not to "use" popular youth culture in the classroom, per se, just as my readings of children's literature do not prescribe strategies or methods of teaching, lessons for reading the books with children as the materials of instruction, but instead to inform the ways we organize and process experiences with our students. By studying the ways that youth work in their everyday lives, we can look for classroom structures that encourage youth to use these same practices and ways of working in school. The goal is to translate the habits of mind and body that enable students to be proficient in crafts outside of school into the school experiences, so that the same habits of mind and body can become part of their life in school. At the same time, even as we celebrate youth cultural practices, we can both recognize those habits that are shared with practitioners of disciplinary ways of working, refine them, and contribute new skills and techniques to students' ways of working outside of school.

In my work at Arcadia University, co-teaching with Leif Gustavson, I have had opportunities to explore this method of *currere*. Each fall, Leif and I teach senior elementary education majors in a seminar that accompanies their work, leading groups of eight to ten children in mathematics and language arts inquiries tied to state standards and the Philadelphia School District benchmark performance objectives. We have developed an effective *infrastructure* that enables these student teachers to learn about the ways in which their students work creatively on their own, to bring those ways of working into the classroom experience and juxtapose them with ways of working as a mathematician and writer, to introduce criteria that promote youth application of creative practices as forms of engagement with the school curriculum, and to document how the students are meeting performance objectives. In the process, I believe, we sanction poaching, weird curriculum, and support improvising by students and teachers, while also enabling teachers to make decisions based on concepts such as identification with the aggressor, the feed, and dark matter.

In our work as teachers and teacher educators, we have met many people who do not think their job involves knowing about their students' lives and thoughts. Their notion of teaching and learning constructs an invisible barrier between the learning that occurs in their classrooms and the world of youth outside of school. They don't see this interesting world in which the students are living as part of what it means to be a student or part of what it means to be in school. The worst-case scenario is when a teacher sees everyday practices of youth as a deficit. For example, a teacher could possibly understand a student's intense interest in basketball as getting in the way of doing homework or occupying too much of his time. A teacher might blame a student's lack of interest in school on watching too much T.V., or call a student a vandal because of his practice of graffiti. In our work with teachers, we have found that these beliefs come from a genuine lack on the teacher's part of understanding the cultural practices in which youth are involved. Not surprisingly, this lack of understanding often stems from a lack of interest in the cultural practice itself as well as an acculturated devaluing of that practice (e.g., the teacher's parents maligned T.V., the teacher never watched T.V., so too much T.V. is not a good thing; a teacher never played basketball while growing up so basketball just isn't that interesting; or the mass media have influenced the teacher's feeling that graffiti – all graffiti – is bad). One of the fundamental challenges of being a teacher is that we need to lay aside our own biases and judgments as best we can in order to comprehend the ways in which our students perceive their world and how they make meaning in it.

If we believe in this one fundamental tenet of teaching – that we must work from the student's strengths and interests (Dewey 1997) – it no longer matters if *we* are interested in any of these cultural practices, if *we* like or dislike any of these practices, or if *we* have a history in any of them. Essentially, the practices are not about us. They are what the youth do, and it is our job to develop a complex sense of how and why they do what they do in order to understand where youth are coming from and what they could potentially bring to the learning environment. We also position ourselves to understand why youth are involved in the cultural practices in the first place.

Another reason why our interest is secondary to the practice itself is that the skills and knowledge that are part of popular culture practices are more important than our own involvement in them. In other words, it doesn't matter if your music of choice is Britney Spears, Jay-Z, Coltrane, Bach, or Pavement; underlying each musical choice, each habit of music listening, is a complex set of skills, strategies, and mechanisms that youth employ to appreciate the music they listen to. It is our job as teachers to understand that complex set of skills. Furthermore, when we make the effort to understand youth cultural practices, we acknowledge the differences between our ways of being in the world and those of our students. We can realize what we don't know, and all of the knowledge that informs these practices. We can also begin to examine how our assumptions about what students would be interested in, which activities would engage them, and which techniques they employ to organize information, are likely very different from those that our students make. The ways in which youth organize information often differ from the ways in which curriculum lays it out. So there is a real tension here and we only recognize it through understanding how youth make meaning through popular culture (how that differs from how we make meaning from popular culture).

How and why you do what you do every day

We (Leif and Peter) often introduce the use of youth culture by asking, "Have you ever thought about how and why you do what you do every day?" For example, have you thought about how and why you watch T.V., or how and why you change what you are wearing when you go out after dinner? On the surface these questions may seem really silly. When viewed in a certain way, they *are* silly. Yet these seemingly silly acts make up our lives. In fact, they occupy a large part of our time. When viewed in this way, they are not so silly any more. We argue that these activities, what De Certeau (1984) calls the "practice of everyday life," are what should be informing the art and craft of teaching.

You may be wondering what youth cultural practices have to do with popular culture. Often, popular culture is defined as the products of entertainment: music, T.V. shows, movies, and so on. We maintain that the everyday practices of youth *are* popular culture. In other words, logging on to

Instant Messenger, playing Madden 2004, choosing a body gel, burning a new CD, adding to your blog, planning how you're going to get down to Bonaroo in Tennessee, are the kinds of practices that create the products of popular culture. It is more useful to think of the *process* of generating popular culture (e.g., youth cultural practices) when it comes to teaching because all of the work and learning involved happens in the process, not in the product.

We find we need to expand on this distinction between process and products. When we ask if you think about how and why you do something every day, the kind of response we are looking for is not,

> yeah, I've got to go to the gas station to fill up on gas because I'm almost on empty; I know why I'm doing this: because I'm almost on empty. How? I'll drive to the station and unscrew the gas cap and....

That kind of response does not get at the how and why of the activity. Such a comment is really a surface answer. A more useful response when connecting the everyday, taken-for-granted cultural practices with learning is one where we tease out the strategies, tactics, mechanisms, and reasoning – the tacit knowledge that's in place – in order for us to do what we do. With our silly example of changing your clothes to go out after dinner, the surface answer might be, "because I need to wear something different." Underneath this surface answer, however, are a host of strategies, tactics, and mechanisms you have in place in order to do what seems to be a simple act:

1. You have a complex sense of your entire wardrobe (shoes, shirts, dresses, skirts, pants, socks).
2. You know where you think you are going to go and the kind of dress that's appropriate for that kind of place.
3. You know the messages that certain clothes send to others.
4. You've weighed the risk of wearing certain clothes, physically (can they get damaged tonight?) and socially (does this call too much attention to parts of my body?).
5. You've thought through the probability of your friends wearing the same thing.
6. You have an appreciation of aesthetics, color schemes, and matchings of clothing styles and types.
7. You know how much the clothes are worth and where they came from.

We belabor the skills and concepts embedded in this seemingly simple task because it is only when we acknowledge the skills and sophisticated problem-solving strategies of a practice that we can then translate that understanding into informing our teaching and the way in which we design learning environments for and with our students. It could be argued that the rest of the world doesn't need to have a meta-awareness of the practices of everyday life. However, teachers do.

How and why you do what you do every day becomes even less of a silly question when we recognize that the things we do every day don't happen in a vacuum. The practices that youth get involved in and the ways in which teachers think about them are influenced by multiple forces in society. For example, there are forces influencing what we decide to wear when we go out: the advertising we watch, what our friends wear, how much money we have, our parents' feelings on clothing, the bands we listen to, the movies we see. All of these forces influence what we decide to put on before we step out of the door to a greater or lesser degree. When we do step out of the door to go out, what we wear is not neutral or meaningless. In a sense, we are saying through our clothes, "This is who I am, and this is what I want to do tonight." We are making meaning through the clothes that we choose to wear.

Making meaning through popular culture is an academic way of describing how people use the resources of their culture to understand themselves, their world, and their lives. By culture, we mean beliefs, values, languages, traditions, symbols, styles, and tastes. (If you are interested in this, check out books written by Paul Willis, James Paul Gee, Michel De Certeau, Angela McRobbie, and John Fiske to get started.) Basically, culture is your family, your friends, the music you listen to, the clothes you decide to put on, and the church, synagogue or mosque you may attend. More specifically, culture is the language you use with your family, the language you use with your friends, the kind of coffee you decide to buy, what you do when you are in school. Why is this culture? It is culture because when you are in a family, your family has particular ways of being and thinking; your family has an implicit and explicit set of values and beliefs that it practices. Sometimes we can see culture manifested in the way families eat together, for example. There may be a particular place where each family member sits. Culture is also apparent in the ways groups of friends talk with one another. They have their own lingo, and so on. Popular culture is further evident in the ways we distinguish between who listened to Fountains of Wayne before they were well known outside of New Jersey, and who listens to them after they have been on MTV. In Sherry Ortner's words, "culture is a product of acting social beings trying to make sense of the world in which they find themselves" (Ortner 1984: 130).

Products are part of culture, too. In other words, culture also produces things like works of art, dance routines, pieces of music, and stuff to buy. Some people use the term "high culture" for fine art, like sculpture, painting, ballet, the kinds of literature that are usually part of the school curriculum (Shakespeare), or documentaries on PBS (Ken Burns' *Civil War*). These are called high culture because they are considered within our society to be elite, special, highly refined, important, and only able to be done by special people who have trained in high art. Often, popular culture is considered to be the products that are not included in high culture. If we can recognize that there are particular cultural forms that are privileged and therefore part of high culture, then the leftovers when we separate high culture from the rest of the cultural world might seem lesser and not nearly as important. Nevertheless, all of this is what we could call "popular culture." The reason why we are making the distinction between high culture and popular culture here is because our society teaches us in many ways to think of high culture as superior. Two ways of reinforcing this idea that there is a hierarchy of culture is to feature only forms of high art in museums and galleries and to study only forms of high culture in school (e.g., in art we study Degas, we do not study the graffiti artist down the street). In turn, because popular culture is not often honored in museums, galleries, and schools, it becomes trivial or merely associated with pleasure and entertainment. This is why it is so easy for us as teachers to say, "Oh, isn't that cute," about a student's interest in popular dance or video games. School is part of the culture that privileges high culture over other ways of making meaning in the world, and as part of that culture we naturally work to maintain the hierarchy. When you have a privileged list of texts for an American lit class, it is hard to see where a youth's Zine would fit in. When you have a scope and sequence for a biology class, it is hard to see where discussions of condom use fit in. How do you see the mathematics of turntablism in a rigid math curriculum? The existence of the idea of high culture influences the way we see the rest of our world, so that the ways we make meaning in and structure school experiences are a reflection of the values implicit in high culture.

In addition, high culture is often viewed purely as a product: something that we go to see and/or hear. People outside of the high culture, for example, painting, are purely spectators of the culture. They are not practicing the culture. They are merely consuming it. If we really think about it, we don't even know how to discuss the practices of our high arts: nobody can really say anything about Van Gogh except that he cut off his ear (unless you are an art historian or painter yourself); all we know about Shakespeare is that he may not have written several of his plays. We know how to recognize high culture, or how to recognize when someone is "gifted" in it, and therefore special. But we don't have a language for how to talk about the practices of any of the arts of culture, unless we are one of the few who are involved in a high art itself. This is one reason why it is so hard to teach people the high culture that makes up the school curriculum or the crafts of our high arts.

In contrast, youth do have the ability to talk about the crafts of popular culture; they are situated within the practices themselves. Youth are involved in popular culture practices in the same ways and with the same intensities that Picasso was involved in painting, or Mozart was involved in composing. They have the kinds of skills that we want them to have in order to be able to work at a high and complex level. For example, if you watch somebody play a video game or choose an outfit, you can see them demonstrating knowledge, comprehension, application, analysis, synthesis, and evaluation, the full range of higher order thinking according to Benjamin Bloom's taxonomy of learning (Bloom 1956).

Placing ourselves in a position to participate in popular culture practices is challenging because the practices are embedded in our everyday lives, right under our noses. Because of its "commonness," popular culture is just not celebrated the way high culture is; it isn't held up for everyone to see and value. On the other hand, school subjects are prime examples of a high culture stance on the world because they name privileged categories of knowledge, and because they make it possible for people to train in them to become specialists or experts. We might say therefore that many forces are working against the inclusion of popular culture in the school curriculum, even though teachers should make efforts to understand the practice of everyday life that characterizes their students' experiences in and out of school. Yet, as Ortner writes, "if *we* are to make sense of a culture, we must situate ourselves in the position from which it was constructed" (Ortner 1984: 130). Ortner is arguing that as teachers we need to be there with our students to see, hear, and therefore understand popular culture in the sophisticated ways that they themselves understand the practice of everyday life.

Using popular culture in the classroom

"How can teachers use popular culture?" Actually, teachers *are* already using popular culture, despite the forces working against this. Using popular culture in school is not a new idea, and we can learn from other teachers' work. Here are some ways we have seen popular culture used in the classroom as teachers ourselves and as teacher educators:

- popular culture as entertainment and a motivating force;
- popular culture as connection to the "real world";
- popular culture as unit of study;
- popular culture as social critique.

In this section we illustrate how teachers use popular culture in these different ways to inform their teaching. We will argue that these practices are worthwhile but do not really enable the teacher to see, hear, and understand popular culture from the perspective of the crafter of the art, namely youth, as suggested by Ortner. We then offer a parallel and independent way of thinking about popular culture growing out of what we have written above. We will then continue to discuss some implications and benefits of using popular culture.

Popular culture as entertainment and motivating force

It is Friday. Ms. Wilson and her fifth-grade students are at the end of their unit on Mesopotamia. They've learned about the Fertile Crescent,

cuneiform, the sexigesimal system, and the modern history of oil production. As a reward for all the hard work that they did, Ms. Wilson has
constructed a *Jeopardy* game. She divides the class into three teams,
checking for gender equity and ability. She has come up with categories
of questions in order of difficulty. Some she has devised out of mini-
lessons she gave in class; others are from the textbook they have been
reading; and some are from a film they watched the previous week. Ms.
Wilson acts like Alex Trebec, and she sets up the room to resemble the
game-show set. She has even taped the theme song. As the students
enter the classroom, lights flash and the music plays. The desks have
been divided so that there are three groups of desks facing the game-
show host. She keeps score on a yellow notepad as the game is played.
The winning team gets the reward of ten extra bonus points on
Monday's test. Down the hall, Mr. Smith has designed and organized a
basketball tournament as a vehicle for the class' study of angles in
geometry (the way the ball bounces off of the backboard, or the floor
when passed), and statistics (they are keeping records of players' performances). In Ms. Flips science classroom, students are making music
videos about mitosis.

Here popular culture is a reward and a motivator. It is driven by the idea
that popular culture is entertainment. It is a break from other things, from
other work perhaps. The question that drives this use of popular culture is,
"How do I get these kids motivated?" Implicit in this question is the teacher's
responsibility to "make" the students interested. Alfie Kohn (1993: 199)
would argue that this is not the right question to be asking.

> It operates within a paradigm of control, the very thing that is death to
> motivation.... The job of educators is neither to make students motiv-
> ated nor to sit passively; it is to set up the conditions that make learning
> possible.

In general these uses of popular culture are mostly "added on" at the
beginning or end of a unit of study, rather than being used to drive the study
itself. Some concerns that teachers have raised about the approach include: in
the long run this approach can work against itself because it teaches students
to expect that the teacher's job is to sell them on school and learning; over
time, students either need more and more incentive to engage with the material, or they may consistently expect extrinsic justifications for learning almost
anything in school rather than seeking to learn on their own. It positions the
students as consumers who sit back and entertain themselves through role-
playing things that happen in popular culture; students lose their sense that
they can control what or how they learn, and conform to passively receiving
information (hooks 1994; Macedo 1994; Freire 2000). In addition, the game

Jeopardy frames the idea of knowledge – understanding through experience and association – in a particular way. Knowledge becomes factoids or titbits of information. It is an object (e.g., the Civil War can be boiled down to these eight categories). Note also that the student shows that she or he knows something by being able to quickly shoot back a one- or two-word answer (Postman 1986; Appelbaum and Clark 2001). The basketball game is a hook or device to pull kids in when it has only a tangential, surface connection to the curriculum content; students are asked to put up with learning mathematics as long as they get to play basketball at the same time. This approach may teach students that fun things only happen when they do not look like school (Appelbaum and Clark 2001).

Popular culture as connection to the real world

At a recent faculty meeting the principal announced that the school needs a website. Mr. Jefferson immediately thinks of a group of six students in his fourth period eighth-grade class who talk about webpages all of the time, and suggests that the website could be designed and maintained by a club that he would advise. He is thinking this would be great because it would capitalize on student strengths and teach important skills and concepts, but would not take up any regular class time. In the high school down the street, two groups of students have been pestering the vice-principal for permission. One group wants to host a big end-of-year rock concert where student and local groups perform; the other group wants to raise awareness of sexually transmitted diseases (STD) through a pamphlet campaign. Ms. Hart, a health teacher, still has one more duty assignment to fulfill for the year, so the vice-principal assigns her to advise and monitor these two groups. She realizes that their concerns could be meshed, and calls a meeting of the two groups to discuss planning a rock concert devoted to STD awareness.

These are great ideas because the school is acknowledging students' interests or passions, and helping to facilitate an enactment of those passions. The school is not only letting students do what they want to do, but helping them to learn important information and life skills through social experiences. Such projects enable students to critically interpret popular media and to find ways to use popular culture forms of expression to influence how they and their peers interpret the world. However, these uses of popular culture do not answer our basic questions about how to use popular culture in the classroom because they place it outside of the regular classroom and the curriculum. Every school has the potential to do a lot of this kind of work; every club, sports team and religious youth group offers socially connected problem-based learning that is meaningful and which connects with everyday life. Outside of the regular school curriculum is a host of rich resources for popular culture sanctioned and supported by school programs. Still, this kind of work is not happening within the school curriculum, which is what we are talking about in this chapter. While we might create a dream school where students take on such projects *as* the curriculum, we recognize that this fantasy is unlikely to be the experience that most of us will have outside of perhaps a really great summer camp (Kenway and Bullen 2001).

Popular culture as a unit of study

> Mr. Salvatore teaches tenth-grade English. He sees that a considerable number of his students are involved in or talk about graffiti all the time. Many mornings when he comes into his room, he finds at least one or two new tags on the desks. He's also seen his students pull out black books and practice their graffiti before, during, and after class. He's pretty sure that some of his students are the ones who are tagging the outside of the building, much to the frustration of the administration. Mr. Salvatore does not know much about graffiti himself; he's never done it before. Nevertheless, he figures his students are not really interested in much of the other things in the curriculum so he designs a unit about graffiti. He checks out books from the local library, walks around the neighborhood and takes pictures of tags and pieces, and sets the tone for the unit by asking his students the broad question, "What is graffiti?" Down the hall, Mrs. Lindstrom is planning her poetry unit and decides that this time they won't only be reading poems by Wordsworth, Dickinson, and Hughes; she will also incorporate lyrics by Bob Dylan and Tupac Shakur. The question she wants to explore with her students is, "What makes this poetry?"

These teachers are informed about popular culture. They value this popular culture as high art and potentially part of the "canon." These teachers are helping their students to see that they can view anything as a source of learning. Placing popular culture at the center of the curriculum legitimates it and allows students to speak about their own experiences within the classroom. Nevertheless, youth do not necessarily want their cultural practices to be legitimated or co-opted by schools. In fact, adult sanctions of popular culture may ironically delegitimate it as an interesting world of experience; it may be the exact opposite of what they "want." Youth may "see through this" as trying to trick them into learning; that is, they may very well interpret this as a manifestation of the first option we describe above: an attempt to motivate them to participate. If the teacher's interest in the practice is merely as a tool of motivation, students will read this as an ultimate dismissal of their interests, rather than as a "cool" way to learn. In addition, not everyone is "into" graffiti, and not everybody needs to be into graffiti. If teachers head down this road, they could be setting up all sorts of obstacles for certain students to get involved with whatever it is that they are exploring in the classroom. Finally, making something a subject of study can "fix it" in such a way that it loses its vitality. In the same way a Shakepearean play can be boring to read, graffiti could be boring if it is something to study rather than something lived.

Popular culture as critical literacy

Students in Mr. Jimenez' history class are interviewing community members as part of their study of the 1960s and 1970s; they are making a video documentary about the history of affirmative action. Mrs. Tyner is watching films about gangs from the 1970s, 1980s and 1990s with her eleventh-grade English class; students are discussing their own experiences of gang life while they also write about how the representation of gangs has changed over time in popular culture. In Ms. Abercrombie's math class, students are doing a comparative analysis of the mathematical concept of *pi* and the way in which it is represented in the film *Pi*. In Mr. Chueng's and Ms. Dimanopolis' combined fourth- and fifth-grade math class, half of the students are counting the number of times children laugh and/or smile in commercials on Saturday mornings; the other half of the class is counting how many times their siblings laugh and/or smile when playing with similar toys. The class will compare graphs of the two results and discuss the meanings behind them.

This form of popular culture as pedagogy teaches students that popular culture is not neutral, and that they can look at it in a critical way. They can, for example, use films to understand the world around them. Popular culture as critical literacy also helps students to see the multiple meanings within "texts"; working this way in school gives students skills that are directly applicable to their everyday lives without translation. As Lankshear *et al.* (1997: 3) explain, critical literacy teaches students about:

what meanings "are," where meanings "come from," how meanings "get fixed," what *authorizes* particular meanings; and in changing notions of how we treat or handle texts so far as meanings and meaning-making are concerned.

However, teachers might be concerned that these approaches run the risk of privileging the teacher's agenda. Doesn't it seem a bit strange that a teacher who is trying to recognize and honor youth cultural practices would end up virtually telling youth how to interpret their own practices? We see this as a central conflict in social justice education, because we ourselves want our students to be able to see things the way we do in order to work for change even as we want to place their own practice at the center of the curriculum (Teaching for Change 1999; Asian American Studies 2000). This does not have to happen if we are careful to organize the ways in which we look at popular culture artifacts and practices together. In the examples given above, the students themselves can be the ones to determine how to analyze what they are investigating. Even so, we may want to expose our students to our own particular, adult agenda (cf., Giroux 1994). Some teachers view a film themselves, see all sorts of examples of how our society misrepresents certain groups of people, or see the potential to apply the representations to a critical social analysis, while their students find entirely different meanings in the film (Giroux 1996; Daspit and Weaver 1998; Dimitriadis 2001). On the other hand, if we can find ways to include our own critical perspectives while valuing those of our students, students may develop a valuable critical understanding of popular culture (Kenway and Bullen 2001).

It is important to note that these ways in which popular culture influences teaching and learning are not mutually exclusive. Making learning fun can motivate certain students to learn. A teacher may attempt to use popular culture as a way of making the learning more relevant in order for his or her students to feel that the class *is* fun. There can be several of these ways happening at once in the classroom. However, none engage in the *practice* of popular culture. Instead, they either look at it from the outside (let's look at graffiti), objectify it to study and control it (critical readings of contemporary films), or turn it into the curriculum (use graffiti as a multiple intelligence ploy). We make this criticism realizing that the distinction we are trying to make is fine-grained. If teachers were using popular culture in the ways described above, learning environments would certainly be more interesting than they usually are in most classrooms. These strategies are not good or bad. For the purposes of this chapter, we find it more useful to stand back from these pedagogical choices and think critically about the advantages and disadvantages of each. What do they contribute to classroom environments in terms of work and learning? How do they get in the way of what we know to be rich kinds of learning experiences? When teachers are careful to avoid the potentially negative outcomes described above, popular culture has the potential to engage students in learning, to introduce critical literacy into the school curriculum, and to challenge societal assumptions about high and popular culture.

The practice of everyday life in the classroom

While we each have had success with these approaches, we have come to realize that together they do not take advantage of what popular cultural practices have to offer: the ways in which youth engage in the practices – how they do what they do. What is missing is Aristotle's idea of tekhne: "the art in mundane skill and, more significantly, in day-to-day life ... an intrinsic aesthetic or crafting that underlies the practices of everyday life ... Call it tekhne, 'a reasoned habit of mind in making something'" (Cintron 1997: xii). To help explain this point, we have developed a continuum of popular culture curriculum. On one end of this continuum is a position in respect to the popular culture artifact or practice that puts it outside the State Standards and school curriculum frameworks. To the right of this approach on our continuum we place classrooms where students take on the roles of someone in popular culture. Students in English may publish their own Zines. Students may *be* filmmakers in history and graffiti artists in math. While there's a fine line that may be hard to see at first, we place ourselves to the right of this stance toward popular culture. We concern ourselves with the artificiality of playing a role. There is a subtle yet significant issue here. Normally students play the role of "student" in a classroom; if we ask them to play the role of "graffiti artist," "fashion critic," or "film director," how is the experience of learning all that different from the same old classroom that doesn't concern itself with popular culture (Appelbaum 2000)? In the classrooms above, the teacher has chosen one popular culture experience, artifact, or set of practices. The teacher must still extrinsically motivate students. In our conception of popular culture in the classroom, we work instead to build on the skills and practices that students use in their engagement with and participation in popular culture, to transport these habits of mind and body into the classroom work at hand. We design an infrastructure for how we will work together in the classroom to support and capitalize on the wealth of skills and concepts that youth bring with them into the learning environment from all of the cultural work they are doing on the "outside."

So let's take our description of how we think teachers should be informed by popular culture in the classroom and lay it on top of the *Jeopardy* game example we describe above. Notice that Ms. Wilson designed the game. She did all of the work. The excitement she brought to the classroom grew out of her own involvement in the design of the game, including all of the choices about questions, difficulties, categories, and rules. In this design, the students experience only game-playing strategies as opposed to game-designing strategies. This characteristic is the rub in terms of the distinction we are making between common uses of popular culture and doing the work as a craftsperson. What if students were studying Mesopotamia and a small group got the idea of creating a *Jeopardy* game? This group would experience the same excitement that the teacher had in creating the game. They would also build skills and conceptual understanding through this work, skills and concepts not developed in simply playing the game. Common uses of popular culture are appealing to teachers because they help the *teacher* to become engaged in a genuine inquiry. Whenever we feel ourselves really enjoying the preparation of class, we step back for a moment and ask ourselves: Should the *students* be doing this instead? The answer usually is "Yes." Yes, the students should design the *Jeopardy* game (with our guidance, perhaps). But this does not mean that we turn around and assign the class to design a *Jeopardy* game. Instead, it's more like approaching the students and saying, "What would *you*

Table 10.1 Mathematics investigation criteria

Problem-posing Document you are posing at least twice per week	Problem-solving Document you are solving at least twice per week
Brown and Walter's techniques • What-if-not • Attribute-listing **Polya's understanding of the problem** • Have I ever seen a problem like this before? • How is what I don't know related to what I do know? • Can I define any variables? **Polya's looking back** • What's the meaning of my answer? • What have I learned? • Can I see an easier way now that I have done all that work? • What new questions grow out of my work so far? **Mason's generalizing** • Turn patterns and categories into conjectures • Identify monster cases that can be barred from a conjecture, and ask what that tells you about the conjecture	**Polya's four phases** • Understand the problem • Plan what you will do • Carry out your plan • Look back **Mason's specializing and generalizing** • Try special cases • Organize your cases in a logical way; try a chart • Look for patterns and/or categories • Look for general ideas that are true for all cases or for categories of cases • Make a conjecture; now find a proof for your conjecture **Brown and Walter** • When does a crazy way of doing a math procedure end up working anyway? • Which what-if-nots change the problem significantly and which only in relatively unimportant ways?

like to do with what you are learning?" If students choose to design a game because they like games, they are wielding their game knowledge in order to dive into Mesopotamia. The openness of the experience, the broad intellectual boundary, enables other students to see how their own engagement with popular culture could be put to good use in the activities of the class. Imagine five to ten different groups in Ms. Wilson's class. One is designing a game. Other students have found various interesting ways of answering the question of what they would like to do.

We argue that youth cultural practices can usefully inform and influence teaching practices – the way we work and learn in the classroom. The way we go about doing this is to get an ethnographic understanding of how youth make meaning in their own lives. Ethnography is a form of qualitative research where the researcher works to understand the lived practices of the people she/he is studying. It is a form of research that involves "looking, listening, collecting, questioning, and interpreting" (Sunstein and Chiseri-Strater 2000: 1). Through this method, ethnographers come to understand how the people they are studying make meaning in the world. Ethnographers approach their phenomena realizing that they know little and the people who are part of the phenomena, the "natives," know a lot (Gallas 1994). With this realization, ethnographers position themselves as the learners, and the people who are part of the phenomena as the teachers. When we make this analogous to teaching, it is our job as teachers to figure out how our students are mathematicians, historians, writers, and scientists, instead of assuming that they are not or that they need to be taught how to be. Therefore, a teacher who is influenced by ethnographic practices would no longer look at a student's interest in popular culture as simply a product. Instead, the teacher would recognize that the student is involved in a practice, a craft, a habit of mind and body, which enables the student to do the work of the popular culture form. From a curriculum standpoint we would call this "experience." The teacher would realize that it is part of her or his job to understand the how and why of the practice because it is one of the ways in which the student makes meaning in the world. Here's how you know when you are to the right of that scraggly line in our diagram: You have a student and she's a poet. She is not just reading Dickinson and Tupac Shakur; she's reading all over the place; watching and thinking in so many seemingly disparate ways that contribute to and make it possible for her to make meaning in this popular culture form. Or you've got a student and she is a mathematician. She is not just doing math homework or number crunching all day; she's thinking in creative, disparate, and diverse ways that inform what she does as a mathematician.

Understanding youth cultural practices as an ethnographer requires that we look at youth as inherently creative problem-solvers, posers, solution-finders, and so on. The teacher enters her or his room assuming that her or his students are already some form of mathematician, scientist, poet, architect. Karen Gallas (1994), a first- and second-grade teacher, writes that she "suspend[s] [her] disbelief as a teacher and [leaves her] judgement in abeyance in service of a child's development" (p. 96). She references her experience with 7-year-old John who, in science class, says that rap is science because "rap is so exciting when you, when you never went to a rap concert, it's so exciting, like micro- and they're electric too." Gallas writes, "Rather than my 'teaching' John what science was, we struggled together to understand his changing picture of science" (p. 96). Edward Said (1994) would describe Karen Gallas as a "professional amateur," someone who doesn't limit herself through her special knowledge of a discipline. Experts, Said contrasts, only feel comfortable approaching problems, issues, ideas, through their rarified knowledge. When someone presents an expert with a problem that grows out of their craft of popular culture, an expert often feels that she or he can't even discuss it because it is beyond the purview of her or his expertise. What they know has nothing to do with the problem. In contrast, teachers often think of themselves or approach their subject as experts. For example, a math teacher may see her or his job as teaching students how to factor polynomials, and therefore cannot afford the time to link mathematics with presidential elections or even be able to entertain a provocative tangent relating to everyday life. Teachers as professional amateurs voraciously pounce on these opportunities to think about things differently and learn from others. They relish the chance to get involved in conversations where they can take what they know and grow new understandings. They see their students as allies in a common project. They expect to learn from their students, not just how to be a better teacher or how to understand fractions in a new way but also about the world in general. In sum, students' experiences in popular cultural practices are resources for the teacher's own understandings of academic subject knowledge in particular and the world more broadly.

Youth involved in popular cultural practices are professional amateurs as well. Consider Karl, a Zine writer we know, whose cultural practice is to write handmade publications that he distributes to friends and through independent bookshops and record stores. What makes Karl a professional amateur is the range and variety of things he does that somehow influence how he writes his Zines. For example, he reads widely and disparately (including *The Economist*, comic books, and *On the road* by Jack Kerouac); he sculpts, makes films, attends rallies, views films, writes music, listens to music, plays pool with friends, and volunteers at a soup kitchen. He does not pursue these experiences because of his interest in Zine writing. Nevertheless, they inform and influence what and how he decides to write. Like Gallas, teachers who understand popular culture as a craft provide a space where students can see for themselves that the skills and concepts they are developing within their popular culture practices are assets in the classroom. All of Karl's varied experiences may be used in the classroom to do the work of the class. Thus we are avoiding a deficit model of teaching. The student is not an empty vessel. Students as professional amateurs see their craft as informing and influencing the way they engage in the work of the class. They see academic disciplines and their popular cultural practices as equal resources for their work.

As teachers, we are always trying to find something to do with our students. The problem is that our search for the best activities is never over, and we are always still hunting for more ideas. Jean Lave (1997) captures this perpetual crisis of teaching by comparing a curriculum that supports the cultural practices of youth with a curriculum which delineates what that practice must be:

> The problem is that any curriculum intended to be a specification *of* practice, rather than an arrangement of opportunities *for* practice (for fashioning and resolving ownable dilemmas) is bound to result in the teaching of a misanalysis of practice ... and the learning of still another. At best it can only induce a new and exotic kind of practice.... In the

settings for which it is intended (in everyday transactions), it will appear out of order and will not in fact reproduce "good" practice.

(Lave 1997: 32)

A curriculum on the right side of the fuzzy line is more sustainable than the kind of curriculum that is built from daily lessons and one-off activities. We are describing a way of being in the classroom, as opposed to a collection of methods of teaching. We find that implementing this sort of curriculum gives teachers a "solution" to the problem of constantly trying to find one day, one month, or one hour of something to do in the classroom. Lemke (1997) reminds us that "practices are not just performances, not just behaviors, not just material processes or operations, but meaningful actions, actions that have relations of meaning to one another in terms of some cultural system" (p. 43). Therefore, we see the value of building a "common culture" of "professional amateurs" in our classrooms in order to enable our students to "learn not just what and how to perform, but also what the performance means" (p. 43). It is in this spirit that we can build with our students a "community of classroom practice" through the conception of popular culture as craft. One must know the meaning in order to appropriately deploy the practice, to know when and in what context to perform.

Maxine Greene (1986: 29) once wrote:

To engage with our students as persons is to affirm our own incompleteness, our consciousness of spaces still to be explored, desires still to be tapped, possibilities still to be opened and pursued. ... We have to find out how to open such spheres, such spaces, where a better state of things can be imagined ... I would like to think that this can happen in classrooms, in corridors, in schoolyards, in the streets around.

When we inform our pedagogy with popular culture practices, we begin to affirm our own incompleteness as well as our consciousness of spaces still to be explored. We are incomplete in that we do not know everything about our students. These realms of popular cultural practices are spaces still to be explored with our students. To support the crafts of youth culture in our classroom is to open up and pursue new possibilities. Perhaps a better state of things can be imagined when we move away from the hierarchy of high culture vs. low culture to a more common culture, where students as professional amateurs seize upon both academic disciplines and popular culture practices as resources for their work. New things might happen in classrooms, corridors, schoolyards, and the streets if the culture of the streets informs the way we work in classrooms. In the same way that our decisions regarding clothes for stepping out declare who we are and what we want to do tonight, youth cultural practices enacted as ways of being in the classroom make each

Table 10.2 Elementary mathematics folder criteria

Criteria for working
My folder includes:

- Work I am not proud of as well as work I am proud of.
- Three charts I have used to further my investigation.
- Notes and suggestions from at least two other students who have helped me with my investigation.
- Work on two questions I invented myself by asking what-if-not.
- A copy of the letter I wrote to another student about their work, including what I thought was most important about their work so far, ideas for how they might do more, and suggestions for making their folder easier to use.
- Two mathematical equations I created to further my investigation.
- My plans for putting my work back out into the world.
- My reflection on what I learned from putting my work back out into the world.

---

student "present" as who they really are, not just in the role of a student but as someone who knows what they want to do today.

Millennial children? Millennial curriculum!

The current generation of *millennial children*, especially in the U.S., is shaped by cultural messages, including "be smart – you are special" (children's T.V., special stores for youth products, special magazines and other media, recreational programs); "leave no one behind" (be inclusive of other ethnicities, races, religions and sexual orientations); "connect 24/7" (it is good to be interdependent on/with family, friends, teachers); "achieve now" (go to the right school, university); and "serve your community" (think of the greater good) (Howe and Strauss 2003; Raines 2002; Oblinger 2003). Experiences should be designed so that they can enact the values of these messages: they feel special and unique, sheltered (others often take the risks for them), confident (they have been told they are great since birth), team-oriented (from group pedagogies in school to participation in team sports to play dates), achievement-focused (need to accomplish something they can point to), pressured (want the experience to contribute to recognition), and conventional (unlike baby-boomers who criticized adults, they share many values with the adults in their lives).

The five-part structure shown in Figure 10.1 centers the above feelings by leading students through investigations of their own design, identifying findings and results by members of the classroom community (of mathematicians, poets, architects, historians). The class serves as a support team that helps individuals think through their ideas and/or leads to small group collaborations, and which facilitates students' making an impact on the larger community based on what they have accomplished. The end of the experience enables them to recognize what they have learned and achieved, and to see

Part 1	Part 2 through Part 4			Part 5
Opening *Creating the issue* *Finding the question* *Generating the interest*	**Doing the investigation** *Three weeks devoted to active engagement in student designed* *investigation around curricular themes, issues, conflicts, problems*			**Archaeology** *Making explicit the* *knowledge gained*
Open-ended activities to elicit student-generated questions about issues or problems related to has been learned, and to disciplinary concepts, curricular topic, or theme	Three parts devoted to investigations. Class time devoted to discussing work done, strategizing next steps, organizing mini-lessons and workshops on ideas generated by students, and putting the work back out into the world in the form of "taking action."			Time devoted in class to look back at the work done, to name what extend into new areas and directions
Materials needed: Working portfolios, Criteria, books, Center materials, films, speakers, field trips, to help stimulate interest	**Materials needed:** Working portfolios; criteria specifications; conference forms; peer feedback; teacher feedback; center materials; new tools and materials as needed for investigations; assessment vehicles.			**Materials needed:** Working portfolios; tests and other evaluation instruments; manipulatives;; new problems
	Envisioned activities: Interviews, experiments, debates, in-class writing and work time, peer review of work in progress, reading discussions, mini-lessons and workshops developed by teacher, initiated by students, guest speakers, planning sessions, and so on.			
Envisioned activities: Quickies; center work modeling ways of working within the discipline; improvise warm-ups; discussions; lists of questions; experiments, background information	**Developing the investigation** **Activities:** Quickies, center work, polya phases, problem-posing; improvise; reflecting on their work; discussions	**Doing the investigation** *Can start this part sooner if students identify their investigation* **Activities:** Quickies, center work, polya phases, problem-posing; improvise; reflecting on their work; discussions of student work on large posters; mini-lessons and workshops as needed	**Taking action** **Activities:** Quickies; improvise; writing about the idea; brainstorming in groups; getting ideas up on big sheets of paper; practice meeting with potential audiences; actually doing the work of putting the work back out into the world.	**Activities:** Quickies; improvise; core curriculum and standards based conversations where investigations are linked to school, city and state expectations; challenges presented by teacher to show students they can utilize skills and concepts developed in their investigations; activities that encourage students to transport the skills and knowledge they learned to other areas
Culmination: Each student identifies interesting and potentially significant ideas they have been working with at a center (e.g., on posters, in discussions, in their portfolios); students identify the center they will return to for their own investigation	**Assessment:** Student work sample analyses; center observation notes; targeted interviews **Culmination:** Peer strategy sessions	**Assessment:** Student work sample analyses; center observation notes; targeted interviews **Culmination:** Students identify a significant idea coming out of their investigation	*Questions guiding the critical activities:* What do you want to do with what you've learned? What *should* you do? Do something that impacts on you, or that impacts on other people. **Assessment:** Student work sample analyses; center observation notes; targeted interviews **Culmination:** Taking the action of putting the work back out into the world; debriefing of the experience	**Culmination:** Class addresses these subjects: What should we do next? Start a new project? Leave taking, goodbyes, and plans for a reunion?

Figure 10.1 Five-part structure

Table 10.3 Mathematician's notebook

For the first part of this course, the main form of work will be to maintain a working mathematical notebook that will enable you to pursue particular mathematical investigations. These investigations will help us do several things: help us work through a provocative mathematical problem; develop an understanding of what it means to be a mathematician; and show us how we can design mathematical inquiries for our students. Your notebook will include things like drawings, writings, and reflections. The contents of your notebook are what you will be evaluated on in the first five weeks of this course.

This notebook may not be like other notebooks you have kept. Think of it as a sort of lab notebook where one keeps systematic records of experiments, or the notebooks photographers keep about lighting, lenses, and settings. Anthropologists keep notebooks; so do cooks and architects. These notebooks all help these professionals keep track of, study, and improve their practice; they simply help them to do their work. You are developing a notebook that supports your working as a mathematician and your learning as a teacher of mathematics.

The goal is to create a usable notebook of your own work as well as your class's accumulating understandings and investigations, our conjectures and arguments. Your notebook will be a place for you to track and record your thinking about issues and ideas. It will also provide an additional avenue of communication between you and us. You will use your notebook to record the work you do within the initial group mathematical investigation and in the design, implementation, and reflection of your own investigation tied to a core curriculum unit.

Below we have listed some specific qualities that distinguish work in notebooks.

Notebook grading criteria

Your notebook should be organized to keep track of your own reactions and thoughts, solutions, and experiments. It should include all work on your inquiry: things and ideas you collect to help you do the work, notes on conversations with others, records of representations and examples, records of trial and error, and plans and reflections for taking action.

Overall quality work within your mathematician's notebook will reflect consistent and repeated use of:

- Polya's four phases
- Specializing and generalizing
- Problem-posing
- Looking back to systematically understand what has been done and what could happen next.

Intellectual practices	Very good	Accomplished *All very good criteria plus:*
Problem-solving strategies	• Reflect complete cycle of Polya's Four Phases at least three times per week • Consistently use pictures, charts, patterns, and application of similar problems	• Develop mathematical importance over time • Reflect repeatedly on use of different strategies • Integrated use of pictures, charts, patterns, and applications similar to problems
Specializing and generalizing	• Record of at least six uses of this technique • At least one reorganization of special cases into a chart to look for a generalization	• Consistent use of these techniques leads to mathematical generalizations that lead to mathematically significant results • Explains significance of generalizations
Problem Posing	• Record of at least six uses of either *what if not* or *changing attributes*	• Questions have a purpose that deepens the investigation or leads to a mathematically significant focus

that they have met goals that adults have set for them. The teacher introduces critical skill and concept goals and ways of working (e.g., as a mathematician: Mason *et al.* 1982; Brown and Walter 1983; Polya 2004; as a poet: Collom and Sheryl 1994) through mini-lessons or "clinics," understood by the students as helping them to accomplish their own investigations.

The specialness of each student is established in tandem with a "team" through *opening* and *developing the investigation*; initial experiences also satisfy conventionality (the topic is chosen by adults) and shelter (impossible to fail at identifying what one wants to accomplish, what one already knows about a topic). We introduce ways of working within the discipline, first, by identifying how students already use these strategies on their own, and then as tools for helping them get unstuck when they do not know what to do next. Classroom conversations elicit ideas from other students as part of the supportive team, and highlight everyone as doing something special contributing to others' learning. Students use Polya's "looking back" to repeatedly identify what they have achieved so far, or Collum's "finding what's right" in each poet's poem. Treating students as mathematicians refining their techniques to further achieve, we are taking advantage of students' confidence in themselves while also helping them to meet pressures for success from family and society. Or, working with students as members of a poetry guild we know that each of us in the class is a publishing author worthy of the esteem such a role carries with it. At the same time taking the accent off mastering prescribed mathematics or languages arts material (for the students, as they are working) and shifting the emphasis to using such material to see what they might be able to do with it (since the teacher is indeed documenting how his or her students are meeting these objectives), we make risk-taking easier, accommodating the need for shelter. Putting the work out into the world helps students use what has been done so far to connect with others outside of the class, working for the good of the larger community. The archaeology phase helps students see that they have indeed achieved, and to apply skills and concepts learned to other contexts beyond the specific investigation carried out.

Weirding and poaching

The common uses of popular culture that we have outlined – as entertaining and motivation, as connection to the "real world," as a unit of study, and as social critique – continue the typical practice of weirding the content in order to attract students' attention, rather than weirding the curriculum. In contrast, the five-part investigation weirds the curriculum as it maintains an ordinary, standards-based set of content objectives; it does so by taking advantage of tekhne, the reasoned habit of mind in making something. Students use clever ideas of their own to invent ways to explore areas of interest, using as bricoleurs the tools of the assigned curriculum along with those funds of knowledge brought to school from everyday life, to help in accomplishing their goals. As we know from Chapter 1, the basic idea guiding a curriculum that sanctions poaching as the spark of life is that the treasure cannot be given to another person; it is in the taking of that treasure that the spark is found, in the poaching that the meaning of the encounter is manifested. In the process, the purpose is immediately transformed away from stealing or redistribution of resources toward the art of poaching itself, the process and method as opposed to the result. In classrooms that use the five-part structure, conversations focus on the ways of working rather than the instructions for what to do. While a teacher may show students a specific way to accomplish certain work, this would only be in a larger context that establishes a community of investigators pursuing important and exciting work. This is why the second part of the infrastructure requires students to take as much time designing their investigations, experimenting with potential inquiries, as they do in actually carrying out the investigation in part 3: the students must feel that they are creative actors pursuing something special and risky in order for them to live the processes of poaching.

The next step weirds the curriculum by avoiding rules for how to carry out the investigation; instead of directions, the teacher presents students with *criteria* for the work that is valued.

In Chapter 1, we discussed how a "generous teacher" tells students what they need to know; then they know. Is it surprising if the students mock or dismiss what the teacher offers? Is it surprising if the child does not take what the teacher offers? If the child cannot take what the teacher offers? Danny didn't want Mr. Hazell's token generosity, because with it came disrespect and physical threats. In our five-part organization, we share ideas that support what the student is pursuing – for example, Danny's father shares outrageous and ingenious strategies for poaching pheasants because they are inspirations for Danny's own future inventions, not to train him in already-known techniques. Similarly, we also shift the focus of discussion from the content to the work at hand, by explicitly discussing the ways of working that are successful or that might be useful in the future, as models. In a mathematics classroom, we talk about Polya's steps for problem-solving, Mason *et al.*'s ideas for specializing and generalizing, and Brown and Walter's ways of problem posing. In our poetry classroom, we experiment with *Oulipo* techniques, read Jack Collum, Mike Cook, Johari Amini, and Gwendolyn Brooks on how they work, and try out the same ideas ourselves. In our history classroom, we discuss methods of oral history, document analysis, identifying cultural symbols in artifacts, and so on. Criteria for the work that is valued are in a sense part of the dark matter in all classrooms; sometimes they are internalized as a component of an implicit or hidden curriculum. Making the criteria explicit actually allows us to play around with what they are, experimenting as teacher-poachers ourselves, and confronting a little bit of the dark matter of teaching.

One resource for thinking about ways of working – as a mathematician, writer, historian, group facilitator – is the field of "academic literacy." This area of scholarship prods the teacher to explicitly make transparent the skills of being a successful student. In some ways this is like clarifying the criteria for the work, yet it also helps educators to see school success as largely determined by cultural capital honed over years and manifested through experiences of acculturation and enculturation. Academic literacy helps us understand the depth of knowledge a student must have about the arts of being a student that some students simply have not had the opportunity to learn, and that others have not been ready to learn before they work with us as their teachers. The skills of being a student can be explicitly named and learned. What exactly does a reader do when he or she reads a math book? Some keep a notebook nearby and work through the ideas as they read, taking an hour or more per page. What do teachers expect students to be thinking about and attending to when they are completing homework problems? In this class, this involves looking back over the processes of working and the results obtained to generate new questions that could be the basis of new investigations, or to brainstorm a list of potentially different strategies of working; it always means describing the implications and meaning of any results or solutions obtained. When a teacher asks you to work in a small group, what is the teacher expecting each member of the group to do? In this class, perhaps, this involves coordinating a range of roles or expectations; in another it might involve monitoring the participation of each group member. Peter started thinking a great deal about these issues when he had the opportunity to visit the Academic Development Department at the University of Cape Town in South Africa, coordinated by Lucia Thesen. After apartheid, as part of the "new" South Africa, UCT, a traditionally White institution, seized upon its commitment to being a school for the new democracy, and developed programs to support the success of all students, especially those who were new to the university from rural, previously non-White "homelands." Students admitted to the university scored well on matriculation exams, so they were clearly qualified for university study according to established criteria; yet they were often unprepared for some of the work at the university. Smart students do not always perform well, and the courses offered by the Academic Literacy Group can make a big difference. By extension, in his classes back in the United States, students who are not performing are, he should assume, often smart students who would benefit from academic literacy work; since there is no special academic literacy group at his school, he looks for ways to build in such experiences as part of his regular classes.

In academic literacy studies, the teacher helps the students to examine the concrete ways of working in academic study, and to adopt these ways of working. For example, successful students often socialize with each other and make studying part of their socializing. They may go out for pizza together, and while they are eating talk about the homework problems, how they each did them, what is important to remember about them, and so on. Some very smart students work for extra hours studying by themselves, redoing the homework, testing themselves on things to remember from the textbook; this studying alone is useful, but the social studying is crucial to performing well in the end. So perhaps we need to help our students to make this way of studying part of their approach to school. It can be quite a challenge, since social time away from school for many students would only be ruined by talking about homework. But we can make the homework be social.

> Tonight, you must telephone or IM at least two people and explain how you approached each of your assigned problems. Turn in tomorrow a print-out of the IM discussion, or a picture that you drew when the other person gave you directions over the phone.

> For homework, decide with one other person what you will do in class tomorrow so that your group is ready for a presentation on Friday; just decide on how you will work together in class; you should not do the work until you come back.

"Compare the methods your group invented with what two adults demonstrate as how they were taught or have figured out on their own." "By next Wednesday, meet with two people and come up with a list of those problems that you still can't do on your own. We will talk about them in class." We can also create social events centered around our classes – parties, field trips, and so on, where students have the chance to develop friendships with others in their class, so that it is easier for them to plan social events on their own. An even better idea would be to provide a criterion and challenge the students to meet it:

> You must do something for homework that requires you to confer with at least one other student in order to make progress on your investigation. How is up to you. Tomorrow you must be ready to explain how what you did met this criterion.

Other aspects of academic literacy involve skills related to the languages that are used in the classroom and in the texts that are used. What goes into a complete explanation of what you were discussing in your group? Many students will benefit from role-playing and experimenting with possible responses to teacher assignments for in-class and outside work. If three volunteers discuss a math problem in front of the class, and then the class notes what they did well that helped the group to move toward a solution, or toward the identification of strategies they could use, then each group can try out these group techniques on their own. The point here is that performance is not always tied to conceptual understanding of the material. In addition, not understanding the ways of working academically can interfere with

Table 10.4 M.Ed. in curriculum studies culminating project guidelines

The culminating project must:

- Evolve out of your passion and interest.
- Be more than an academic paper.
- Be large enough in scope to keep you engaged for the equivalent of three credits of course work.
- Represent a synthesis of your master's program course work.
- Connect you in some way to a world outside of Arcadia.
- Raise consciousness about some issue or idea.
- Connect you with someone else you confer with over the semester.
- Include a list of at least five references that informed and helped shape your project.
- Be useful or make an impact on at least one of the following: your current job; a prospective job; other people.
- Include a public presentation about the project.

All work must be original and of advanced degree quality. Presentation form will vary as appropriate for the project.

producing what the teacher wants. Peter couldn't help wondering about this as he was reading Lew Romagnano's wonderful self-reflection on how so many fantastic ideas for exploration fell flat in his class. Would it have helped if he had made the expectations explicit, instead of wondering why they were losing interest? We can only guess. But we personally believe that he might have been happier with the outcomes if he had described the kinds of things that he wanted them to have ready after cutting paper and making boxes to fill with rice. We know why he didn't do this: he had good pedagogical reasons for thinking that too much information would spoil the surprise. And the surprise was the punch line for the investigation: there is a functional relationship between the length of the square you cut out of each corner of the paper before folding up the sides and the eventual volume that the box can hold. But in this case the punch line and the purpose of the activity were too intertwined, so that holding back on the punch line meant holding back on the purpose, and students felt aimless.

Ways of working

We strongly suggest the use of "classic good problems" like Romagnano's box volume problem as examples for academic literacy work within mini-clinics on ways of working. That is, instead of making such teacher-assigned challenges the center of the work in the classroom, use them as asides, as the focus of mini-clinics or short, guided instruction lessons that are targeted toward particular discussions about ways of working. One might say,

> This next week we are going to work on understanding what you are expected to produce in this class and in other mathematics classes when you are presented with a certain kind of ambiguous and open-ended

situation instead of a formulaic task. First, you have to find a way to collect enough data to form the basis of an analysis that could produce a pattern. You may find this aimless and you may feel like you are losing interest. This is only natural, and part of the work of being a mathematician. Sometimes the collection of enough special cases gets boring and you forget why you are doing it. But keep in mind what we are trying to find: a pattern or relationship, which means first a range of data that we can organize into a table.

As the students work, we might keep the purpose in the front of their minds:

Remember, we are collecting data to see if there is something worth exploring. I could tell you what to pay attention to but we are practicing what mathematicians do, which is figure out what to look for themselves. Let's not spend too much time redoing what everyone else is doing. If one group is trying small cuts for the squares, can another group try large cuts? What about in-between?

Fifteen or twenty minutes later:

Do we have enough data to start suggesting a pattern? If we want to make the biggest volume box, should we use small, large, or medium cuts for the squares? We can't go on to make these boxes for our packages that we're sending to our partner school in Managua until we figure out how we want to make the boxes.

Rather than getting frustrated with students' disinterest I would just not let them fall into that state:

OK, so after working for one day on this, what can we say that we know? What can we say that we still do not know? Remember, as mathematicians, we are expected to find a pattern, to write an equation if we can, that fits our data, so what might we do tomorrow in collecting data, to look for a pattern within the first fifteen minutes of class?" Then tomorrow: "Did our plan for today help us within our goal of fifteen minutes? Why? Or, Why not?"

Now, in order to concretize the literacy skills:

Look at how Mr. Romagnano's class used their table in studying the coin toss game; can we use a table in the same way for our reports on the box problem, or do you think we should organize our data differently for this investigation?

If we put the table at the top of the page, how will we explain what we are saying to the reader who hasn't looked there yet? (Write a note to the reader to look at the next page?) How should we start a paragraph that is going to introduce an equation for the relationship between the length of the side of the square and the volume? How can we explain to the reader why this is so surprising, or otherwise interesting? What is useful about this result? Why should the reader care? Each of these things must be communicated in our report.

And so on. Finally, because this is important, we suggest asking students to identify several new questions that they want on some level to know the answer to, and to which they agree ahead of time to be willing to work on with others. Form groups based on their questions and ask them to pursue their own investigations. Before they actually get started on this, again orient them to the idea that interest is not always automatic, and that mathematicians use clever tricks to keep going and maintain their attention long enough for them to become absorbed in their work. We will have regular, brief, whole-class chats about what works for various members of the class in maintaining interest, creating interest, and sustaining interest, because, as we know, even when we care about the answer we sometimes find our mind wandering to other things. In this way, losing interest and finding a way back in are both part of important contributions to the class.

Language and being: a pedagogic creed

As Dwayne Huebner (1999) noted, the task of the curriculum theorist includes laying bear the structure of being-in-the-world and articulating this structure through the language and environmental forms one creates. We can take seriously Heubner's notion that the descriptive and controlling functions of language are significant vehicles for developing and introducing new conditions into the environment. In this book, such a new language led to startlingly different forms of classroom organization, growing simply out of the reading of youth culture texts and children's literature as curriculum theory. Huebner further considered the ways that curricular practice goes beyond concern for the construction of the educative environment, also addressing the human events that occur within that environment. Thus, as we imagine whole-class discussions, small group strategy sessions, and conversations among members of the classroom community (as mathematicians, poets, historians, architects, fund-raisers, publicity managers), we should examine those ways in which the theoretical problem becomes, in the words of Huebner, "one of finding, creating, or borrowing a language that can be used to describe and explain human events in educative situations" (1999: 225).

I believe we should strive to design learning environments where students and teachers act as poachers. We should *sanction* poaching in curriculum theorizing; in doing so we would thereby sanctify time. This makes it possible for school experience and curriculum practice to be at once the "spark" of being in time and the poaching of time itself, avoiding the reification of time as a spatial object, and enabling the experience of time to dissolve into the life project. There is a kind of cleverness of violating or circumventing rules and structures of which poaching is centrally formed. By making this cleverness the feature of curriculum theorizing and curriculum practice, we have the opportunity to release poaching from its currently telescoped construction into a foundational precept of curriculum practice.

I believe we should weird curriculum and not the content of curriculum. To weird the content is to fall into the trap of motivation and attention, a peculiarly twentieth-century phenomenon likely tied to modernist world-views. When we weird curriculum, we unrest rather than preserve categories and binaries. We take curriculum as an experience of mirroring, one that is both familiar and strange, but neither familiar nor strange, making it uncanny. Curriculum becomes the experience of those dark spaces that hide fears and fantasies yet in doing so contains them and makes them potentially "visible." Yet even as we use the metaphor of dark matter, we unrest those categories of light and dark with all of their problematic colonialist connotations, and consider the ways in which technologies of vision have cast us into a world split from ancestry, manipulating our notions of that very "real world" we seem to think we see so clearly, so that everything ends up being something that we know because we "see it." Indeed, so often our clouded technologies of vision mislead us into thinking that knowledge is caring for us, when in fact it is a tool of power.

One example of those tools of power is the commodification of knowledge so eagerly challenging our efforts to structure differences differently; this is what makes it so hard to avoid the collapse of diversity into an individualizing and psychologizing form. Desires are produced in the struggles against disparities of injustice, mobilized and frustrated in the pedagogical encounter with difference. Our relationship with the *Mhondoro* leads us to see that desire itself can be our Deleuzian, independent term, referring to that which ceaselessly circulates through the unsaid, manifesting itself in expectations, hopes, visions, and fears (even as it intersects with the symbolic and spoken discourses uttered by teachers and students). Consumer culture, object relations, and the ideology of perception are embraced but also left to do what they wish, while other important conceptual work is accomplished by recognition of difference, disparity, and desire. Disparities are enunciations.

Sometimes we wish for the secret treasure; indeed, the search for it by both teachers and students has become a distracting fantasy of learning itself. But we must not confuse this false dark matter with the potentially tangible ways in which curriculum as experience can be a holding environment for students who practice identity design. We are left with tales of the rite of passage, hybridity of identity constituted as Other, and identification with the aggressor. In our postmodern or supermodern times, we are tempted to think of identity as something we construct, invent, or buy. School as either the rite of passage or preparation for the rite of passage is a counterpoint to the notion that one can reinvent oneself, come up with a new, desirable identity, and purchase the garments, accessories, and other symbols of the identity, and then strut or perform for Others. I argued for a shift from thrownness to using the material and tools at hand to do something that one can positively value at the heart of the design process, both in terms of our conception of the student and the teacher in the teaching–learning process, and in leading to the pedagogical notion of criteria for the ways of working. The good designer does not deny constraints, nor does she allow herself to be trapped or paralyzed by them; instead, she finds a new way of looking at them, a new language that shows the possibilities for response, i.e., for design. Within this method of *currere*, reading children's literature and youth culture texts as curriculum theory, we are led to a new language that shows one potential set of possibilities for such a response, the five-part infrastructure for an investigation-based classroom.

Huebner describes six functions for language: *the descriptive*, for talking about what goes on in a classroom; *the explanatory*, for establishing causes, giving reasons for what occurs, and explaining why or how something occurs; *the controlling*, for constructing and manipulating things, events, phenomena, and people, predicting what might happen and thus determining events that become part of a cause-and-effect chain (bringing together the descriptive and the explanatory); *the legitimating*, used to rationalize action, serving to establish the claim that one knows what one is doing, or that one has the right, responsibility, authority, or legitimacy to do it (as in an appeal to some social group for acceptance of the rightness or appropriateness of action undertaken); *the prescriptive*, convincing or influencing others to undertake similar actions (carrying a political quality, as in an imperative or command that imposes a course of action); and *the affiliative*, serving as a vehicle or token of cohesion (as in the initiation that transpires through mastering the language) (Huebner 1999: 214–216). The *currere* of children's literature and youth cultural practices is in each of these senses a language, as is the particular language of weirding and poaching that grew out of the illustration of this method in the previous chapters of this book. As a form of human praxis, this particular manifestation of *currere* shapes a world. We can describe instances of identification with the aggressor, use the concept to explain encounters, establish causes, or to predict what might happen, perhaps to explain to ourselves or others the appropriateness of a particular action or plan; and this idea certainly serves as a token of affiliation for those who make it a part of their practice. The point would not be to make such identification happen or to work to avoid it, but to recognize the centrality of this human experience within the educational experience. I am led to the relations among authority, knowledge, and mystery in my own working out of these issues, because, as we have seen, authority derived from expertise denies mystery, or hides it in a secret place that no one dare enter. This type of authority manufactures dark matter out of thin air, perpetuating the colonialist baggage of darkness versus enlightenment, and working as the evil villain so necessary for the secret treasure fantasy to unfold. In the process, mystery is precluded, poaching is undermined, weirding is applied to content rather than curriculum, and disappoint ensues on all sides. This is the predicament of education. The presentation of criteria establishes the pulse against which improvisation can begin. Criteria for the work that is valued, and explicit discussions of ways of working *as* a mathematician, writer, scientist, and so on, weird curriculum rather than content, making the instructional act a design process. We can't plan in advance what exactly will be produced; if we could we would merely be repeating something that had been done before. What we *can* plan is the *gap* into which the new thing will fit. That new thing might be knowledge, the question, the frame; weirding curriculum makes it most likely to be a new invention, a new way of doing things.

Education is not to be confused with prosthetic enhancement. While new tools of perception can hone and extend perception, the *Mhondoro* of curriculum is present in the intergenerational, which distinguishes the picaresque adventure from the educational encounter. One version of this is found in thinking about the relationship between problems that seem to need a solution and the contexts in which these problems are articulated. Another is in doing something other than solving problems. Once problems are set by either a teacher, the students themselves, or others, we seem to be trapped in the praise singer's quest, the pedagogical act of sending students off on a journey to perceive new things. Intergenerationality as a mode of *currere* in this sense is not a technology of vision or a tool of power; when none of the previous forms of generationality are adequate to the task at hand, we improvise; training in one of the previous forms, however, may lead us to a point of paralysis rather than to mystery. Such paralysis is often associated with an experience of identification with the aggressor. Education is present, in all of its glory as potential futures, when poachers weird curriculum, when surprise humor and mystery travel with improvisation; when ways of working become the counterpoint to the pulse of criteria, the work that transpires is valuable.

11
Afterword:
Zoom Re-Zoom

Zoom in – What do you see?
Two children playing on a farm.
Zoom out – What do you see?
One child playing with a toy farm,
But don't stop Zooming yet.
Just when you think you know where you are,
Guess again.
Nothing is as it seems –
And there's nothing to do but hang on tight
As this tilt-a-whirl world goes
Zooming by.

Banyai 1995b: book jacket

When I first discovered Istvan Banyai's (1995) books, *Zoom* and *Re-Zoom*, I immediately thought, "great visual narratives for ratio and proportion!" We can see now that I had begun, like most of us, in the mode of reading the books as curriculum materials, not as *currere*. We read the books literally as texts to be plugged into the classroom, losing the jazz of curriculum in the dust. These books are very cool; they lead readers through delightful surprises as each turn of the page requires them to step back and see the previous page in a new context. What first looks like two children on a farm is now seen as a larger child playing with a toy farm of which those two previous children are a part. That child playing with a toy farm turns out to be nothing more than a picture on the cover of a catalog, held by a boy on a ship. Which is simply a picture of a ship on the outside of a bus, in a scene of a city, on a television, viewed by a cowboy, all in a little stamp, on a letter being mailed from somewhere in the South Pacific, seen from an airplane, and so on. Startling transformations of meaning occur with each new page. My students created their own Zoom books. We drew pictures, stepping back a predetermined distance each time. We changed the distances using different formulas, such as twice the distance each time, or three times the distance each time, or increasing the distance by the numbers in the Fibonacci sequence, and so on. We video-taped and photographed scenes, stepping back by varying distances. In this way, we developed visual notions of ratio and proportion, and represented them with drawings, videos and photographs, with algebraic notations, with number patterns, and with fractions. Re-Zoom offered newer ideas, because it is clearer in this second book that the perspective of each new page is not just one of stepping back, zooming out, but also turning: one could trace a trajectory path along a complicated hypothetical curve from start to finish. Here, too, we experimented: Can we draw the curve? How do we represent a curve in three dimensions on a piece of paper? Can we use string or pipe cleaners floating in space? (Wikki Stix® worked best.) If we start with pictures, what strategies help us to figure out the curved path in space? If we start with a path, how can we predict what the pictures will look like?

The classroom experience with Banyai's books was a good one. It led me further into the field of visual literacy and a search for techniques that would help my students develop fluency in new media (e.g., Kress *et al.* 1996, 1998 New London Group 1996). However, it did little to help me rethink my fundamental beliefs about teaching and learning. It simply inspired a reasonably interesting set of tasks for the students, with possible opportunities for individual questions and investigations to pop up. Then, at some point after many readings of the book, one of my students noted that things move in *Zoom*, but not all things, only some of them. We dove back into the original images. Did Banyai mess up? Or did he do it on purpose? Assuming the author had a purpose in mind for every detail, we eventually came up with an explanation: the things that move are only those things that exist in the real world and can move, and they move about as much as they should in the time it takes to zoom out. That is, objects that turn out to be merely parts of pictures would not move, but people folding envelopes and flying airplanes are alive and really move. The movement could help in thinking about how long it took in-between pictures, and could be related to the distance of the zoom. The books were no longer static reflections of plodding steps dictated by ratios and proportions. They were now calling us to experiment with the ways in which series of images might tell similar and different stories when controlled by particular patterns, when only slightly deviating from patterns, when patterns change or slowly transform over time, or when a plot need dictates a change in the pattern. We were now mathematical artists using mathematics to improvise interpretations of events, to suggest possibilities, and to explore unpredictable interactions.

Our attempts to explain how and why these books were similar to and different from our own static and less interesting visual texts based on careful ratios and proportions forced us to think in new ways. The books were no longer "implemented" in order to meet prescribed instrumental objectives in language arts and mathematics. They became instead the metaphor for a new way of thinking about thinking itself, and, in this transformational act of becoming something other than what they had originally been, they made it possible for the teacher and the students to experience "becoming" themselves, to change the way they changed as they changed. For us, *Zoom* and *Re-Zoom* were no longer "books"; the presence of these books made it possible to have an experience of reading them in order to rewrite who we are and what we are doing, much as Dennis Sumara (2002) and his students pay attention to certain details (and not others) in order to gain insight into themselves, their relations with others, and their contexts. That "gap or pause displacing the usual action of our classroom" instantaneously became the stuff of a line of flight. The books miraculously shifted, like the string in a game of cat's cradle, from stories told into *literature.*

Since that experience with *Zoom* and *Re-Zoom* I have witnessed similar cat's cradle moments through children's literature. Some found their way into this book. I have also noticed how the "training" that such readings of children's texts as curriculum theory provided has led me to find such metaphorical uses of a more generalized notion of text in the same ways as the children's books. Just as some of my students (pre- and in-service teachers, and graduate students in education) have initially found children's literature more accessible for these purposes than, say, cooking or television, only later to see how they might use cooking or television in analogous ways, to reconceptualize teaching and learning, so too have I returned over and over again to the notion that anything in my world may be used as a text for such purposes.

More importantly, though, is the ways the concepts constructed through these readings play back upon themselves as a new discourse. And even more important than the conceptual discourse are the interwoven strands of connection that link the concepts in ever-increasing ways. It behooves us to reflect one last time on poaching and weirding before this book runs its course. *Zoom* and *Re-Zoom* can help us to do this by asking us to think about looking back in ways that are not purely linear. They ask us to break out of assessment understood as "stepping back to examine." When we perform assessment of any kind, we are not merely looking at what just happened from a distance; we are moving through multiple standpoints along a curve that may be so complicated as to be impossible for us to represent to ourselves as a three-dimensional image. Indeed, curves may even be knots in time and space that can never be unraveled. So our paths of assessment may be something quite different from what we imagine them to be.

I am reminded of sociologist Allan Johnson's (1997) discussion of unraveling the "gender knot," in which he described the complexity of patriarchy as a system, and argued that the undoing of the knot requires undoing the knot of paralysis in the face of the knot. I find many parallels in his discussion of patriarchy and my relationship with schools, probably because schools are reflections and tools of the patriarchal social structures in which they find themselves. Lines of flight like those released by encounters with children's literature require the dissolution of two kinds of myths: (1) things have always been a certain way and can never change; and (2) our own individual efforts make little difference in the end. These are myths, writes Johnson, and therefore we can move past their paralyzing effects. Oppressive systems often seem stable, because they limit our loves and imaginations so much that we can't see beyond them. But this masks a fundamental long-term instability caused by the dynamics of oppression itself. Any system organized around control is a losing proposition because it contradicts the essentially uncontrollable nature of reality, and furthermore because it does such violence to basic human needs and values.

To get past the paralyzing myth that we cannot be effective as individuals in making changes in the discourse and practice of education demands of us that we reframe how we see ourselves in relation to long-term, complex change. We have to rethink, as Banyai does, what it means to see ourselves as reframed, even as we question whether "seeing" ourselves in new frames is the right language to understand the processes involved. For one thing, we need to re-understand time, not as a thing comparable with space, but as a relationship with poaching. A goal such as ending gender inequality takes more than one minute or one day, but is also happening even when we do not "see" it, because time in which change is happening is not a hypostasized thing that we see. Johnson advocates that we work on our time constancy, a concept analogous to the psychological term "object constancy." Babies lack object constancy; if you hold something in front of them and then hide it behind your back, they act as if the object has disappeared. As we get older we develop the skills to believe the object still exists even when we no longer see it. In the same way, we have to learn how to see processes of change even when they are not visible.

My final image for thinking about knots comes back to cat's cradle, where a seemingly complex knot of string is entirely transformed in a fleeting moment into an entirely different constellation. In cat's cradle, the necessity of more than one person in the constantly shifting formulations and patterns becomes crucial to the image. One can play with string designs all by oneself, but this experimentation, while good practice for cat's cradle, does not hold the social nature of the multi-person game. This came up in our classroom work with Wikki Stix® and paths of stepping back, as our teams of students produced interwoven lines of flight and paths of standpoints that knotted within each other. Similarly, this comes up when we think about the nature of assessment as a knotted string of pathways.

A mathematician would describe a knot as some sort of embedding of a circle in three-dimensional space. The questions she would ask have to do with whether or not two knots are pretty much the same – they would be if you could smoothly slide one on to the other without making fundamental changes in it or cutting it in any way; if not, then the two knots would have to be classified as different from each other. When we see "looking back" or assessment metaphorically as a theoretical knot, we might want to consider similar questions. We might also wonder how the analogy would extend to the idea of combining more than one form of assessment, so that each knot gets tied up with the others, or as moving through a knotted pathway to look back upon more than one concept or event at a time, so that, again, multiple knots are co-existing at one and the same time. Mathematicians think about adding or combining knots together as well. But classifying, untying, and combining knots is pretty much a solitary single standpoint theory, which does not incorporate the collaborative element of cat's cradle.

Some of the more interesting advancements in knot theory have to do with complementary spaces – what's not a knot. Profound theorems of recent mathematics show that most known complements carry the structure of hyperbolic geometry, a geometry in which the sum of three angles of a triangle is always less than 180 degrees. In other words, by stepping out of the Euclidean one-dimensional world of the knot, into the complementary world of everything that is not that knot, we enter a kind of world that is entirely different from the one we have been trained to live in, where things are not what they seem. Just like *Zoom*.

6 Harry Potter's World

1. After weeks on the *New York Times* bestseller list, the *Harry Potter* books found themselves on the newly created list of "Children's Bestsellers." Thus *Harry* ushered in a new awareness of the field of children's literature and the need to pay attention to the field as a major market niche. But more importantly, the *Harry* books found themselves as markers of a new boundary, effectively denying it "real" status even as it was celebrated as a cultural phenomenon. No longer a book for adults, it continued to be read by many "older" readers.

2. Filk are new words to well-known songs, sung together by fans at gatherings.

3. *Gundam* is a term from Japanese animation for the hero who dons technology in order to fight the unleashed threats resulting from previous human efforts with technology and science.

4. How do you cope with the aggravation from strongly religious people against witchcraft? J.K. Rowling:

   "Well, mostly I laugh about it I ignore it … and very occasionally I get annoyed, because they have missed the point so spectacularly. I think the Harry books are very moral but some people just object to witchcraft being mentioned in a children's book unfortunately, that means we'll have to lose a lot of classic children's fiction." (Comic Relief 2001)

   Q: What are your feelings toward the people who say your books are to do with cults and telling people to become witches ? (reader's question, didn't give name)

   A: Alfie. Over to you. Do you feel a burning desire to become a witch?

   Alfie: No.

   A: I thought not. I think this is a case of people grossly underestimating children. Again.

   (Southwest News 2000)

5. "Any smoothly functioning technology gives the appearance of magic." Quote attributed to Arthur C. Clarke (Jacobs 2000).

6. ***Hogwarts School Song****: Hogwarts, Hogwarts, Hoggy Warty Hogwarts/Teach us something, please/Whether we be old and bald/Or young with scabby knees/Our heads could do with filling/With some interesting stuff/For now they're bare and full of air/Dead flies and bits of fluff/So teach us things worth knowing/Bring back what we've forgot/Just do your best, we'll do the rest/And learn until our brains all rot.* ("And now, before we go to bed, let us sing the school song! Everyone pick their favorite tune and off we go!")

7. Toys in Dudley Dursley's spare bedroom: computer, PlayStation, two televisions, racing bike, video camera, remote control airplane, large numbers of computer games (including MegaMutilation Three), VCR, gold wristwatch, working model tank, bird in a cage, air rifle, tortoise, sports bag, books (unused), computerized robot.

7 Cyborg Selves

1. Dividing into categories, or an act of *triage*. *Triage* in a different sense, but also compatible in its pursuit of a moral context and the social and cultural values communicated through representations of education, may be found in Sue Books' article, "Literary journalism as educational criticism" (1992).

2. This work begins with an embrace of concepts found in the work of Michel Foucault (see, e.g., Foucault 1980; Martin *et al.* 1988). For another discussion of self, subjectivity, and power see Henriques, *et al.* 1984.

3. Within these daily spaces, clearings forged in the midst of permission slips and mandated curriculum and computer print-outs of test scores, educators do recognize that the fissures of teaching and research, theory and practice, public and private, are artificial distinctions that separate us from ourselves and from the relationships in which knowledges about self and about our worlds are generated (Miller 1990: 172).

   The issue of knowledge control moves us into a direct confrontation with teacher power. We cannot maintain a view of students as democratic participants and teachers as disempowered technicians. Over sixty years ago, Dewey argued that teachers must assume the power to assert themselves on matters of educational importance with the assurance that this judgment will affect what happens in schools. Current technicist models of teacher education do not accept this argument, often teaching novices not to seek empowerment, not to think in an independent manner. Indeed, the hidden curriculum of technicist teacher education promotes a passive view of teachers; they are seen as rule-followers who are rendered more "suspensable" with their standardized lesson plan formats and their adaptations of technical evaluation plans (Kincheloe 1993: 35).

4. It should be mentioned that viewing habits have changed somewhat since the original publication of this material. In addition, children enjoy viewing some programs not discussed in this chapter. Teachers mentioned, for example, *Bill Nye the Science Guy, Wishbone, and Animaniacs*. However, the children I spoke with did not suggest these programs in my interviews. Even those children who later agreed that these programs would be worth my time viewing did not include such programs in their recommendations.

5. The issue of difference between children's and adults' epistemological *triage* of cyborg opens up a host of dilemmas. I want to avoid reifying the distinctions in a backhanded age-ist construction of "adult" and "child" through my descriptions of these meaning-making activities. Yet there are important constellations of cyborg as "power" versus cyborg as "sex" in these discourses (see, e.g., Freudian analyses of cinematic cyborgs, virtual sex, cyborgs and goddesses...). This is an area that requires a great deal of synthesis, ranging from Foucault's work on the care of the self (Foucault 1978) to the work of Evelyn Fox Keller (1985) on the sexual metaphors of knowing and knowledge. The links become clearer to me when I think in terms of the Foucauldian collapse of power/knowledge. But there is much to be done here in respect of curriculum research and theory.

6. Much work has been done in this area of curriculum. For exemplary work see Noel Gough's (1993) *Laboratories of Fiction*.

7. Kincheloe (1993: 115) suggests that this is an example of post-formal teaching.

Bibliography

Adas, Michael. 1989. *Machines as the Measure of Man: Science, technology, and the ideologies of western dominance.* Ithaca, NY: Cornell University Press.

Amazon.com a. *The Bear Comes Home.* www.amazon.com/exec/obidos/ASIN/0393040372/qid=1000750886/sr=1–1/ref=sc_b_1/107–5462734–7080564. last visited September 23, 2006.

Amazon.com b. *Girl in Landscape.* www.amazon.com/exec/obidos/ASIN/0375703918/qid=1000751465/sr=1–1/ref=sc_b_1/107–5462734–7080564. Last visited September 23, 2006.

American Psychological Association. 1993. *Violence and Youth: Psychology's response.* Washington, DC: American Psychological Association.

Anderson, M.T. 2002. *Feed.* Cambridge, MA: Candlewick Press.

Anno, Mitsumasa. 1992. *Anno's Magic Seeds.* New York: The Putnam & Grosset Group.

Aoki, Ted. 2005. *Curriculum in a New Key: The collected works of Ted Aoki.* Mahwah, NJ: Erlbaum.

Appelbaum, Peter. 1995a. Making "sense" of curriculum as commodity or cultural resource. American Educational Studies Association, Cleveland, OH, November 1–5.

Appelbaum, Peter. 1995b. *Popular Culture, Educational Discourse, and Mathematics.* Albany, NY: State University of New York Press.

Appelbaum, Peter. 1998. Cyborg selves: Saturday morning magic and magical morality. In Toby Daspit and John Weaver (eds), *Popular Culture and Critical Pedagogy: Reading, constructing, connecting.* New York: Garland Press, pp. 83–115.

Appelbaum, Peter. 2000. Performed by the space: The spatial turn. *Journal of Curriculum Theorizing* 16 (3): 35–53.

Appelbaum, Peter. 2001. Can a game-show host become a talk-show host? Can a day-trader become a reality provocateur? *Taboo: The Journal of Culture and Education* 4 (2): 125–127.

Appelbaum, Peter. 2002a. *Hopping Back – How much?* Newton, NJ: Abaton Books.

Appelbaum, Peter. 2002b. *Multicultural and Diversity Education: A reference handbook.* Santa Barbara, CA: ABC-CLIO.

Appelbaum, Peter. 2003. Poaching; Sanctifying time. In Donna Trueit, William Doll, Hongyu Wang, and William Pinar (eds), *The Internationalization of Curriculum Studies.* New York: Peter Lang, pp. 15–33.

Appelbaum, Peter and Clark, Stella. 2001. Science! Fun? A critical anlaysis of design/content/evaluation. *Journal of Curriculum Studies* 33 (5): 583–600.

Applegate, Katherine. *Animorphs.* The series is published by Scholastic Books, New York.

Artext. Undated. www.digitalxpression.co.uk/dwheel.swf. Last visited September 23, 2006.

Asian American Studies. 2000. Teaching for social change. www.sscnet.ucla.edu/aasc/classweb/spring00/webmag_197j/loyola.html. Last visited September 23, 2006.

Babbitt, Natalie. 1987. *Tuck Everlasting.* New York: Dell.

Banyai, Istvan.1995a. *Re-Zoom.* New York: Puffin Books.

Banyai, Istvan.1995b. *Zoom.* New York: Puffin Books.

Bartz, Dean. 1999. Father and son face $3,276 in fines for turkey poaching. WON Richland Center. www.up-northoutdoors.com/outdoornews/WI/5–19–99/poaching.html. Last visited August, 2006.

Baudrillard, Jean. 1990. *Seduction.* New York: St. Martin's Press.

Belenky, Mary Field, Clinchy, Blythe McV., Goldberger, Nancy R. and Tarule, Jill M. 1986. *Women's Ways of Knowing: The development of self, voice, and mind.* New York: Basic Books.

Bell, Beverly. 1993. *Children's Science, Constructivism and Learning in Science.* Australia: Deakin University Press.

Benjamin, Walter. 2006. *A Berlin Childhood Around 1900.* Cambridge, MA: Belknap Press.

Bingham, Charles. 2001. What Friedrich Nietzsche cannot stand about education: Toward a pedagogy of self-reformation. *Educational Theory.* 51 (3): 349.

Block, Alan. 1988. The answer is blowin' in the wind: A deconstructive reading of the school text. *Journal of Curriculum Theorizing* 8(4): 23–52.

Block, Alan. 1995. *Occupied Reading: Critical foundations for an ecological theory.* New York: Garland Press.

Block, Alan. 1997. *I'm Only Bleeding: Education as the practice of violence against children.* New York: Peter Lang.

Block, Alan. 1998. Curriculum as affichiste: Popular culture and identity. In William Pinar (ed.), *Curriculum: Toward new identities.* New York: Garland Press, pp. 325–341.

Block, Alan. 1999. Curriculum from the back of the bookstore. *Encounter* 12(4): 17–27.

Block, Alan. 2001. Personal communication. Department of Education, School Counseling, and School Psychology, University of Wisconsin-Stout, Menomenie, WI, 5475, USA.

Books, Sue. 1992. Literary journalism as educational criticism: A discourse on triage. *Holistic Education Review* 5 (3): 41–51.

Boundas, Constantin. 1993. *The Deleuze Reader.* New York: Columbia University Press.

Bourdieu, Pierre. 1977. *Outline of a Theory of Practice.* Oxford: Cambridge University Press.

Britzman, Deborah. 1996. On becoming a "little sex researcher": Some comments on a polymorphously perverse curriculum. *Journal of Curriculum Theorizing* 12 (2): 4–11.

Britzman, Deborah. 1998. *Lost Objects; Contested Subjects.* Albany, New York: State University of New York Press.

Britzman, Deborah. 2003. *After-Education: Anna Freud, Melanie Klein, and psychoanalytic histories of learning.* Albany, New York: State University of New York Press.

Britzman, Deborah. 2006. *Novel Education: Psychoanalytic studies of learning and not learning.* New York: Peter Lang.

Brown, Stephen I. 1973. Mathematics and humanistic themes: Sum considerations. *Educational Theory* 23: 191–214. Reprinted in Stephen I. Brown and Marion I. Walter (eds) (1988), *Problem Posing: Reflections and applications.* Hillsdale, NJ: Erlbaum.

Brown, Stephen I. 1984. The logic of problem generation: From morality and solving to deposing and rebellion. *For the Learning of Mathematics* 4(1): 9–20.

Brown, Stephen I. 2001. *Reconstructing School Mathematics: Problems with problems and the real world.* New York: Peter Lang.

Brown, Stephen I. and Walter, Marion. 1983. *The Art of Problem Posing.* Philadelphia, PA: The Franklin Institute Press.

Brunner, Diane Dubose. 1998. *Between the Masks: Resisting the politics of essentialism.* Lanham, Maryland: Rowman & Littlefield.

Buber, Martin. 1965. *Between Man and Man.* New York: Macmillan.

Butler, Judith. 1989/2000. *Gender Trouble: Feminism and the subversion of identity.* New York: Routledge.

Butler, Judith, Laclau, Ernesto, and Žižek, Slavoj. 2000. *Contingency, Hegemony, Universality: Contemporary dialogues on the left.* London: Verso.

Butler, Octavia. 1997. *Xenogenesis Trilogy.* New York: Warner Books.

Calabrese Barton, Angela *et al.* 2003. *Teaching Science for Social Justice.* New York: Teachers College Press.

Chiseri-Strater, Elizabeth and Sunstein, Bonnie 2000. *Fieldworking.* New York: Bedford-St. Martin's Press.

Cintron, Ralph. 1997. *Angels' Town: Cheroways gang life and rhetorics of the everyday.* Boston, MA: Beacon Press.

Collom, Jack. 1985. *Moving Windows: Evaluating the poetry children write.* New York: Teachers and Writers Collaborative.

Collom, Jack and Noethe, Sheryl. 1994. *Poetry Everywhere: Teaching poetry writing in school and in the community.* New York: Teachers and Writers Collaborative.

Comic Relief. 2001. Live Webchat March 21, 2001. www.comicrelief.com/harrysbooks/pages/transcript.shtml. Last visited September 23, 2006.

Coville, Bruce. *My Teacher is An Alien.* The series is published by Pocket Books.

Crary, Jonathan. 1999. *Suspensions of Perception: Attention, spectacle, and modern culture.* Cambridge, MA: MIT Press.

Dahl, Roald. 1975. *Danny, the Champion of the World.* New York: Puffin Books.

Dahl, Roald. 1982. *The BFG.* New York: Puffin Books.

Daspit, Toby and Weaver, John (1998) *Popular Culture and Critical Pedagogy: Reading, constructing, connecting.* New York: Garland Press.

Davis, Belinda and Appelbaum, Peter. 2001. Post holocaust science education. In Marla Morris and John Weaver (eds), *Difficult Memories: Talk in a (post) holocaust era*: 171–190. New York: Peter Lang, pp. 171–190.

Davis, Brent. 1996. *Teaching Mathematics: Towards a sound alternative.* New York: Garland Press.

Davis, Brent. 1997. Listening for differences: An evolving conception of mathematics teaching. *Journal for Research in Mathematics Education* 28(3): 355–382.

Davis, Brent, Luce-Kapler, Rebecca, and Sumara, Dennis. 2000. *Engaging Minds: Learning and teaching in a complex world.* Engelwood Cliffs, NJ: Erlbaum.

De Certeau, Michel. 1984. *The Practice of Everyday Life,* trans. Steven Rendall. Berkeley, CA: University of California Press.

Deleuze, Gilles and Guattari, Felix. 1991/1996. *What is Philosophy?* New York: Columbia University Press.

Deleuze, Gilles, and Félix Guattari. 1991. *What is Philosophy?* New York: Columbia University Press.

Deleuze, Gilles. 1986. *Foucault.* Minneapolis: University of Minnesota Press.

Deleuze, Gilles. 1993. *The Fold: Leibniz and the baroque.* Minneapolis: University of Minnesota Press.

Deleuze, Gilles. 1994. He stuttered. In Constantin V. Boundas and Dorothea Olkowski (eds), *Gilles Deleuze: The theatre of philosophy.* New York: Routledge.

Deleuze, Gilles. 2001. *Pure Immanence: Essays on a life.* New York: Zone Books.

Dennett, D. C. 1991. *Consciousness Explained.* New York: Little, Brown, & Company.

Dewey, John. 1902. *The Child and the Curriculum.* Chicago, IL: University of Chicago Press.

Dewey, John. 1915. The psychology of occupations. Chapter 6 in *The School and Society* (revised edn). Chicago, IL: University of Chicago Press, pp. 131–137.

Dewey, John. 1997. *Experience and Education.* New York: Macmillan.

Dimitriadis, Greg. 2001. *Performing Identity Performing Culture: Hip hop as text, pedagogy, and lived practice.* New York: Peter Lang.

Doll, Mary Aswell. 1998 Queering the gaze. In William Pinar (ed.) *Queer Theory in Education.* Mahwah, NJ: Erlbaum.

Doll, Mary Aswell. 2000. *Like Letters in Running Water: A mythopoetics of curriculum.* Mahwah, NJ: Erlbaum.

Doll, William. 1993. *A Post-Modern Perspective on Curriculum.* New York: Teachers College Press.

Donald, James. 1992. *Sentimental Education: Schooling, popular culture, and the regulation of liberty.* London: Verso.

Eco, Umberto. 1979. *The Role of the Reader: Explorations in the semiotics of texts.* Bloomington, IN: University of Indiana Press.

Egan, Kieran. 1986. *Teaching as Storytelling: An alternative approach to teaching and curriculum in the elementary school.* Chicago, IL: University of Chicago Press.

Elbow, Peter. 1986. *Embracing Contraries: Explorations in learning and teaching.* New York: Oxford University Press.

Electronic Arts. 2000. *The Sims.* Computer game. Electronic Arts, Inc.

Ellison, Ralph. 1972. *The Invisible Man.* New York: Vintage Books.

Ellul, Jacques. 1967. *The Technological Society.* New York: Random House.

Farmer, Nancy. 1994. *The Ear, the Eye and the Arm.* New York: Puffin Books.

Ferenczi, Sander. 1988. *The Clinical Diary of Sandor Ferenczi.* Cambridge, MA: Harvard University Press.

Feyerabend, Paul. 1988. *Against Method.* London: Verso.

Feyerabend, Paul. 1995. *Killing Time: The autobiography of Paul Feyerabend.* Chicago, IL: The University of Chicago Press.

Field, Joanna. 1957. *On Not Being Able to Paint.* Los Angeles, CA: J. P. Tarcher.

Fiske, John. 1987. British cultural studies and television. In Robert Allen (ed.), *Channels of Discourse*. Chapel Hill, NC: University of North Carolina Press, pp. 254–289.

Fiske, John. 1989a. *Reading the Popular*. New York: Routledge.

Fiske, John. 1989b. *Understanding Popular Culture*. New York: Routledge.

Flake, Sharon. 1998. *The Skin I'm In*. New York: Hyperion.

Fleener, Jayne. 2002. *Curriculum Dynamics: Recreating heart*. New York: Peter Lang.

Foucault, Michel. 1977. *Discipline and Punish: The birth of the prison*. New York: Pantheon Books.

Foucault, Michel. 1978. *The History of Sexuality: An introduction*. New York: Vintage.

Foucault, Michel. 1980. *Power/Knowledge: Selected interviews and other writings*. Brighton, England: Harvester Press.

Foucault, Michel. 1988. Technologies of the self: A seminar with Michel Foucault. In Luther H. Martin, Huck Gutman, and Patrick Hutton (eds), *Technologies of the Self*. Amherst, MA: The University of Massachusetts Press.

Fraiberg, Selma. 1989. Tales of the discovery of the secret treasure. *Psychoanalytic Quarterly* 58: 218–241.

Freire, Paulo. 2000. *Pedagogy of the Oppressed*. New York: Continuum.

Freud, Anna. 1995. The ego and the mechanisms of defense. In *The Writings* 1936. Madison, WI: International Universities Press, Inc.

Freudenthal, Hans. 1978. *Weeding and Sowing: Preface to a science to mathematical education*. Dordrecht, Holland: D. Reidel.

Gadamer, Hans G. 1989. *Truth and Method*. New York: Continuum.

Gallas, Karen. 1994. *The Languages of Learning: How children talk, write, dance, draw, and sing their understanding of the world*. New York: Teachers College Press.

Gallas, Karen. 1995. *Talking Their Way into Science: Hearing children's questions and theories, responding with curricula*. New York: Teachers College Press.

Gallas, Karen. 1998. *Sometimes I Can Be Anything: Power, gender and identity in a primary classroom*. New York: Teachers College Press.

Gee, James Paul. 1996. *Social Linguistics and Literacies: Ideology in discourses*. London: Falmer Press.

Giroux, Henry. 1994. *Disturbing Pleasures: Learning popular culture*. New York: Routledge.

Giroux, Henry. 1996. Hollywood, race and the demonization of youth: The kids are not alright. *Educational Researcher* 25 (2): 31–35.

Giroux, Henry. 2000. *Stealing Innocence: Corporate culture's war on children*. New York: Palgrave.

Giroux, Henry and Simon, Roger. 1989. Popular culture and critical pedagogy. In Henry A. Giroux and Peter McLaren (eds), *Critical Pedagogy, the State, and Cultural Struggle*. Albany, New York: State University of New York Press.

Goodlad, John. 1984. *A Place Called School*. New York: McGraw Hill.

Goodlad, John. 1994. *Educational Renewal: Better teachers, better schools*. San Francisco, CA: Jossey-Bass.

Gough, Noel. 1991. An accidental astronaut: Learning with science fiction. In George Willis and William H. Schubert (eds), *Reflections from the Heart of Educational Inquiry: Understanding curriculum and teaching through the arts*. Albany, NY: State University of New York Press, pp. 312–320.

Gough, Noel. 1993. *Laboratories in Fiction: Science education and popular media*. Geelong, Victoria, Australia: Deakin University Press.

Greenburg, Dan. Recent. *Zack Files* books. New York: Grosset & Dunlap.

Greene, Maxine. 1973. *Teacher as Stranger*. Belmont, CA: Wadsworth.

Greene, Maxine. 1982. Public education and the public space. *Educational Researcher* 11 (6): 4–9.

Greene, Maxine. 1986. In search of a critical pedagogy. *Harvard Educational Review* 56 (4): 427–441.

Grossberg, Lawrence. 2003. Animations, articulations, and becomings: An introduction. In Jennifer Daryl Sacks (ed.), *Animations (of Deleuze and Guattari)*. New York: Peter Lang, pp. 1–8.

Grumet, Madeleine. 1988. *Bitter Milk: Women and teaching*. Amherst, MA; The University of Massachusetts Press.

Guattari, Felix. 1995. *Chaosmosis: An ethico-aesthetic paradigm.* Bloomington, IN: Indiana University Press.

Gutman, Amy. 1987. *Democratic Education.* Princeton, NJ: Princeton University Press.

Haraway, Donna. 1985/1990. A manifesto for cyborgs: Science, technology, and socialist feminism in the 1980s. *Socialist Review* 80: 65–107. Reprinted (1990) in *Feminism/Post-Modernism,* edited by Linda J. Nicholson. New York: Routledge, pp. 190–233.

Haraway, Donna. 1992. Situated knowledges: The science question in feminism and the privilege of partial perspective. In Haraway, *Simians, Cyborgs, and Women: The reinvention of nature.* New York: Routledge, pp. 183–202.

Haraway, Donna. 1997. *Modest Witness: Second millennium female man meets OncoMouse: Feminism and technoscience.* New York: Routledge.

Hargreaves, Andrew. 1994. *Changing Teachers, changing times.* Toronto: OISE Press.

Hawkins, David. 1980a. I, Thou, and It. In David Hawkins, *The Informed Vision.* New York: Pantheon, pp. 48–62.

Hawkins, David. 1980b. *The Informed Vision.* New York: Pantheon.

Hendrix, Air. 2001. Off to Be a Wizard. *GamePro* June, 2001: 36–41.

Henriques, Julian, Holloway, Wendy, Urwin, Cathy, Venn, Couze, and Walkerdine, Valerie. 1984. *Changing the Subject: Psychology, social regulations and subjectivity.* London: Methuen.

Herz, J.C. 1997 *Joystick Nation: How Videogames Ate Our Quarter, Won Our Hearts, and Rewired Our Minds.* New York: Little, Brown.

Heschel, Abraham J. 1951. *The Sabbath: Its meaning for modern man.* New York: Farrar, Straus & Giroux.

Heschel, Abraham J. 1966/1959. *The Insecurity of Freedom: Essays on human existence.* Philadelphia, PA: Jewish Publication Society.

Hesse, Hermann. 1969. *The Glass Bead Game: Magister Ludi.* New York: Rinehart & Winston.

Hoban, Tana. 1970. *Shapes and Things.* New York: Simon and Schuster.

Hobsbawm, Eric. 1959. *Primitive Rebels: Studies in archaic forms of social movement during the nineteenth and twentieth centuries.* Manchester: Manchester University Press.

Hobsbawm, Eric. 1969. *Bandits.* Harmonsworth: Penguin books.

hooks, bell. 1994. *Teaching to Transgress: Education as the practice of freedom.* New York: Routledge.

hooks, bell. 1996. *Reel to Reel: Race, sex and class at the movies.* New York: Routledge.

hooks, bell. 2000. *Where We Stand: Class matters.* New York: Routledge.

Howe, Neil and Strauss, William. 2000. *Millennials Rising. The next great generation.* New York: Vintage.

Huebner, Dwayne. 1999. *The Lure of the Transcendent: Collected essays by Dwayne Huebner,* ed. Vikki Hillis. Mahwah, NJ: Erlbaum.

Jacobs, Alan. 2000. Harry Potter's magic. *First Things: The Journal of Religion and Public Life* 99: 35–38.

Jardine, David, Friesen, Sharon, and Clifford, Pat. 2003. *Back to the Basics of Teaching and Learning: Thinking the learning together.* Mahwah, NJ: Lawrence Erlbaum Associates.

Jardine, David, Friesen, Sharon, and Clifford, Pat. 2006. *Curriculum in Abundance.* Mahwah, NJ: Lawrence Erlbaum Associates.

JCTBergamo. Undated. www.jctbergamo.com. Last visited July 19, 2005.

Jenkins, Henry. 1988. Star Trek rerun, reread, rewritten: Fan writing as textual poaching. *Critical Studies in Mass Communication* 5 (2): 85–107.

Johnson, Allan. 1997. *The Gender Knot: Unraveling our patriarchal legacy.* Philadelphia, PA: Temple University Press.

Jones, Gwyneth. 1992. *White Queen.* London: VGSF.

Joseph, Pamela Bolotin and Burnaford, Gail E. 1994. *Images of Schoolteachers in Twentieth-Century America.* NY: St. Martin's Press.

Keller, Evelyn Fox. 1985. *Reflections on Gender and Science.* New Haven, CT: Yale University Press.

Kenway, Jane and Bullen, Elizabeth. 2001. *Consuming Children: Education, entertainment, advertising.* Buckingham, and Philadelphia, PA: Open University Press.

Kincheloe, Joe. 1993. *Toward a Critical Politics of Teacher Thinking: Mapping the postmodern.* Westport, CT: Bergin & Garvey.

KISS Institute for Practical Robotics. 2001. Botball Technology Education website: www.kipr.org/botball/index.html. Last visited September 23, 2006.

Klein, Julie Thompson. 2005. Integrative learning and interdisciplinary studies. *AAC&U Peer Review* summer/fall: 8–10.

Kohl, Herb. 1991. *I Won't Learn From You: The role of assent in learning.* Minneapolis, MN: Milkweed Editions.

Kohn, Alfie. 1993. *Punished by Rewards: The Trouble with Gold Stars, Incentive Plans, A's, Praise, and Other Bribes.* New York: Houghton Mifflin.

Kress, Gunther and van Leeuwen, T. 1996. *Reading Images: The grammar of visual design.* New York: Routledge.

Kress, Gunther, Ogborn, John, and Martins, Isabel. 1998. A satellite view of language: Some lessons from science classrooms. *Language Awareness*, 7(2 and 3): 69–89.

Ladson-Billings, Gloria. 1997. *Dreamkeepers: Successful teachers of African-American children.* San Francisco, CA: Jossey-Bass.

Lalami, Laila. 2006. "The missionary position," *The Nation*, June 19. Available online at www.thenation.com/doc/20060619/lalami.

Lankshear, Colin, Gee, James Paul, Knoble, Michele, and Searle, Chris. 1997. *Changing Literacies.* Buckingham: Open University Press.

Lave, Jean and Wenger, Etienne. 1991. *Situated Learning: Legitimate peripheral participation.* Cambridge: Cambridge University Press.

Lave, Jean. 1997. The culture of acquisition and the practice of understanding. In David Kirshner and James Whitson (eds), *Situated Cognition: Social, semiotic and psychological perspectives*, Cambridge: Mahwah, NJ: Lawrence Erlbaum, pp. 17–36.

LeGuerer, Annick. 1992. *Scent: The essential and mysterious powers of smell.* New York: Kodansha International.

LeGuin, Ursula (1989) *Languages of the Night: Essays on science fiction and fantasy.* London: Women's Press.

Lemke, Jay. 1997. Cognition, context, and learning: A social semiotic perspective. In David Kirshner and James Whitson (eds), *Situated Cognition: Social, semiotic and psychological perspectives.* Mahwah, NJ: Lawrence Erlbaum, pp. 37–55.

Lethem, Jonathan. 1999. *Girl in Landscape.* NY: Random House.

Letts, William and Sears, James. 1999. *Queering Elementary Education.* New York: Rowman & Littlefield.

Levi, Antonia. 1996. *Samurai from Outer Space: Understanding Japanese animation.* New York: Open Court.

Levin, Diane E. and Carlsson-Page, Nancy. 1995. The mighty morphin power rangers: Teachers voice concern. *Young Children* September: 67–72.

Lionni, Leo. 1967. *Frederick.* New York: Alfred Knopf.

Lionni, Leo. 1978. *Nicolas, Where Have You Been?* New York: Alfred Knopf.

Lowe, Donald. 1982. *History of Bourgeois Perception.* Chicago, IL: University of Chicago Press.

Lowry, Lois. 1993. *The giver.* New York: Houghton Mifflin.

Macdonald, James. 1995a. A transcendental developmental ideology of education. In Bradley J. Macdonald (ed.), *Theory as a Prayerful Act: The collected essays of James B. Macdonald*, with an introduction by William F. Pinar. New York: Peter Lang.

Macdonald, James. 1995b. *Theory as a Prayerful Act.* New York: Peter Lang.

Macedo, Donald. 1994. *Literacies of Power. What Americans are not allowed to know.* Boulder, CO: Westview Press.

Macedo, Donaldo, and Bartolomé, Lilia. 1999. *Dancing with Bigotry: Beyond the politics of tolerance.* NY: Palgrave.

MacIntyre, Alasdair. 1984. *After Virtue: A study in moral theory.* Notre Dame, IN: University of Notre Dame Press.

MacLean, French. 1998. *The Cruel Hunters: SS-Sonderkommando Dirlewanger Hitler's most notorious anti-partisan unit.* Atglen, PA: Schiffer Publishing.

Mahalingham, Ram and McCarthy, Cameron. 2000. *Multicultural Curriculum: New directions for social theory, practice and policy.* London: Taylor & Francis.

McRobbie, Angela. 1994. *Postmodernism and Popular Culture.* New York: Routledge.

Marcuse, Herbert. 1964. *One Dimensional Man.* New York: Ark Paperbacks.

Martin, Emily. 1995. Citadels, rhizomes, and string figures. In Stanley Aronowitz, Barbara Martinsons, and Michael Menser (eds) *Technoscience and Cyberculture: A cultural study.* New York: Routledge, pp. 97–110.

Martin, Luther H., Gutman, Huck, and Hutton, Patrick (eds) (1988) *Technologies of the Self: A seminar with Michel Foucault.* Amherst, MA: University of Massachussetts Press.

Mason, John, Burton, Leone, and Stacey, Kaye. 1982. *Thinking Mathematically.* New York: Addison-Wesley.

Mazlish, Bruce. 1993. *The Fourth Discontinuity: The co-evolution of humans and machines.* New Haven, CT: Yale University Press.

Mead, Margaret. 1970. *Culture and Commitment: A study of the generation gap.* New York: Doubleday.

Mellin-Olsen, Stieg. 1987. *The Politics of Mathematics Education.* Dordrecht, Holland: D. Reidel.

Menser, Michael. 1996. Becoming – Heterarch: On technocultural theory, minor science, and the production of space. In Stanley Aronowitz, Barbara Martinson, and Michael Menser (eds), *Technoscience and Cyberculture.* NY: Routledge, pp. 293–316.

Merleau-Ponty, Maurice. 1964a. The primacy of perception and its philosophical consequences. In *The Primacy of Perception.* Evanston, IL: Northwestern University Press.

Merleau-Ponty, Maurice. 1964b. The film and the new psychology. In *Sense and Non-Sense.* Evanston, IL: Northwestern University Press.

Miller, Janet. 1990. *Creating Spaces and Finding Voices: Teachers collaborating for empowerment.* Albany, New York: State University of New York Press.

Minha, Trinh T. 1989. *Woman, Native, Other: Writing, postcoloniality, and feminism.* Bloomington: Indiana University Press.

Morris, Marla. 1996. Toward a ludic pedagogy: An uncertain occasion. *Journal of Curriculum Theorizing* 12 (1): 29–33.

Morris, Marla. 1998. Unresting the curriculum: Queer projects, queer imaginings. In William Pinar (ed.), *Queer Theory in Curriculum in Education:* 275–286. Mahwah, NJ: Erlbaum, pp. 275–286.

Morris, Marla. 2004. Stumbling inside dis/positions: The (un)home of education. In William Reynolds and Julie Webber (eds), *Expanding Curriculum Theory.* Mahwah. NJ: Erlbaum, pp. 83–104.

Mu, Queen and Sirius, R.U. 1989. Editorial. *Mondo 2000:* 7.

Nachmanovitch, Stephen. 1990. *Free Play. Improvisation in life and art.* New York: Penguin Putnam.

Napier, Susan. 2001. *Anime: from Akira to Princess Mononoke.* New York: Palgrave.

National Anti-Poaching Foundation. *Sportsmen aren't Poachers, Poachers aren't Sportsmen.* http://colorado.on-line.com/ogt/naws.htm. Last visited August, 2006.

National Association for the Education of Young Children. 1985. NAEYC Position Statement on media violence in children's lives. *Young Children* 45 (5): 18–21.

National Council of Teachers of Mathematics. 1989. *Curriculum and Evaluation Standards for School Mathematics.* Reston, VA: NCTM.

National Council of Teachers of Mathematics. 1991. *Professional Standards for Teaching Mathematics.* Reston, VA: NCTM.

National Council of Teachers of Mathematics. 1995. *Assessment Standards for School Mathematics.* Reston, VA: NCTM.

National Council of Teachers of Mathematics. 2000. *Principles and Standards for School Mathematics.* Reston, VA: NCTM.

New London Group (1996) Pedagogy of multiliteracies: Designing social futures. *Harvard Educational Review* 66 (1): 66–92.

Noddings, Nel. 1985. Formal modes of knowing. in Elliot Eisner (ed.), *Learning and Teaching the Ways of Knowing.* Chicago, IL: University of Chicago Press/National Society for the Study of Education, pp. 116–132.

O'Har, George. 2000. Magic in the machine age. *Technology and Culture* 41 (4): 862–864.

Oblinger, Diane. 2003. Boomers, Gen-Xers and Millennials: Understanding the new students. *EduCause* July/August: 37–47.

Ohanian, Susan. 1992. *Garbage Pizza, Patchwork Quilts, and Math Magic: Stories about teachers who love to teach and children who love to learn.* New York: W. H. Freeman.

Ortner, Sherry B. 1984. Theory and anthropology since the sixties. *Comparative Studies in Society and History* 26: 126–166.

Osborne, Margery. 1999. *Examining Science Teaching in Elementary School from the Perspective of a Teacher and Learner.* New York: Falmer Press.

Paul, Jim. 1991. *Catapult: Harry and I build a siege weapon.* New York: Avon Books.

Panshin, Alexi. 1968. *Rite of Passage.* New York: Ace Science Fiction.

Pazsaz Entertainment Network. 1991–2006. www.pazsaz.com/zackfold.html. Last visited September 23, 2006.

Pereira, Joseph. 2000. Caution: 'Morphing' may be hazardous to your teacher. *Wall Street Journal* 7 (December), 224 (111): 1, 8.

Piercy, Marge. 1991. *He, She, and It.* New York: Knopf.

Pinar, William (ed.). 1975. *Curriculum Theorizing: The reconceptualists.* Berkeley, CA: McCutchan.

Pinar, William. 1978. The reconceptualization of curriculum studies, *Journal of Curriculum Studies* 10 (3): 205–214.

Pinar, William. 2004. *What is Curriculum Theory?* Mahwah, NJ: Erlbaum.

Pitt, Alice. 2003. *The Play of the Personal: Psychoanalytic narratives of feminist education.* NY: Peter Lang.

Plant, Sadie. 1997. *Zeros and Ones: Digital women and the new technoculture.* New York: Doubleday.

Poitras, Gilles. 2000. *Anime Essentials: Everything a fan needs to know.* New York: Stone Bridge Press.

Polanyi, Michael. 1958. *Personal Knowledge: Towards a post-critical philosophy.* Chicago, IL: University of Chicago Press.

Polya, Georg. 2004. *How to Solve It.* Princeton, NJ: Princeton University Press.

Postman, Neil. 1986. *Amusing Ourselves to Death: Public discourse in the age of show business.* NY: Penguin Books.

Provenzo, Eugene. 1991. *Video Kids.* Cambridge, MA: Harvard University Press.

Pullman, Philip. 1982. *Count Karlstein.* New York: Knopf.

Pullman, Philip. 1996. *The Golden Compass.* New York: Knopf.

Raschka, Chris. 1992. *Charlie Parker Played Be-Bop.* New York: Scholastic Books.

Raschka, Chris. 1997. *Mysterious Thelonius.* New York: Scholastic Books.

Raines, Claire. 2002. Managing millennials. *Generations at Work.* www.generationsatwork.com.

Ritchart, Ron. 1997. *Through Mathematical Eyes: Exploring functional relationships in math and science.* Portsmouth, NH: Heinemann.

Romagnano, Lew. 1994. *Wrestling with Change: The dilemmas of teaching real mathematics.* Portsmouth, NH: Heinemann.

Rorty, Richard. 1981. *Philosophy and the Mirror of Nature.* Princeton, NJ: Princeton University Press.

Rosen, Charles. 1995. Beethoven's triumph. *New York Review of Books* XLII (14): 52–56.

Ross, Andrew. 1991. *Strange Weather: Culture, science and technology in the age of limits.* New York: Verso.

Rousseau, Jean-Jacques. 1979. *Emile, or Education.* Introduction, translation, and notes by Allan Bloom. New York: Basic Books.

Rowling, J.K. 1999a. *Harry Potter and the Chamber of Secrets.* New York: Scholastic.

Rowling, J.K. 1999b. *Harry Potter and the Prisoner of Azkaban.* New York: Scholastic.

Ruitenberg, Claudia. 2003. From designer identities to identity design: Educating for identity de/construction. In *Philosophy of Education Yearbook.* Champaign, IL: PES Publications, pp. 121–128.

Rushkoff, Douglas. 1996. *Playing the Future: How kid's culture can teach us to thrive in an age of chaos.* New York: HarperCollins.

Rutherford, John. 1990. *Identity: Community, culture, difference.* London: Lawrence & Wishart.

Said, Edward. 1994. *Representations of the Intellectual.* New York: Pantheon Books.

Sartre, Jean-Paul. 1969. *Being and Nothingness: An essay on phenomenological ontology.* New York: Washington Square Press.

Sciesczak, Jon. *Time Warp Trio*. The series is published by Puffin Books.

Serres, Michel. 1998. *The Troubadour of Knowledge*. Ann Arbor, MI: University of Michigan Press.

Shor, Ira. 1987. *Critical Teaching and Everyday Life*. Chicago, IL: University of Chicago Press.

Shor, Ira. 1996. *When Students Have Power: Negotiating authority in a critical pedagogy*. Chicago, IL: University of Chicago Press.

Southwest News. 2000. Webchat July 8, 2000. website: www.southwestnews.com/rowling.htm. last visited September 23, 2006.

Stine, R.L. 1994. *The Scarecrow Walks at Midnight*. New York: Scholastic, Inc.

Sumara, Dennis. 1993. Of seagulls and glass roses: teachers' relationships with literary texts as transformational space. *Journal of Curriculum Theorizing* 10 (3): 153–182.

Sumara, Dennis. 2002. *Why Reading Literature in School Still Matters: Imagination, interpretation, insight*. Mahwah, NJ: Erlbaum.

Sunstein, Bonnie and Chiseri-Strater, Elizabeth. 2000. *Fieldworking: Reading and writing research*. New York: Bedford/St. Martin's Press.

Teaching for Change. 1999. Welcome to teaching for change: Building social justice, starting in the classroom. www.teachingforchange.org/.

Thomas, Sheree. 2000. *Dark Matter: A century of speculative fiction from the African diaspora*. New York: Aspect/Warner Books.

Tierney, John. 2001. Here come the alpha pups. *New York Times Magazine*. August 5: 38–43.

Tisch, Chris. 1997. *Crafty Animal Poachers Now Going to the Dogs*. Bradenton Herald Internet Plus. www.bhip.com/news/9dogs.htm.

Todd, Sharon. 1997. Looking at pedagogy in 3-D. In Sharon Todd (ed.), *Learning Desire: Perspectives on pedagogy, culture, and the unsaid*. New York: Routledge, pp. 237–260.

Truiet, Donna, Doll, William, Wang, Hongyu, and Pinar, William. 2003. *The Internationalization of Curriculum Studies: Selected proceedings from the LSU Conference 2000*. New York: Peter Lang.

Tyler, Ralph. 1949. reprint 1969. *Basic Principles of Curriculum and Instruction*. Chicago, IL: University of Chicago Press.

Vander Ark, Steve. 2000. *Harry Potter Lexicon*. www.i2k.com/~svderark/lexicon/w_spells.html. Last visited September 23, 2006.

Vidler, Anthony. 1994. *The Architectural Uncanny*. Cambridge, MA: MIT Press.

Waught, Coulton. 1947. *The Comics*. Jackson, MS: University Press of Mississippi.

Weaver, John. 2001. Introduction. In John Weaver, Marla Morris, and Peter Appelbaum (eds) *(Post) Modern Science (Education): Propositions and alternative paths*. New York: Peter Lang, pp. 1–22.

Weems, Lisa and Lather, Patti. 2000. A psychoanalysis we can bear to learn from. *Educational Researcher* 29 (6): 41–42.

Weisglass, Julian. 1990. Constructivist listening for empowerment and change. *Educational Forum* 54: 351–370.

Weisglass, Julian. 1994. Changing mathematics teaching means changing ourselves: implications for professional development. In Douglas B. Aichele and Arthur F. Coxford (eds), *Professional Development for Teachers of Mathematics, 1994 Yearbook*. Reston, VA: National Council of Teachers of Mathematics, pp. 67–78.

West, Cornell. 1994. *Race Matters*. New York: Vintage.

Westfahl, Gary. 2000. *Science Fiction, Children's Literature and Popular Culture: Coming of age in fanstasyland*. Westport, CT: Greenwood Press.

Williams, Vera. 1986. *Cherries and Cherry Pits*. New York: Mulberry Books.

Willis, Paul. 1990. *Common Culture: Symbolic work at play in the everyday cultures of the young*. Philadelphia, PA: Open University Press.

Winfield, Ann. 2005. Eugenics, education, and scientific curriculum: Definitions of ability and the role of science. Paper presented at the annual meeting of the American Educational Research Association, Montreal, Canada.

Winnicott, Donald W. 1971. *Playing and Reality*. New York: Routledge.

Winnicott, Donald W. 1984. *Aggression and its Roots in Depression and Delinquency*, Ed. by C. Winnicott, R. Shepherd, and M. Davis. London: Tavistock Publications.

Wolmark, Jenny. 1994. *Aliens and Others: Science fiction, feminism, and postmodernism.* Iowa City: University of Iowa Press.

Wright, Bradford. 2001. *Comic Book Nation: The transformation of youth culture in America.* Johns Hopkins University Press.

Yolen, Jane. 1991. *Wizard's Hall.* New York: Harcourt.

Zabor. Rafi. 1997. *The Bear Comes Home.* New York: W.W. Norton.

Zack Files Fan Club. 1998. Available online at http://us.penguingroup.com/static/packages/us/yreaders/zack/fanclub.

The Zack Files Official Fanclub. 1998. *Out-Of-This-World Fanclub Newsletter.* http://us.penguingroup.com/static/packages/us/yreaders/zack/newsletter.htm. Last visited September 23, 2006.

Zaragoza, Nina. 2002. *Rethinking Language Arts: Passion and practice.* New York: Routledge.

Index